Granddady - Grandday granddady---
(your name all over it)

Y0-DKP-560

Granddady - Grandday granddady---
(your name all over it)

WASHINGTON REDSKINS

THE AUTHORIZED HISTORY

THOM LOVERRO

TAYLOR PUBLISHING COMPANY
DALLAS

Published by Taylor Publishing Company
1550 West Mockingbird Lane
Dallas, Texas 75235

Scott Cunningham: page i, ii, vi, ix, x center, xi, xii, xiv, xv. Al Messerschmidt Photographs: xvi
Washington Redskins: iv, viii, x

Designed by David Timmons

Library of Congress Cataloging-in-Publication Data

Loverro, Thom.
    Washington Redskins / by Thom Loverro.
        p.   cm.
    ISBN 0-87833-136-0 (cloth).—ISBN 0-87833-137-9
(limited).—ISBN 0-87833-138-7 (collector)
        1. Washington Redskins (Football team)—History.
    I. Title
    GV956.W3L68 1996
796.332'64'09753—dc20   96-41453
                                             CIP

Printed in the United States of America
10   9   8   7   6   5   4   3   2   1

To Andy and Irene, who showed me that success was just a matter of getting up just one more time than you fall down; to my wife, Liz, who gave me a sense of purpose and dedication with her honesty and character; and to my two sons, Rocco and Nick, who provide me with the compass to find my way through this life.

CONTENTS

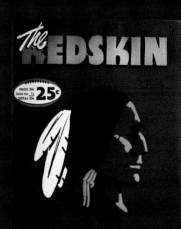

The REDSKIN

PRICE 24c
Sales tax 1c
TOTAL 25c

25c

OPENING GAME · 1950
GRIFFITH STADIUM · WASHINGTON, D. C.

SALESMANSHIP CLUB PRO FOOTBALL CLASSIC

Detroit Lions
vs
Washington Red Skins

37

50c

OFFICIAL PROGRAM
AUGUST 30, 1950

COTTON BOWL · DALLAS, TEXAS

OFFICIAL
PROGRAM

NATIONAL
FOOTBALL
LEAGUE
★★★
Season
1938

PRICE 10¢

Pittsburgh Pirates
versus
Washington
Redskins

GRIFFITH STADIUM
WASHINGTON, D.C.
League of the World's Greatest Football Players

NEXT GAME—DECEMBER 4th
GIANTS at NEW YORK

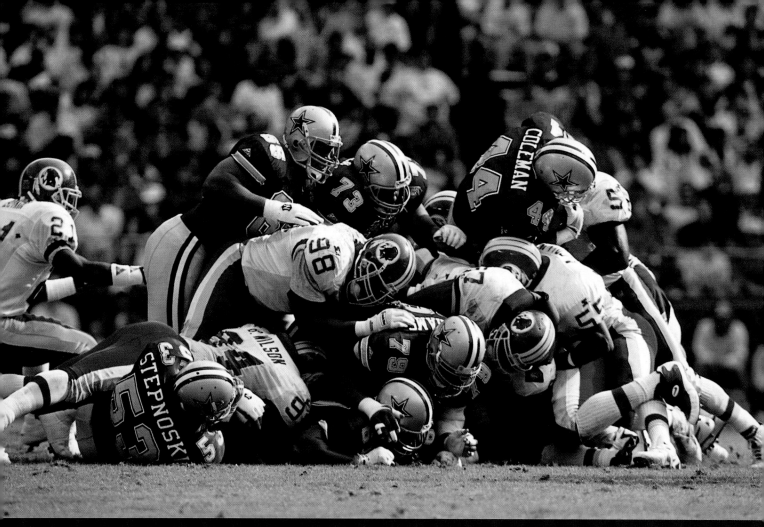

ACKNOWLEDGMENTS

It is no small task to put together a history of one of the most tradition-rich teams in the National Football League. It requires a lot of help—and now, many thanks to many people.

First of all, thanks to all the Washington Redskins players, coaches, and officials, and to the Cooke family, who cooperated with this venture. This is their story.

Particular thanks goes out to former Redskins public relations director Rick Vaughn and current public relations director Mike McCall for their support and help in compiling information for this team history. Thanks also goes out to the staff at the Library of Congress for their help in my research.

My thanks also goes out to my wife Liz and my two boys, Rocco and Nick, for their support while I was buried in my office, and to my friend Pete, who came over and cooked steaks when I needed it.

Special thanks goes to Jake Elwell, a first-class agent and friend. And finally, thanks to Scott Cunningham for his photo work and to Mike Emmerich, Bruce Corey, and all the people at Taylor Publishing for their faith and their quality work.

THOM LOVERRO

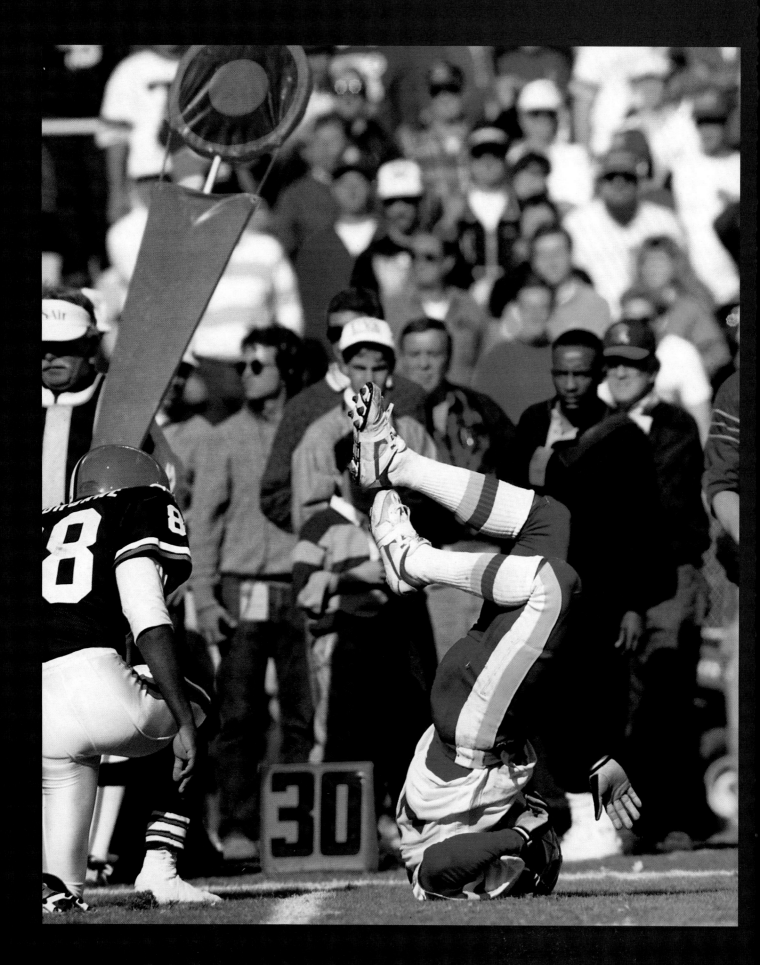

INTRODUCTION

"You couldn't ask for a better place to play."

That's what Sonny Jurgensen said about playing for the Washington Redskins, and he has had a lot of company over the years.

The Washington Redskins and their fans have had a very special relationship throughout the history of the franchise. The Redskins came to Washington in 1937 after five seasons in Boston, where they received little attention or acclaim.

But they were embraced, even smothered, by Washington fans in their first season—a championship season. On the day of an important game against the Giants in New York to decide the Eastern Division title, between ten and twelve thousand fans filled the trains running from Union Station to New York to show their support for their team and even paraded up the streets of Manhattan. It was a display of fan devotion rarely seen in the National Football League.

Forty-five years later, it was a little bigger show—more than five hundred thousand fans lined the streets of Washington to show their appreciation for the 1982 World Champion Redskins in a parade through the city.

Like any love affair, this one has had hot and cold times. But when it's hot, Washington's like no other place in the league. A city full of elected leaders, dignitaries, and other powerful figures join with the taxi drivers, waitresses, and construction workers to go "Hog" wild over their Redskins.

That is the common thread that runs through the years of the Redskins. Sammy Baugh still marvels in amazement at the reception they received their first year in Washington and the army that went to New York with them. "Those fans were great," he said. "I never thought we'd have anything that big."

Even through losing seasons, players felt they had a special relationship with Redskin fans. "They backed us when we tried our best," said Bob Pelligrini, a linebacker who played on several losing Redskin teams in the 1960s. "I really enjoyed playing there. The town was great."

In 1966, the relationship with the fans escalated to a new level. That was the beginning of the sellouts that have continued to this day. Redskin tickets are left in wills. They are contested in divorces. They are simply prized possessions.

During the research for this book, nearly everyone—former players, coaches, and club officials—made a point of saying, in one form or another, what Jurgensen said: What a great place Washington was to be a football player.

Hall of Fame coach Joe Gibbs counted on the fans as part of his team, literally. "I always felt we had an advantage playing at RFK [Stadium] because of our fans," Gibbs said. "You say fans are the same all over, but they're not. Redskin fans, I don't care if it was twenty below, our fans are going to be there. You don't have no-shows. They were there, they were vocal, and helped us emotionally. I think the reason for that is that they were not Johnny-come-lately fans. The people that have tickets in that stadium go back twenty years or more. I think it takes that to be a great fan. You

have to go through the bad times, the good times, and be battle tested.

"Those fans cheered special teams," Gibbs said. "They understood what good defense was. It's a knowledgeable fan in Washington. It's not somebody who just buys a ticket and shows up for the game and doesn't understand the past heritage of the Redskins. That's what's so special about Redskin fans."

Sammy Baugh. "Hail to the Redskins." Hugh Taylor. The Redskins Marching Band. Eddie LeBaron. Sonny and Sam. Vince Lombardi. The Over the Hill Gang. Pat Fischer. The Hogs. Art Monk. Norv Turner.

And the fans. Washington Redskin fans. These are some of the components that make up one of the richest traditions in the National Football League.

One

BEGINNING IN BOSTON

The arrival of a National Football League franchise these days is greeted with tremendous hoopla, with a barrage of copy on the sports pages.

Not so in Boston, 1932. When George Preston Marshall's Boston Braves arrived for their first workout, the new NFL franchise barely got a mention in the local papers.

Actually, they began their practices in nearby Lynn, Massachusetts, on September 7, and buried at the bottom of one of the pages of the *Boston Globe* was a story four paragraphs long about the Braves' arrival and a preview of their first workout. The article was barely longer than a report on the second day of racing at the Lancaster, New Hampshire, Fair.

Even on their first day, Marshall's Braves were having front-office problems. They were in a battle with the New York Giants over the services of a player.

"Members of the Braves professional football team arrived in Boston yesterday and, with Head Coach Lud Wray in command, will have their first practice session today at Lynn Stadium.

"More that forty men will take the field to condition themselves and perfect team play.

"Though Ernie Pinkert, who was claimed by the New York Giants, did not report yesterday, his case has been definitely disposed of by the president of the league, who awarded him to Boston. Therefore he will play with Boston or be absent from organized professional football.

"President George Marshall of the Braves has been in Boston the past several days to prepare for the coming of the team and to confer with Judge Fuchs concerning Braves Field arrangements."

In other words, where the Braves would play had not yet been finalized. They would play that first season at Braves Field, home of the baseball Boston Braves. Marshall used the familiar name of the baseball team as his own, a practice often used by NFL teams at the time, to capture the attention of fans.

This was the beginning of what has since become one of the most storied franchises in the history of the league. There were no indications in those early days that the Boston Braves would someday become the tradition-rich Washington Redskins.

Actually, there were no indications that the NFL would become the success that *it* has. The league was still in its infancy, born in Canton, Ohio, in 1920 as the American Professional

1932 BOSTON BRAVES "PRO" FOOTBALL TEAM

Before moving to Washington in 1937, the Redskins were known as the Braves and played in Boston. The Braves, shown here in their first season, debuted in 1932 and were coached by Lud Wray. They played their home games at Braves Field. The next year owner George Preston Marshall changed the team's address and name, moving them to Fenway Park, still in Boston, and calling them the Redskins. (Pro Football Hall of Fame)

Football conference and two years later renamed the National Football League.

Franchises came and went in cities like Akron (the Pros), Racine (the Tornadoes), and Buffalo (Bisons), among others, failing and disappearing or moving. But under the leadership of George Halas, owner of the Chicago Bears, and others who would soon join him, like Art Rooney, Wellington Mara, and eventually Marshall, the league achieved stability.

When Marshall's Braves joined the league in 1932, there were only eight teams, down from eighteen just ten years earlier. Actually, the Braves were begat from the old Duluth Eskimos. Marshall knew

Halas and NFL president Joe Carr from his earlier venture in the National Basketball League and was convinced to purchase the bankrupt Duluth franchise for $100. The NFL wanted to move into Boston, and Marshall got three investors—Vincent Bendix, an auto supplier in South Bend, Indiana; Larry Doyle, a New York stockbroker; and Jay O'Brien, a New York investment banker—to go in with him on setting up the franchise in Boston. It would prove to be a tough sell.

Boston appeared to be fertile territory. It was a good sports town, with two baseball teams (the Braves and the Red Sox), pro hockey and soccer franchises, big-time college football and semipro

Marshall Takes on the Colleges

George Preston Marshall was looking for ways to attract attention to his new venture, the Boston Braves, in their first NFL season in 1932. When Harvard University officials offered to make Harvard Stadium available to the mayors of Boston and Cambridge for a charity football game to raise money for depleted unemployment funds, they didn't have the Braves in mind. After all, college football was the biggest game in town, followed by tremendous interest in the various semipro football clubs in the area.

But Marshall made the following offer in a letter to both mayors, published in the local newspapers:

"Dear Mr. Mayor:

"The recently announced offer of Harvard University authorities to grant the use of their stadium for a football game, the proceeds of which are to be devoted to relieving suffering among the unemployed of Boston and Cambridge, influences me in writing this letter.

"Two years ago, the New York Giants, member team of our National League, donated their services to Mayor Walker's Unemployment Fund. He, in turn, had a team assembled by Knute Rockne which was composed of former stars of Notre Dame and the players graduated that year.

"This game netted the largest amount of any of the various contests staged for the purpose, paying into the unemployment more than $150,000. It was played on Sunday, December 10.

"I propose that under your leadership a team be assembled of the boys who finish their football careers by December 1 at Boston College, Tufts, Brown, Boston University, Harvard, Yale, Dartmouth, and Holy Cross.

"This team could be assembled along the lines of the team Tad Jones took to the Olympic games, and I feel sure Messrs. McKinney, Manly, McLaughry, Lane, Casey, Stevens, Cannell and Captain McEwan would be glad to offer their services to so worthy a cause.

"This team would be opposed by the Boston Braves, all services to be donated absolutely free. As president of the Boston Braves team I am making this gesture in gratitude to you and the people of Boston for the support they have given professional football in your city.

"I sincerely believe a game such as this, if handled properly, would draw at least 50,000 attendance and raise a large amount for your fund and at the same time provide the patrons a sterling contest and a happy afternoon.

"I believe this suggestion to have great merit and ask your consideration of it in all sincerity.

"Very truly yours, George Marshall, President, National League Club of Boston."

The game was never played.

The 1932 team had several stars in the making who would become important parts of the Redskins' early history. One of them was tackle Turk Edwards, from Washington State, who played for the club until 1940 and would later coach the team from 1946–48. Edwards was inducted in the Pro Football Hall of Fame in 1969. (Pro Football Hall of Fame)

football, and it was a big fight and wrestling town. Yes, professional wrestling dominated the sports pages those days, with far more coverage than pro football would receive.

But Boston's passion for sports would never translate into professional football during those days, much to Marshall's chagrin. As it turned out, this was a blessing in disguise. At the time, though, Marshall's foray into the NFL did not seem like it would result in success, but not for a lack of trying by the owner.

He hired Lud Wray, a former NFL player who had coached at the University of Pennsylvania, to coach the Braves and put the team together.

Wray signed forty players, and they all were on hand on September 8 in Lynn for the second workout. Among those players were several who would later be enshrined in Canton in the Pro Football Hall of Fame—including Turk Edwards, a huge tackle, and Cliff "Gip" Battles, a running back from West Virginia Wesleyan College.

A newspaper article reported on Wray's first meeting with the full squad. "Routine training regulations have been established, and in addition to pep talks, Coach Wray has outlined the whats and what nots of their behavior programs."

To prepare for the season opener against the Brooklyn Dodgers on October 2, Wray lined up several exhibition games against local semipro teams. Those games also served to put the Braves in the spotlight, because there was much more interest in the Boston area in those teams than there was in NFL football, as the semipro clubs had established a tradition in the region, using local players.

The Braves faced the Quincy Trojans for their first contest, drawing more than three thousand people in Quincy, Massachusetts, and they came away with a 25–0 win. Local favorite Tony Plansky, a former member of the popular Pere Marquette football club, ran for one touchdown, and running back Jim Musick scored two.

But Wray apparently was not pleased with the performance, and he put his team though five hours of workouts in its next practice. "The Braves coach told the players they had to reach major league perfection if they hoped to meet Benny Friedman and his Brooklyn Dodgers on even terms.

"After the workout, Coach Wray and his men were confident the Braves would be far better next Sunday against the Providence Steam Rollers at Providence," the newspaper report said.

So much for confidence. The Steam Rollers, a member of the NFL until it dropped out after the 1931 season, defeated the Braves 9–6. This was one time when the Braves were thankful for being ignored by the Boston media, as the embarrassment of losing to the Steam Rollers earned just five paragraphs in the *Boston Globe*. The game was overshadowed by the preview of the first game of the season for Boston's pro soccer team, as pro football took a backseat to soccer. The fortunes of the two sports have obviously since reversed, as pro soccer battles for any coverage today, while pro football dominates the sports media.

The Braves would get no time to rest, as they played another exhibition game the following day, this time faring better with a 31–0 win over the Beverly Pros at Lynn Stadium before a crowd of about fifteen hundred. The following week was their scheduled regular season opener against the Dodgers, and Wray shook the squad up during the week by releasing several players and adding some others, including John Spellman, a former college star at Brown University who had been earning money as a pro wrestler.

Marshall put on a publicity push for the opening game. He took out newspaper advertisements trumpeting "Big League Football" at Braves

Field on October 2, with the game to be played "rain or shine." Ticket prices were $1.50 for box seats, $1.25 for reserved grandstand, $1 for grandstand, and fifty cents for bleacher seats, "plus ten percent government tax."

To show that Marshall knew what was important to Boston sports fans, he promised to air updates of the World Series game between the New York Yankees and the Chicago Cubs, which would be going on as the football game was played.

The Braves owner also set up a dinner for sportswriters and other local sports dignitaries to promote the home opener.

He didn't get a return on his investment, as just six thousand showed up for the contest against the Dodgers, featuring quarterback Benny Friedman, one of the game's best throwers. It wasn't a

With the arrival of coach Ray Flaherty in 1936, the Boston Redskins finally found on-field success. Don Irwin (above) scores one of two Boston touchdowns in the Redskins 14-0 victory over the New York Giants at the Polo Grounds, which clinched a Boston berth in the NFL championship game. Success at the box office, however, eluded Marshall, who opted to play the title game against the Green Bay Packers in New York, instead of Boston, marking the end of the franchise's stint in Beantown. (Acme)

success on the field, either; the Braves lost 14–0, as Friedman tossed two touchdown passes to Jack Grossman.

Wray was not pleased by the performance. One newspaper reported that at the next day's practice, the coach "read the riot act to the Braves, and four players received the blue envelope," the 1930s version of the pink slip. One of the players released was Plansky—his status as local hero was not enough to save him.

Things did not look much better going in to the next game against the New York Giants, with several injuries to key players. But the Braves, behind a larger crowd of eight thousand at Braves Field, managed to win the franchise's first game, with a 14–6 victory over the Giants. It was the first victory of what later would become the Washington Redskins franchise that would go on to win three Super Bowls over ten seasons.

The Braves carried a 7–6 lead into the fourth quarter, when Meyer Clarke sealed the win by grabbing a Giants lateral and racing fifty yards for the second Braves touchdown. And the play of the Braves received a positive review and a sort of a seal of approval from the local media when a column in the *Globe* called "Live Tips and Topics" written under a pseudonym led with an item about the Braves-Giants game:

"The Boston Braves yesterday scored an impressive victory in their second league game on a Sunday, beating the New York Giants despite the presence of 'Red' Cagle, 'Shipwreck' Kelly, and the other metropolitan stars.

"Yesterday's crowd was larger than the one of the previous week, and again the spectators saw high-grade football."

The team would continue to play as it had in the first two games, going back and forth between wins and losses, ending the year with a 4-4-2 record. Off the field, the results were hardly break-even, as Marshall's team wound up losing an estimated $46,000.

Those losses were too much for Marshall's partners to endure, and the three dropped out. However, Marshall, convinced that there was a big future for professional football, vowed that he was in for the long haul.

After the final game of the 1932 season—a 7–0 win over the Dodgers in Brooklyn, avenging

the Braves' opening game loss—the players said good-bye to each other on "disbanding day." The players presented Wray with a hand-carved pipe with an Indian head forming the bowl. Marshall declared he was "pleased" with his team's first season, but also said he would "immediately apply himself to making necessary changes." Those changes were to include delivering the proverbial "blue envelope" to Wray, but the coach took his pipe and beat Marshall to the punch, quitting to become coach of the new Philadelphia franchise in the NFL.

Another change would be moving the home field of the Braves to Fenway Park, and with the change in location came a change in name. The team left the name of the Braves behind at Braves Field but continued with the Indian theme, changing the name to the one that still identifies the franchise—the Redskins.

The changes, though, failed to produce any success either on the field or at the box office, and Marshall went through two coaches, William "Lone Star" Dietz, a full-blooded Indian who played with Jim Thorpe at Carlisle, and Ernie Casey, a former head coach at Harvard.

In 1936, though, Marshall finally found the right man for the job—Ray Flaherty, a former All-Pro tight end for a the New York Giants. Flaherty would prove to be one of the franchise's most successful coaches, with an overall record of 54-21-3 and two world championships. And Flaherty and Marshall brought several new faces to the 1936 squad that would propel the Redskins to their most successful—and, as it turned out, their last—season in Boston.

The Redskins drafted All-American tailback Riley Smith of Alabama to play quarterback and then got someone for him to throw to—another All-American, former Notre Dame end Wayne Millner, who would also end up representing the Redskins in the Pro Football Hall of Fame.

The newcomers, along with Flaherty's presence as coach, brought optimism and enthusiasm to the team. In their final practice before their opening game against the Pirates football team in Pittsburgh, newspaper reports cited the high spirits of the squad. "Coach Ray Flaherty sent his men through a spirited half-hour scrimmage with Riley Smith and Kim Karcher, two of the latest collegiate

The First Redskins (Braves)

Numerous great players have been part of the Washington Redskins franchise, going way back to the days in Boston. The following are the originals, the first ones to report for the first training camp in 1932 in Lynn, Massachusetts.

Backs—Reggie Rust, Oregon State; Henry Hughes, Honolulu; Jim Musick, Southern California; Jack Roberts, University of Georgia; Cliff Battles, West Virginia Wesleyan; Ken Goff, Rhode Island State; Meyers Clark, Ohio State; Marion Dickens, University of Georgia; Oran Pape, University of Iowa; Fait "Chief" Elkins, ex-Chicago Cardinal and Frankford Yellow Jacket; Larry Dullaire, ex-Salem High star; and L.T. "Cowboy" Woodruff, University of Mississippi.

Ends—Paul Collins, Pittsburgh; George Kenneally, ex-St. Bonaventure player; Jim MacMurdo, Pittsburgh; Dale "Muddy" Waters, University of Florida; Dick Murphy, New York University; Jim Sofish of Keisterville, Pennsylvania; Fred Belber, University of North Dakota; Kermit Schmidt, Olympic Club of San Francisco; and Basil Wilkerson, Oklahoma University.

Tackles—Al Pierotti, Washington and Lee; C.W. Artman, Stanford; Glen "Turk" Edwards, Washington State; Hugh Rhea, University of Nebraska; Milton Rehnquist, Providence Steam Rollers; Russell Peterson, University of Montana; and Basil Wilkerson, Oklahoma University.

Centers—Tony Siano, Fordham; "Bank" Barber, Dartmouth; Henry "Babe" Frank, Syracuse; Andrews Anderson, Cambridge; Lavon Zakarian, University of Maine; and Ken "Buck" Hammer, Oregon State.

Guards—Jim Wigmore, University of Maryland; George Hurley, Washington State; Jack Cox, Oregon State; and Hilary Lee University of Missouri.

Utility men—W.A. Boyd, Louisiana; and C.C. Belden, Chicago.

importations to arrive, taking part in the play...Coach Flaherty was enthusiastic in his praise."

That enthusiasm must have been left behind in Boston, because the new-look Redskins went down to defeat, 10–0, before a crowd of 15,622 in Pittsburgh. Boston's Ed Smith fumbled near the end of the first half with the game scoreless, and a backup guard and kicker for the Pirates, George Kakasic, picked up the ball and ran it in for a touchdown. He would also kick a field goal, scoring all of his team's points.

"We have no alibis to offer," Flaherty said after the game. "We outgained them two to one, but fumbles put the skids under us." Flaherty, putting his best spin on the game, said he was disappointed to lose his first game as coach of the Redskins, "but he looked at it as possibly a good omen which will do the team more good than harm when the bigger teams are encountered later on in the season," the *Boston Globe* reported.

Flaherty must have seen something in that loss, because the Redskins came back strong the following week in Philadelphia against the Eagles, rolling up a 26–3 win for Flaherty's first victory as head coach, with Cliff Battles scoring two touch-

George Preston Marshall

It took certain types of men to be involved in professional football back in the 1930s. It was a game in its infancy, taking a backseat to the more popular college game. During tough economic times, with the stiff competition for the American public's entertainment dollar, it took confident individualists to embark on this new venture. Therefore, it was right up George Preston Marshall's alley.

Marshall was born in Grafton, West Virginia, on October 13, 1897. He would attend Randolph Macon College and flirt with show business briefly, a passion that would resurface time and time again while he was owner of the Washington Redskins.

In 1918 he inherited the Palace Laundry in Washington, D.C., from his father and built it into a profitable business. But his desire to be on stage and his interest in sports would push him into other endeavors. He was part of a professional basketball league in the 1920s and would make the contacts there—NFL president Joe Carr and Chicago Bears owner George Halas—that would lead him to the NFL.

He, with several partners, would purchase the old Duluth franchise and move it to Boston, starting out as the Boston Braves in 1932, playing at Braves Field, then moving to Fenway Park and becoming the Boston Redskins in 1933. After five years of poor attendance, Marshall moved the team to Washington, where it won a league title in its first year, in 1937, and would win another one in 1942. The franchise would go through some lean times on the field from 1945—when the team lost to the Cleveland Rams 15–14 in the league title game—until Marshall had to step aside in 1963 due to ill health. But he influenced the game both on and off the field with rule changes and the use of promotions. He always made his teams interesting and evoked strong opinions from both admirers and critics, particularly those who would take him to task for being the last NFL owner to have a black player on his roster.

Even his close associates, at times, would be exasperated by him. "There were so many times I wanted to quit him because he made me angry," said his attorney, Bernie Nordlinger.

George Preston Marshall was one of the pioneers of the National Football League, a venture that required foresight and guts. Marshall and several partners purchased the Duluth franchise in 1932 and moved it to Boston. Under the auspices of Marshall, the Redskins would evolve into one of the most tradition-rich teams in the league.
(Pro Football Hall of Fame)

"But there were so many other times that he made up for it."

"He was a dynamic, forceful, volatile man," Nordlinger said. "He was also an intensely loyal man. Very few people who stayed around Marshall left him, because he was so darn interesting."

Marshall also had a big impact on the growth of the league. "He [Marshall] and [Wellington] Mara and [Art] Rooney and Halas really ran the league," Nordlinger said.

One change that Marshall pushed for involved the rule that required the quarterback to be at least five yards behind the line of scrimmage when he passed. "In order to make Sammy Baugh more effective, because he could run so well, too, Marshall got the league to change the rule so that the quarterback could pass anytime up to the line of scrimmage," Nordlinger said.

"That was very important to the growth of the league," Nordlinger said. "The entire movement of the game would be different."

On August 9, 1969, Marshall passed away at his home at the age of seventy-two. NFL Commissioner Pete Rozelle recognized the owner's accomplishments at his funeral. "Mr. Marshall was an outspoken foe of the status quo when most were content with it," Rozelle said. "We are all beneficiaries of what his dynamic personality helped shape over more than three decades."

downs before a good-sized crowd of twenty thousand at Municipal Stadium.

On the road for the third straight week, the Redskins won their second straight with a 14–3 victory over the Brooklyn Dodgers at Ebbets Field. The remainder of the season, the team would play well enough to be in the running for the top spot in the Eastern Division, taking over first place on November 29 at Fenway Park, gaining revenge on the Pirates with an impressive 30-0 victory.

"Capitalizing on every break that came their way, rolling up 227 yards by rushing, and holding their vaunted foemen to a net loss of two, the Marshall Mohawks played the best game ever produced by a Boston professional eleven and became top heavy favorites for a divisional championship," wrote Paul Craigue in the *Globe*.

Hanging over the team's success on the field, though, was Marshall's frustration over the team's lack of success at the box office. The big game against the Pirates drew just 4,800 people and gained little attention in the local media. In five years, his football team had made little progress, taking a backseat to nearly every other sports

endeavor in Boston when it came to media attention.

So, in the week leading up to the final game of the season against the Giants in New York—one that the Redskins needed to win in order to face the Green Bay Packers for the NFL championship—the portable stands for football at Fenway were being torn down, and the team's offices in Boston were closed.

No official word had come yet, though Marshall had made statements during the season that he would consider moving the team if attendance did not improve. The Boston media was writing that the Redskins would be leaving town and would likely not even play the title game in Boston, as the Redskins would have the home field in the game.

But even local writers had a difficult time condemning Marshall for his move. "It's hard to feel any resentment against a guy who has stayed in there trying for five years and spent $100,000 in vain pursuit of a championship," wrote Paul Craigue in the *Globe*. "Marshall would have been satisfied with an even break financially, and he

After the team struggled under several coaches, the Redskins discovered a winner in Ray Flaherty, a former All-Pro tight end for the New York Giants, who, in his first season, led the club to the 1936 championship game, where it lost to the Packers. The next year, the Redskins' first in Washington, they captured the 1937 NFL title. Flaherty's reign endures as one of the franchise's most successful, with two world championships. He was inducted into the Pro Football Hall of Fame in 1976. (Pro Football Hall of Fame)

went through a long siege without cracking."

The Redskins, before a crowd of about nineteen thousand at the Polo Grounds under rainy skies, clinched their berth in the league championship game with a 14-0 win over the Giants. However, the news of the win was tempered in Boston by the anticipated departure of the team

and by the plans for the championship game against the Green Bay Packers to be played back in New York, on a neutral field, instead of back home in Boston, where it had been scheduled to take place.

"I couldn't help being impressed by today's splendid turnout in the miserable weather," Marshall said, getting a dig in at Boston fans.

In the end, Marshall's frustration was just as strong over the lack of newspaper coverage that his franchise received as it was over the poor attendance. At one point in that final season, he fumed when a win by the team was buried deep in one sports section in favor of a story about the Radcliffe girls hockey team.

"Marshall said he wasn't going to play football in a place that gave more publicity to a girls hockey team than football," said Bernie Nordlinger, Marshall's longtime attorney.

So the morning after defeating the Giants, Marshall met with league president Joe Carr to discuss plans to play the title game at the Polo Grounds in New York rather than at Fenway in Boston. After the meeting, Carr made the announcement, which was, for all intents and purposes, the end of the Redskins in Boston.

"The decision to play the game in New York was reached following a canvas of the club owners involved and of the players of the two teams," Carr said. "Since the playoff game is largely one in which the players are rewarded for winning the divisional titles and their sole remuneration is from the players' pool made up from the gate receipts of the playoff, it was decided that New York was the place in which the players would benefit to the greatest degree possible under existing conditions.

"New York is not only the most centrally located spot, but the danger of bad weather appears less here than in any other spot, with the Polo Grounds offering the best equipment for inclement weather, with its covered stands and lighting system."

Players did profit from the move, as the agreement to play in New York called for sixty percent of the proceeds of the game to go to the players, twenty percent to the league, and ten percent to each club.

"We'll get a much bigger gate in New York

Flaherty's presence wasn't the only reason for the Redksins' turnaround in
1936. The infusion of new talent such as
Riley Smith, the All-American tailback
from Alabama, contributed in no small
part. (Pro Football Hall of Fame)

than in Boston," Marshall said. "We certainly don't owe Boston much after the shabby treatment we've received. Imagine losing $20,000 with a championship team."

Marshall was proven right, at least at the gate, as thirty thousand fans turned out for the game, double the best crowd to watch the Redskins in Boston. But the results on the field were disappointing, as the Packers, led by Don Hutson, won the 1936 NFL championship 21-6.

Hutson caught one touchdown pass, and Johnny Blood caught another from quarterback Arnold Herber. The Packers also blocked two Redskins punts, one of them leading to a touchdown.

The score at the gate? The reported total in receipts was $33,471, with each Green Bay player receiving $250 and each Redskin player pocketing $180 for the game.

Marshall had already made plans to move to Washington, where his Palace Laundry business was based. He formed a new corporation, Maryland Pro Football, and signed a lease with Clark Griffith to play in Griffith Stadium.

On December 17, 1936, Marshall made it official to the city of Boston: The Redskins were moving to Washington. The item was buried at the bottom of the page deep in the sports section of the *Boston Globe*.

Two months later, on February 13, 1937, the league officially approved the transfer, and the Washington Redskins were born.

A HOME IN WASHINGTON

I

f George Preston Marshall had any doubts that Washington would be more receptive to his team than Boston had been, they were erased in the first game the Washington Redskins played at Griffith Stadium on September 17, 1937, when 24,942 showed up, watching the Redskins get off on the right foot with a 13–3 win over the New York Giants.

It was a big change from the indifference that greeted the franchise in Boston, and the players were excited over the response.

"We just can't get over it," said Redskins lineman Turk Edwards. "The fans of Washington have been wonderful to us, and we'd like to let them know that every one of us appreciates their treatment from the bottom of his heart."

The Redskins show also got rave reviews in the press and far more attention in the Washington newspapers that it had in Boston. "As for the near 25,000 crowd, methinks the patrons were more than satisfied with professional football's debut and believe that the pros, like the talkies, are here to stay," wrote Bill Dismer, Jr., in the *Washington Evening Star*.

It was Marshall's flair for showmanship that helped establish the success of the franchise in Washington. First, he hired a public relations man, Jack Espey, who had been the publicity man at George Washington University. He also began using a marching band that eventually would evolve into the legendary Redskins Marching Band.

But the biggest touch of entertainment that Marshall brought to the team also turned out to be one of the greatest players in the history of the franchise.

Marshall made Sammy Baugh the team's first-round draft pick for 1937. The Texas Christian University quarterback had been the best passer and punter in college, and Marshall saw the possibilities of having such an exciting player to kick off his franchise in Washington, capturing the attention of the fans right from the start.

Marshall also tried to package Baugh off the field as a Texas cowboy type. The story goes that Marshall convinced Baugh to wear a ten-gallon hat and cowboy boots when he arrived by plane in Washington after being signed. Baugh did, but he later said that he wore that kind of stuff anyway and that writers embellished the story.

Baugh may have needed off-field embellishment. But on the field he was one of the most exciting players the league had ever seen. "Sammy Baugh was a dynamic personality on the football

Fanaticism took on new meaning when the Redskins moved to Washington. More than 10,000 Redskins backers traveled by train to New York to support their team in the Eastern Division title game against the New York Giants. Led by their owner, George Preston Marshall, and the Redskins Marching Band, fans marched up Seventh Avenue in an impromptu parade. (Pro Football Hall of Fame)

field," said Bernie Nordlinger, Marshall's attorney. "He was a great leader and an exciting ballplayer."

He was also supremely confident. He arrived late to training camp in 1937 after working out his contract with Marshall. On his first day of practice, Baugh was on target with his passes as about three thousand people showed up to watch. As the story goes, Coach Ray Flaherty and Baugh went to the coach's office to go over some plays. When Flaherty drew a big X on the blackboard, he told Baugh, "When the receiver reaches here," he said, pointing to the X, "you hit him in the eye with the ball."

Baugh responded, "Which eye?"

Then, on opening day, in the style of a star, Baugh, on the first play from scrimmage for the Redskins, completed a five-yard pass to Erny Pinckert.

Riley Smith carried the attack the rest of the day for Washington, kicking two field goals and running sixty yards on an interception for a touchdown, then kicking the point after for all thirteen points. "Slinging Sammy" completed eleven out of sixteen passes for 115 yards and impressed Flaherty with his running ability. "He was a much better runner than I had ever imagined," Flaherty said.

Griffith Stadium was usually full in those first heady days in Washington. And the fans developed an immediate, irreversible dislike for the New York Giants, who became the Redskins' first bitter rival and victim in the 1937 Eastern Division title game. More than 35,000 fans turned out at Griffith Stadium the following season for this hard-fought 10-7 loss to the Giants. (Pro Football Hall of Fame)

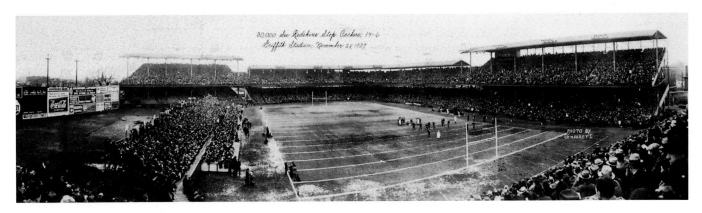

More than 30,000 fans were on hand for this 14-6 win over the Packers in 1937, a victory all the sweeter since Green Bay had throttled the Redskins the year before in the league championship game. (Pro Football Hall of Fame)

Everything that year was much better than Marshall, Flaherty, or Redskins fans could have imagined. The Redskins lost their second game of the year, 21–17, at home to the Chicago Cardinals. But they would go on to win five of their next seven games before their final home game of the season, when they faced the team that had defeated them the year before in the NFL championship game, the Green Bay Packers.

With almost thirty thousand fans filling Griffith Stadium, Baugh led the Redskins to a comeback win. With the Packers leading 6–0 in the third quarter, Baugh threw a touchdown pass to Cliff Battles, with Riley Smith kicking the point after to give Washington a 7–6 lead. Baugh then sealed the victory with a touchdown pass to Charley Malone, as the Redskins took a 14–6 victory.

The win gave Washington a record of 7-3. The Redskins trailed a few points behind the division leader, the New York Giants, who would be their opponent for the final game of the season at the Polo Grounds.

What happened in New York that Sunday was the inauguration of the fan devotion that would become part of the Redskins tradition over the years. Between ten thousand and twelve thousand fans boarded trains at Washington's Union Station early that morning for the trek to New York to support their team. Marshall also brought a band up with him—150 strong, according to some estimates—laying the groundwork for the official team band.

Arriving in New York, the Washington army of supporters, lead by Marshall himself and his marching band, took over Seventh Avenue with an impromptu parade to Columbus Circle, the crowd singing the tune that would soon become the Washington anthem, "Hail to the Redskins."

"At the head of a 150-piece band and twelve thousand fans, George Marshall slipped unobtrusively into town," one newspaper report said of the Redskins entourage.

Even the Redskins players were taken aback by the display of support. "Those fans were great that year," Baugh said. "I never thought we'd see anything like that."

The players gave Washington fans more than they could have hoped for. Baugh completed eleven of fifteen passes, and Battles rushed for an astounding 170 yards, leading the Redskins to a 49–14 win.

When the Redskins arrived back in Washington, they found another crowd of five thousand fans waiting to greet them. "The Redskins caught on like wildfire," Nordlinger said. "They became enormously popular."

There was only one more hurdle to overcome to complete this storybook season. The Chicago Bears lay ahead in the NFL championship game.

The Redskins would be going against the master, George Halas. He would not make the same mistake that Giants coach Steve Owen had made before his game with the Redskins. Earlier that week, when reporters asked Owen to pick an all-NFL team, he did not name one Redskin to the

"Hail to the Redskins"

When George Preston Marshall decided to move his team from Boston to Washington for the 1937 season, one Washington fan was so inspired that he wrote a team song for the new football club.

"Hail to the Redskins" would become one of the most recognized fight songs in professional football.

Bernard "Barnee" Breeskin, who wrote the song, knew Marshall before he moved the team to Washington. The owner lived at the city's famous Shoreham Hotel, where Breeskin was the bandleader.

"When I heard the team was coming to Washington, I decided to write a song," he said. "I used to sit with him [Mr. Marshall] every night between sets at the Shoreham."

The song was first copyrighted as "The Redskins March" and later changed when Marshall's wife, silent film star Corrine Griffith, came up with the lyrics.

"Corrine loved it so much that she said, 'I've got to write words for this,' and she did. It didn't take her long either," said Breeskin, who would lead the famous Redskins Marching Band from 1938 to 1951.

George Preston Marshall always had a flair for show business, and he was a pioneer in his belief that the fans would enjoy entertainment that complemented the games. His zest for showmanship inspired his friend, Barney Breeskin, a bandleader at Washington's Shoreham Hotel, to write a song for the team called "Hail to the Redskins." Marshall's wife, Corrine Griffith, wrote the lyrics. Here the famed Redskins Marching Band plays the song at halftime. (Nate Fine)

The song became the city's unofficial anthem, sung and played all over town, sometimes in unusual places. Once, during a National Symphony Orchestra performance, conductor Mstislav Rostropovich turned to the crowd before the final scheduled song and said, "Ladies and gentlemen, we know about Chopin, Mozart, and the rest, but right now I would like you to meet my favorite composer, Barnee Breeskin, the man who wrote 'Hail to the Redskins.'"

The symphony orchestra, in the hall of the Kennedy Center, then played the Redskins fight song, and, of course, the crowd sang along.

squad. When reporters made the same request of Halas, he named Redskins to every position. "Please see that these selections get in the paper before Sunday," he told reporters, smiling.

But the Bears were an all-pro team themselves, with a huge offensive line to lead the way for the legendary Bronco Nagurski, the feared runner and blocker who averaged 4.4 yards rushing over his NFL career and each off-season became a world champion professional wrestler.

It was a frigid Chicago day, and the Redskins wore sneakers to get better footing on the field. Ironically, eight years later they would lose a championship as a result of another decision about wearing sneakers.

The brutal weather kept the crowd down to about fifteen thousand, and again Redskins fans came through with a testament to their support, as about three thousand of them made the trip to Chicago.

After the teams took the field, the Bears, who also opted for sneakers, had possession of the ball first. The Redskins defense stopped Nagurski, and Chicago punted. Both sides traded possessions again until Baugh handed off to Battles on a reverse play near the Chicago end zone for the first touchdown of the game. Riley Smith kicked the extra point for a 7–0 Redskins lead.

The Bears marched down the field with their running game to tie the score at 7–7 before the end of the first quarter. Soon after, Chicago took a 14–7 lead when Baugh was intercepted, and the Bears

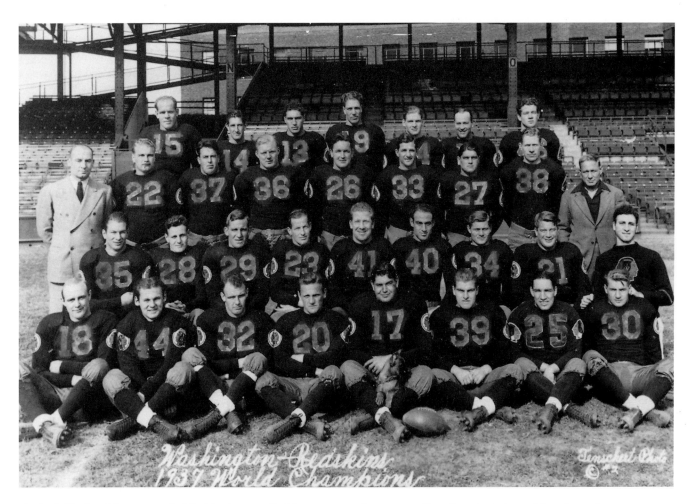

The Redskins' maiden voyage in Washington resulted in an 8-3 regular season. More than 25,000 vocal fans turned out for the team's debut. One Washington reporter wrote, "The pros, like the talkies, are here to stay." (Pro Football Hall of Fame)

The Redskins beat the Chicago Bears 28-21 in the 1937 league championship game, Washington's first title. The 'Skins had to stop legendary Chicago Bears fullback Bronco Nagurski, here bulling his way through a trio of Redskins defenders: Turk Edwards (17) Les Olsson (21) and Jim Barber (15) in pursuit. (Pro Football Hall of Fame)

moved the ball down the field, with running back Jack Manders scoring his second touchdown.

The game took an even worse turn for Washington when Baugh hurt his knee in the second quarter and went to the bench. He stayed there as Chicago took their 14–7 lead into halftime.

At the start of the second half, the Redskins offense remained sluggish without Baugh, but the cowboy rode in off the bench, injured knee and all, and first time he had the ball he connected on a fifty-five-yard touchdown pass to Wayne Millner.

The battle was on, and fans were treated to a classic heavyweight fight. The Bears quickly took back a 21–14 lead on a pass from Bernie Masterson to Manders, and Baugh threw to Millner again for another touchdown, this one a seventy-seven-yard score, and it was now a 21–21 game.

Even though Baugh had a sore knee, he had the hot hand, and the next time he had the ball, he tossed another touchdown, a thirty-five-yard pass to Ed Justice, Washington's third touchdown in ten minutes. Baugh, on one leg, had passed for three touchdowns in one quarter against the tough Chicago defense. And, in the end, it was the Washington defense that turned stingy, holding the Bears scoreless for the rest of the game. But there were some tense moments, none more so that at the end of the game when, with less than a minute remaining, Masterson threw a pass to a wide-open Ed Manske. But Riley Smith preserved the Redskins win with an interception, and the Redskins, in their first season in Washington, were champions of the National Football League.

"If there have been games marked by higher standards of play, there have been few more thrilling," Francis Stan wrote in *The Evening Star*. "Four times the lead changed hands in a bruising, bloody battle, featured by one of the great passing exhibitions of all time."

Baugh made his mark that season—and in that game—as a legendary football figure, playing as well as he did while he was hurt, completing seventeen of thirty-four passes for 352 yards, four yards more than the entire Chicago offense netted.

"He was the difference between the winning and the losing team," Nagurski said.

"He's the best I've ever seen," his teammate Battles said.

The next day, Flaherty made a point of sum-

The lead changed hands four times in the Redskins-Bears 1937 league championship game. "If there have been games marked by higher standards of play, there have been few more thrilling," one Washington reporter wrote. (Pro Football Hall of Fame)

ming up his team's feeling about the Redskins fans. "It's not merely the contrast between Washington and Boston fans," he said. "It's the fact that the sentiment in Washington is a thing apart, something which couldn't have been imagined. Believe you me, this has been the happiest football season of my life. Even if we had lost yesterday, the memory of those Washington fans would have been sufficient to cheer me through the next nine months until we return."

When the Redskins did return for the 1938 season, there were some changes on the team. They added running back Andy Farkas from the University of Detroit through the draft, but lost a key figure in Cliff Battles, who had won the league rushing title in 1937. Battles got into a contract dispute with Marshall. Battles wanted his salary hiked from $2,800 to $4,000. Marshall refused to meet the demands, and Battles simply quit, taking an assistant coaching job at Columbia University.

Marshall did manage to add another talented player, though, in a deal with Pittsburgh, landing

rookie quarterback Frank Filchock from Indiana.

With hopes of defending their championship, Washington opened the 1938 season with a 26–23 win over the Philadelphia Eagles on the road. In their first home game of the year, they tied Brooklyn 16–16 but bounced back with an impressive 37–13 win over the Rams at home. But they lost to the Giants the following week 10–7 in their third straight home game.

The Redskins would lose only once again during the season before the final game, putting together a record of 6-2-2 even though Baugh was injured for a good portion of the season. They were on the way to winning back-to-back titles. All that stood in their way of winning a division crown was one of the two teams that had defeated them during the season, the New York Giants, in the final game of the season.

This one would be played in the Polo Grounds, and, just as they did for this key game the year before, thousands of Redskins fans filled the trains the morning of Sunday, December 4, with the hope that the outcome would be the same as it had been in 1937.

But the game couldn't have been more different. The Giants devised a defensive plan to stop the Redskins' running and Baugh's passing, as the Washington offense made it past the fifty-yard line just three times in a 36–0 loss.

After the season was over, Marshall decided that one of the changes he wanted to make was the site of their training camp. In their first two years in Washington, the Redskins had their summer camp in the hot, humid climate of Virginia. But in 1939, they began what would be a tradition of West Coast training sessions. Marshall found a small college in Washington state for camp that year.

Wayne Millner was a large part of the Redskins success during their early championship run. The Notre Dame end came to the Redskins in 1936 (their final year in Boston) and played through the 1941 season before leaving to join the service. He returned for one season in 1945. Millner was inducted into the Pro Football Hall of Fame in 1968. (Pro Football Hall of Fame)

Flaherty again would lead the Redskins to an outstanding season, with a record of 8-2-1. And again, like the previous two years, the success or failure of the team would come down to a confrontation with its rival, the New York Giants.

The Redskins opened the season struggling offensively, managing to come away with a 7–0 win over the Eagles in Philadelphia. The following week they would meet the Giants at home, and in the mud and rain of Griffith Stadium, Washington would play the only 0–0 tie game in the history of the franchise.

The Redskins reeled off three straight wins before losing their first game of the season, 24–14, to the Green Bay Packers. But then Washington went on a tear, winning four straight and not allowing as many points in those four games combined as they did in the loss to Green Bay. During that stretch, they beat the Eagles 7–6, Brooklyn 42–0, the Cardinals 28–7, and the Lions 31–7. They were primed again for yet another showdown with the Giants in New York in the final game of the

season to decide the division champion.

Again, Redskins fans made what had become their annual trip to New York in December, and, if anything, were greater in numbers this time, with an estimated fifteen thousand showing their support.

It would turn out that none of these three season finales would be the same. Washington dominated the 1937 game with a 49–14 win, and the Giants did the same the following season, shutting out the Redskins 36–0. The 1939 game would not be a blowout on either side, but it would prove to be the most controversial of these contests.

In a defensive struggle, the Giants took a 9–0 lead on three field goals going into the last quarter. Tackle Willie Wilkin blocked a New York punt, and two plays later Filchock completed a touchdown pass to Bob Masterson, who also kicked the extra point, to make it a 9–7 game. The Redskins kept the pressure on, getting the ball back to move it down to the Giants' seven-yard line with less than two minutes to play.

The time had come for Bo Russell to put the game away for Washington. Russell, who took over the kicking duties after the team released kicker Tillie Manton before the start of the season, had not missed a field goal through his first ten games. With fifty thousand fans looking on, it appeared that the Redskins would soon win yet another division title and a shot at the NFL crown.

With seven seconds left, the ball was snapped, and Russell boomed it. It glided past the right goalpost. The Redskins saw it go through the goalposts for the game-winning score and began celebrating. Some of the Giants also saw it go through and began walking off the field, believing they had lost.

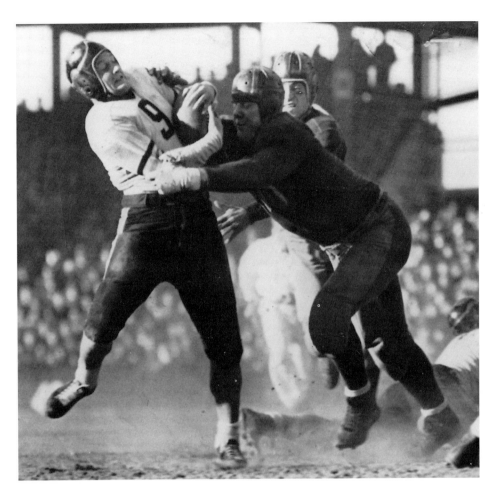

No one could have foreseen the beating the Redskins would take in the 1940 championship game, when the Chicago Bears recorded a historic 73-0 win, catching the Washington defense off guard with the T-formation. The Bears scored so many points officials ran out of game balls, forcing them to use practice balls for the last few snaps. (Pro Football Hall of Fame)

Referee Bill Halloran, though, saw it differently. He ruled that the ball went to the right of the goalpost and was not good, which gave the Giants a 9–7 victory and sent the Redskins to an angry frenzy directed at Halloran.

"What do you mean, no good?" Flaherty screamed at the referee. "Everyone in the stadium knows it was good, including the Giants."

Halloran's call stood, but it would be the last NFL game Halloran would work. Varying reports say that Marshall made sure Halloran would not return to the officiating ranks for the 1940 season.

More Redskins fans would be able to watch their team in the 1940 season, as seating at Griffith Stadium would be expanded to handle forty thousand fans. And they would be treated to yet another terrific Flaherty team, starting the season with a 24–17 victory over Brooklyn at home. The Redskins would go on to win their next six games, posting a record of 7–0, before losing to Brooklyn on the

road 16–14. But Washington bounced back to beat the powerful Bears 7–3 at Griffith Stadium, a win that would ultimately cost the Redskins because of the confidence it would bring them the next time they faced Chicago that season—in the NFL championship game.

There would be no showdown with the Giants this season in the final regular season contest. Washington lost to New York 21–7 at the Polo Grounds in the next-to-last game of the season, but that dropped the Redskins' record to only 8–2, and the win would give the Giants a record of 6–3–1, short of Washington's mark. The following week at home, Washington would clinch the division crown with a 13–7 victory over Philadelphia. Now they would face the Bears again for the league title.

After Washington's 7–3 win over the Bears earlier in the season, Marshall, buoyed by the victory, made some comments that the entire fran-

Sammy Baugh, Hollywood Star

Washington Redskins

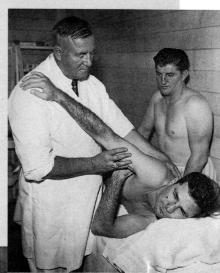

Nate Fine

"Slinging" Sammy Baugh captured the attention of the sports public with his daring play for the Washington Redskins and with his cowboy image straight from Texas. Hollywood was paying attention, too, and in 1941 Baugh starred in a Republic Studios film, *King of the Texas Rangers.*

According to the book, *The Pro Football Chronicles,* Baugh played Slinging Tom King, the quarterback of the Texas All-Stars. His father, a sheriff, is killed by outlaws, and Baugh, seeking to avenge his father's death, trades the pigskin for some iron and becomes a lawman to hunt down the killers.

Baugh was afraid that his Hollywood work would make him a target for ribbing from some NFL defenders. "I can see it coming already," he said. "Some big guy is going to knock me down and then give me a hand and say, 'Mr. Barrymore, can I assist you to your feet?' "

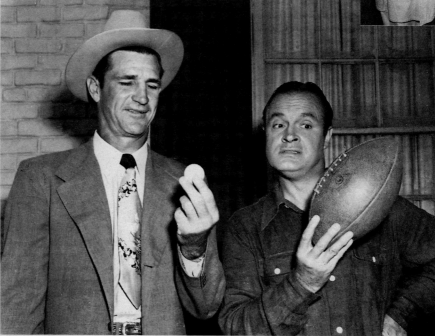

Pro Football Hall of Fame

The Redskins trained on the West Coast for years, most of the time in the Los Angeles area (at Occidental College from 1946–62), and often found themselves a part of the Hollywood scene. Here the squad visits the Nellie Thursday Home for Old Dolls in Hollywood in 1941. At the time, there was no NFL franchise in Los Angeles. (Pro Football Hall of Fame)

(Below): Few coaches would work as well as Ray Flaherty (right) did with George Preston Marshall (left). Marshall was a demanding owner who sought excellence on the field, and Flaherty delivered with two World Championships. (Pro Football Hall of Fame)

chise would regret. The Bears would make sure that no one would forget that championship game, one that would turn out to be history-making, for all the wrong reasons for Redskins fans. Certainly the crowd of more than thirty-six thousand at Griffith Stadium would never forget what they saw.

After the Redskins' regular-season win over the Bears, Marshall declared that Chicago was a team of quitters. "The Bears are a team that folds under pressure against a good team," he said. "They are a team that must win by a big score. Don't ask me why they lose the close games, except that they do. If I were to guess why, it would probably be that there is not too much harmony on that team. Too many stars, and stars are inclined to beef at one another when the going gets tough."

Well, Marshall's comments gave the Bears whatever harmony they needed, and they also took the owner's comments about a big score to heart. Halas used those comments, and an innovative offensive plan known at the T-formation, to embarrass the Redskins in a 73–0 win.

The Bears opened up the game quickly with a touchdown within the first minute on a sixty-eight-yard run by Bill Osmanski, with Jack Manders kicking the point after to stake Chicago to a 7–0 lead.

At the time, there was no indication that the Redskins were in for a historic beating. They nearly came right back with their own score when Max Krause returned the kickoff for Washington fifty-six yards to the Bears' forty-yard line. Several plays later, Baugh would unleash a pass to Charlie Malone that bounced off his chest. It would have surely been a touchdown if caught.

After the game, a reporter asked Baugh what the outcome would have been if Malone had caught that pass. Baugh replied jokingly, "73–7."

The Chicago offense was simply unstoppable. The Bears scored twenty-one points in the first thirteen minutes of the game and carried a 28–0 lead into halftime. Then it really got out of hand.

The 1942 Redskins would be the last to call themselves NFL champions until 1983. Their 10-1 title season was sweetened by the fact that they defeated the Chicago Bears in the championship game, avenging the 1940 title loss to the "Monsters of the Midway." (Pro Football Hall of Fame)

Washington defenders Fred Davis (17), Ray Hare (42), Dick Poillon (25), and Bob Titchenal (18) pursue Cleveland Rams tailback Parker Hall (32) in a 33-14 victory during the 1942 season. Sammy Baugh called this squad perhaps the best Redskins team he had played on. (Pro Football Hall of Fame)

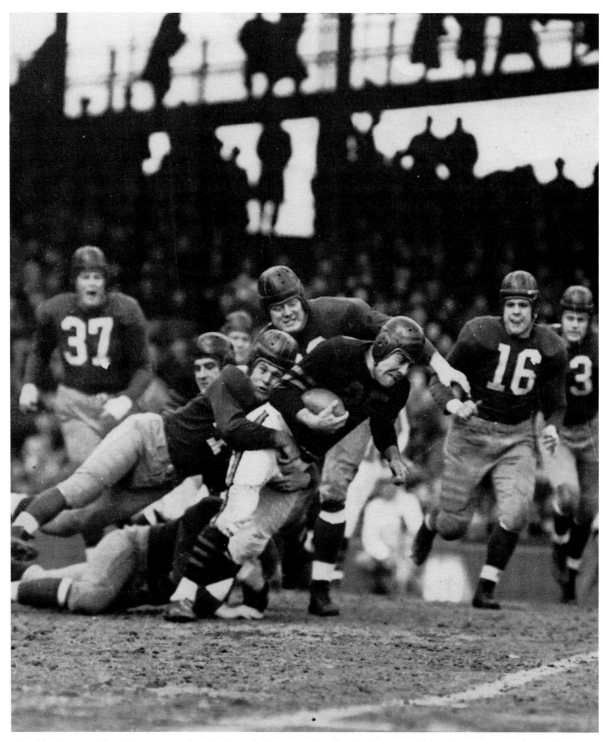

Washington would get its revenge for that humiliating 73-0 beating in the 1940 championship game by outlasting the Bears 14-6 in the 1942 championship tilt. Griffith Stadium could barely contain the 36,000 revenge-seeking fans who attended the game. Here Redskins defensive back Andy Farkas tackles Chicago's Ray Nolling. (Pro Football Hall of Fame)

Gotta Be the Shoes

The 1945 NFL championship game between the Redskins and the Cleveland Rams was like something out of a Nike commercial.

It was a frigid day, with a slick field at Municipal Stadium in Cleveland, and the footing was treacherous. The Redskins planned accordingly and brought sneakers with them to wear. The Rams had no sneakers.

So Cleveland coach Adam Walsh met with Washington coach Doug DeGroot before the game and pleaded with him not to let his players wear the sneakers. "If you use them and we don't, then you get an unfair advantage," Walsh said. "I'd appreciate it if we could play this game on even terms."

DeGroot, in a move that would hardly make George Allan proud, agreed not to let his players use the sneakers,

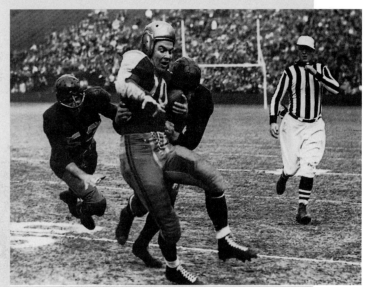

Al DeMao makes a tackle—even without sneakers —in the 1945 championship game. (Washington Redskins)

even after his team, seeing how slippery the field was during warmups, tried to convince him to allow the sneakers.

Redskins owner George Marshall, watching the first half, wondered why his team was not wearing the sneakers and visited the clubhouse at halftime, telling DeGroot to use the sneakers. Center Al DeMao remembers what happened next:

"DeGroot said, 'Mr. Marshall, we made a gentlemen's agreement that we wouldn't use the sneakers,'" DeMao said. "Mr. Marshall hit the ceiling. He said, 'Since when did this game become a gentlemen's game?' We didn't use the sneakers, though, and DeGroot was, in essence, fired right then and there."

Washington went on to lose 15–14.

The Bears intercepted two passes for touchdowns on their way to a 48–0 lead after three quarters and then poured it on in the fourth with the final twenty-five points, the last of eleven touchdowns coming on a one-yard run by Harry Clark after the Chicago defense intercepted a pass from Filchock.

When the final gun sounded, the Redskins had been beaten 73–0 in a game still held up today

as the standard for a one-sided loss. It was so bad that the teams ran out of footballs to use and had to resort to using a practice ball for the final plays of the game.

Marshall's comments had come back to haunt him, although they alone could not account for such a defeat. Still, after the game, the players believed their fate had been sealed before they ever

Ray Flaherty celebrates the Redskins win over the Bears in the 1942 championship game. As it turned out, this was the last Flaherty-coached Washington team. The next year he joined the armed forces and never returned to the Redskins. (Pro Football Hall of Fame)

took the field.

"There was a lot of stuff in the newspapers that Mr. Marshall had put in there about the Bears," Baugh said. "I think any team would have beaten us that day. The team was mad at Mr. Marshall, because he said some awful things about the Bears."

The Redskins would return in the 1941 season for their worst year under Flaherty, putting together a record of 6–5. They played strong after an opening-season loss at home to the Giants, 17–10. Washington then ran off five straight victories, and halfway through the year the Redskins led the Eastern Division with a 5–1 record.

But the team was hurt by a series of injuries. Backs Wilbur Moore and Dick Todd missed play-

ing time, and Washington dropped four in a row. They managed to save a winning season by stopping the Eagles 20–14 on the last game of the season at Griffith Stadium, but the win was dwarfed by the tragic events of the day—December 7—and the memories of the stadium that day are of military and government officials leaving as word came in about the Japanese attack on Pearl Harbor.

The following season the Redskins would bounce back with perhaps their best team yet, though it got off to a shaky start. After a home-opening 28–14 win over Pittsburgh, the Redskins would drop the next game at Griffith Stadium, 14–7, to the New York Giants. But it would turn out to be their only loss of the season.

Washington started its regular-season nine-game winning streak with a 14–10 win over the Eagles in Philadelphia, and it culminated with a 15–3 victory in Detroit over the Lions. Over eleven games, the Redskins offense scored a total of 227 points and held the opposition to just 102 points, with two shutouts, allowing just thirteen points over the final four games of the year.

The 1942 championship game would be a rematch of the 1940 contest, with the Redskins facing the Bears again. And it matched up as one of the best in recent memory—Chicago had an even better record than Washington, going 11–0 and scoring a remarkable 376 points, with an offense again led by quarterback Sid Luckman. The Bears managed this with their leader, George Halas, gone from the sidelines, serving in the U.S. Navy.

More than thirty-six thousand people would come to Griffith Stadium on December 13 for that championship contest. And although the NFL had been broadcasting championship games on radio on a limited basis for several years, this one, with Russ Hodges and Harry Wismer at the microphone, went out to a record 178 stations.

Baugh was the key figure for the Redskins this day, as they upset the powerful Bears 14–6. But it wasn't his passing that proved to be the difference. It was Baugh's kicking ability. The Bears took an early 6–0 lead, as running back Dick Todd fum-

One of Ray Flaherty's key players was Hall of Fame tackle Turk Edwards, on the right here talking to Flaherty. After eight years with the Redskins, Edwards joined the 'Skins coaching staff in 1943. (Pro Football Hall of Fame)

The core of the success of the early Redskins, on the field and in the front office, from left to right: running back Dick Todd, quarterback Sammy Baugh, Redskins owner George Preston Marshall, and coach Ray Flaherty. (Pro Football Hall of Fame)

bled the ball and Chicago tackle Lee Artoe picked it up and ran it in for a fifty-yard touchdown.

Near the end of the first quarter, down deep in his own territory, Baugh surprised the Bears defense with a quick kick that wound up going eighty-five yards, burying Chicago near its own end zone.

"That turned out to be a big play," Baugh said. "When I quick-kicked, I had the wind to my back, and that's why I did it. If the quarter had run out and we had to punt, we would have had to do it against the wind."

After Wilbur Moore intercepted a Luckman

Sports of the TIMES

Washington's defeat of the Chicago Bears in the NFL championship game in 1942 was perhaps the sweetest win in the early days of the game. The Redskins were more than three-touchdown underdogs against the powerful Bears, but they shocked the sports world on December 13 with a 14–6 victory.

New York Times columnist Arthur Daley captured the essence of the day in his column the following day:

"By way of supplying a final madhouse touch to a football season that was noted for its lunacies and upsets, the Redskins soundly trounced the supposedly invincible Bears before an incredulous and deliriously happy gathering of 36,036 spectators in Griffith Stadium today to win the world professional championship.

"This was a team that was so much an underdog that the gamblers stopped giving 7–1 odds and handed out as much as 22 points. This also was largely the team that had been beaten 73–0 in the playoff two years ago. Yet it cracked into the mighty Bears with disregard of the Chicagoans' reputation and handled them as easily as if the Monsters were only P.S. 9."

pass, Baugh connected with Moore for a touchdown, and the point after gave the Redskins a 7–6 lead. Later, in the third quarter, Washington scored again on a one-yard run by Andy Farkas to extend the Redskins lead to 14–6. Washington held on to win its second NFL championship and also to gain some measure of revenge on the team that had embarrassed them in the title game two years before.

However, the win marked the end of an era, as Flaherty left the team to join the Navy in the war effort. Nor would he return after his service time, as he opted to coach the New York Yankees in the All-America Conference. Baugh would miss Flaherty. "He was one of the better coaches I ever played for," Baugh said. "Everybody respected him as a coach."

Replacing Flaherty for the 1943 season was Arthur "Dutch" Bergman, a former coach at Catholic University who had been a scout for Washington in 1942. The team did not seem to miss a beat, at least in the first part of the season.

They started with an opening-day 27–0 shutout of Brooklyn at Griffith Stadium and won their next three before winding up in a 14–14 tie with the combination Philadelphia-Pittsburgh Steagles franchise. Washington won its next two, running up an undefeated record of 6–0–1 before losing the final three games of the regular season. The first loss came to the Philadelphia-Pittsburgh combo, 27–14. Then, in a quirk of the schedule, the Redskins would play their rivals, the Giants, twice in a row, losing the first game 14–10 at the Polo Grounds and getting beat badly in the second game at home 31–7. That loss left the Redskins and Giants tied at 6–3–1 for the Eastern title, setting up a third straight meeting between Washington and New York, this one a playoff game for the division crown.

This game, played in New York before a crowd of forty-three thousand, would have a totally different outcome, thanks to the franchise and Sammy Baugh. He completed sixteen of twenty-one passes for 199 yards and led the Redskins to a

28–0 victory, sending them into the championship game against the Chicago Bears for the third time in four years, with the passing wizards, Baugh and Luckman, dueling it out in the Windy City.

But that duel never materialized. Baugh missed most of the game after he was kicked in head trying to make a tackle. His loss was too much to overcome, and Chicago went on to a 41–21 win for the NFL title.

Having the use of Baugh for the entire game might have made the difference for Washington. He had completed perhaps his finest season, lead-ing the league in passing, with twenty-three touch-downs and 1,754 yards; in interceptions, playing defense, with eleven, which he returned for 112 yards; and in punting, with a 45.9-yard average.

But in the limited time he played in the 1943 title game, he threw just twelve times, completing eight, for 123 yards and two touchdowns. Luckman completed fifteen of twenty-six for 286 yards and a record-setting five touchdowns.

Despite the successful season, Bergman opted not to come back to coaching, instead taking a job in broadcasting, and Marshall hired his second

Under former Catholic University coach Arthur "Dutch" Bergman, the 1943 Redskins managed to return to the cham-pionship game, thanks to Sammy Baugh's near spotless performance against New York in the playoffs. Baugh com-pleted 16 of 21 passes for 199 yards to lead the Redskins to a 28-0 win. Here Baugh and his teammates rock the locker room following the game. (Pro Football Hall of Fame)

Two significant changes occurred in 1944: the arrival of a new head coach, former Rochester University head man Doug DeGroot; and the installation of the T-formation offense. The first year under DeGroot was bumpy as the team struggled to learn the new offense. The next season, however, the offense hummed and the defense, which held opponents to 121 points, hissed. (Pro Football Hall of Fame)

coach in two seasons, Doug DeGroot, head coach at Rochester University.

Another key change also took place—the installation of the T-formation into the Redskins offense. The man who refined it in Chicago, Clark Shaughnessy, was now coaching at the University of Maryland. Baugh was unable to spend much time practicing that season, because he was forced to spend more time as a cattle rancher during the season because of the demands for beef during the war. But Filchock worked with Shaughnessy on the

T-formation for much of that season and wound up getting more playing time. He even led the NFL in passing with 1,138 yards and thirteen touchdowns.

But the new system had its share of kinks to work out, and Washington, after yet another strong start—winning five straight after an opening-season 31–31 tie with the Eagles in Philadelphia—lost three of its last four games, including the final two to the Giants, for a record of 6–3–1—not good enough for championship play.

(*Above*): Coach Doug DeGroot and his Redskins squad celebrate in the locker room after their impressive 17-0 victory over the New York Giants at Griffith Stadium, sending Washington to the 1945 NFL championship game. (Washington Redskins)

(*Left*): Wayne Millner and rookie Al DeMao helped DeGroot guide the Redskins to the league championship game, where they lost 15-14 to the Cleveland Rams. (Pro Football Hall of Fame)

The 1945 championship game was the Redskins' last until 1972. (Pro Football Hall of Fame)

The 1945 championship game in Cleveland was played on a Municipal Stadium field that was frozen and slick, making the footing abysmal. The Redskins brought sneakers to wear; the Rams didn't. Foxy Cleveland coach Adam Walsh, though, persuaded DeGroot to shun the sneakers, a decision many believe cost the Redskins the game –and DeGroot his job, which according to some players was yanked from DeGroot at halftime when Marshall learned of his coach's fatal promise. (Pro Football Hall of Fame)

Conditions at Municipal Stadium were so dreadful that officials covered the playing surface with hay; Redskin players used, mostly in vain, that hay and blankets to stay warm in the frigid weather. Footing was tough for ball carriers and tacklers alike (*Top*); Washington's Ki Aldrich (55) slips and slides to stop Cleveland's Jim Gillete (*Above, left*); Redskins halfback Steve Bagarus skates for a second quarter score after catching a 38-yard toss from quarterback Frank Filchock. (*Above, right*). (Pro Football Hall of Fame)

The Redskins suffered many heartbreak plays against the Rams. But the most wrenching was a 31-yard field goal attempt by Joe Aquirre in the fourth quarter. The kick had the distance, but the strong wind off Lake Erie blew the ball away from the goal post, and with it the Redskins' chances for a championship. (Pro Football Hall of Fame)

Baugh came back in 1945 to master the new system, and he credits it with prolonging his career. "It probably added five years to my career," he said.

He wound up setting an NFL record by completing 70.3 percent of his passes. And he had some strong offensive support, like Frank Akins, who gained 797 yards rushing that season, the most since Cliff Battles rushed for 897 eight years before.

Washington opened the 1945 season with a 28–20 loss to the Boston Yankees, who had joined the league the year before, as Marshall had to suffer the indignation of having his team lose in the town that had ignored him during the first five years of the franchise. But little else went wrong

for Marshall and his team for the rest of the regular season.

The team was strengthened by the return of a number of players who had been out during wartime, such as end Wayne Millner, halfbacks Dick Todd and Cecil Hare, and linemen Al DeMao and Fred Davis. They went on a six-game winning streak, starting off with a 14–0 shutout of the Steelers on October 14, and didn't lose again until November 25, when the Eagles stopped them 16–0. Washington won its final two games of the year, holding the opposition scoreless—24–0 over Pittsburgh and 17–0 over New York—for a record of 8–2 and another shot at an NFL championship, but his time it wouldn't be played against the

Bears. The Redskins opponents would be the Cleveland Rams, who put together a record of 9–1, led by another future Hall of Fame player, rookie quarterback Bob Waterfield.

It was a brutally cold day in Cleveland on December 16, 1945, and the field at Municipal Stadium was frozen and slick, and the footing was poor. The Redskins brought sneakers with them. The Rams didn't have any sneakers. On a day like this, with temperatures barely above zero as the wind blew off Lake Erie, it would seem simple enough: The team with the sneakers would have a good chance of winning.

But in one of the more bizarre chapters of

Redskins history, DeGroot listened to the pleas of Rams coach Adam Walsh, who asked that Washington players not use their sneakers. The Redskins coach complied, even after his players insisted they needed the sneakers because of the slick footing.

"From twenty yards into the end zone it was frozen like a sheet of ice," Al DeMao said.

The decision by DeGroot was a sign of the bad things to come. A crossbar would also prove to stand in the way of a Washington championship.

In the first quarter, Baugh went back to pass in his own end zone to Millner, who was wide open on the play. But when Baugh threw the ball,

A spate of changes following the 1945 season inaugurated a downward spiral that took years to reverse. The most significant: DeGroot's dismissal, end Wayne Millner's retirement, and the trade of quarterback Frank Filchock to the New York Giants. (Pro Football Hall of Fame)

it hit the crossbar on the goalpost and then hit the ground. At the time, league rules dictated that it be ruled a safety, and so what might have been a touchdown and a Washington lead turned out to give the Rams a 2–0 lead.

Then the worst happened. Baugh hurt his ribs and would not throw another pass in the game.

Filchock took over the offense, and after Ki Aldrich intercepted a Waterfield pass, Filchock completed a thirty-eight-yard scoring pass to Steve Bagarus, staking Washington to a 7–2 lead. Waterfield answered back with a touchdown pass to Jim Benton, and again the crossbar would be the Redskins' enemy. When Waterfield kicked the extra point, the ball teetered on the goalpost bar, looking as if it could fall back or go over. It went over for the extra point, which would prove to be a crucial point.

"It was the battle of the crossbars," DeMao said. "It was very frustrating."

In the third quarter, both Waterfield and Filchock connected on scoring passes, and Cleveland took a 15–14 lead going into the fourth

quarter. With time ticking away, the Redskins had one shot left, a field goal attempt by Joe Aguirre from the thirty-one-yard line. But with Baugh holding, the kick missed, and Cleveland came away with a win and an NFL title.

It would be DeGroot's last game as a Redskins coach, as Marshall fired him—some believe at halftime—for his decision not to use sneakers. Marshall would make another change, lobbying the league to change the safety rules. "It was the first time we've ever been licked by a goalpost," Marshall said.

But the biggest change would come in the success—or lack of it—of the Washington Redskins franchise, because for the Redskins, after riding a wave of glory from the time they moved to Washington in 1937, with two NFL championships and five trips to the title game—the good times on the field were about to end. The team would suffer a run of frustration that would last nearly twenty-five years. But that doesn't mean there weren't some spectacular moments and interesting times along the way.

Three

The Long, Lean Years

There was no reason to believe the good times that had accompanied the Redskins in their first nine years in Washington would not continue. Sammy Baugh was still leading the team, and though Doug DeGroot had been fired, Marshall believed he was putting the team into capable hands when he named as head coach legendary Redskins defensive tackle Turk Edwards, who had become an assistant coach after retiring in 1940 after eight illustrious years anchoring the Redskins defense. The players were familiar with Edwards and respected him, as did Marshall.

But Edwards was unable to make the transition to head coach, and, after three seasons and a record of 16–18–1, Marshall, not wanting to dismiss one of the mainstays of the franchise in its early days, moved Edwards into the front office before the start of the 1949 season.

"Turk was a hell of a football player and a good line coach," Al DeMao said. "But he never did make a good head coach."

In fact, Marshall would spend the rest of his life trying to find the right head coach who could win and coexist with the demanding owner. After the 1945 title game, the Redskins would go through nine head coaches, amassing a total record of 85–126–2 before they hired a coach who put them back on to the right track—Vince Lombardi. It was in 1969—the same year that Marshall passed away.

Edwards did have to deal with some tough personnel changes before the 1946 season began. Wayne Millner, a future Hall of Fame receiver, retired, and quarterback Frank Filchock was traded to the New York Giants and would later come back to haunt his old team. And the 1946 team had a number of injuries to key players like Steve Bagarus and Wilbur Moore.

The Cleveland Rams—Washington's nemesis in the 1945 title game—moved to Los Angeles in the off-season. The Redskins had been training on the West Coast since 1939, most recently in California, and they set up a charity game against the Rams, sponsored by the *Los Angeles Times.* The first such game, played in the preseason of 1946 at Memorial Coliseum, netted $96,711 for the *Times* Boys Club. The Redskins would lose 14–6.

The season began with a 14–14 tie against the Steelers at Griffith Stadium. Then Edwards' team would win their next three games, including a 24–14 win over the New York Giants at home. The rest of the season would be up and down, as they finished with two straight losses for a record of 5–5–1.

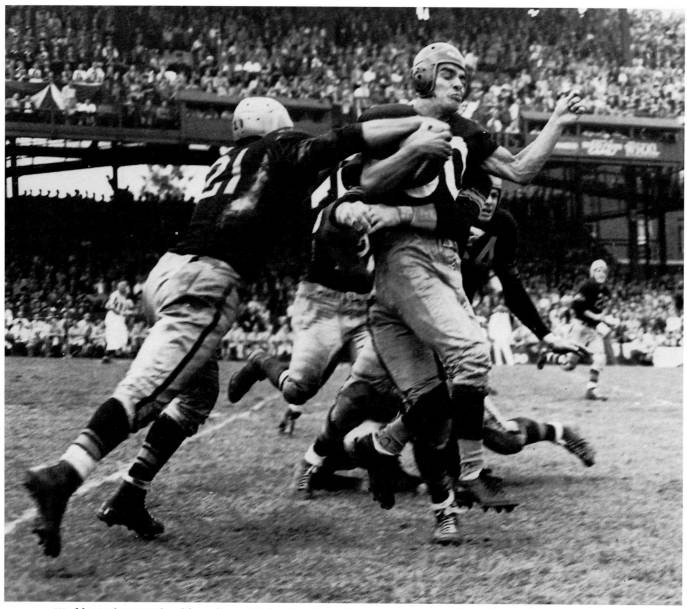

Washington's 14-14 tie with mediocre Pittsburgh in the 1946 opener was a foreshadowing. Under new coach Turk Edwards, the Redskins skidded to 5-5-1 and began a slide that would last for nearly three decades. (Pro Football Hall of Fame)

The final game of the year was against the Giants in New York, and Washington still had a shot at the Eastern Division crown going into that last game. But not even the usual parade of Redskin fans going to New York and the Redskins Marching Band could overcome the revenge sought by a former teammate, as Filchock led the Giants to a 31–0 win.

The following year would be even worse, even though Marshall made a number of changes, adding thirteen rookies to the roster, including an end named Hugh Taylor, who would go on to be the Redskins' star receiver over the next eight seasons. He would catch 272 passes for 5,233 yards and fifty-eight touchdowns for Washington, and Baugh called him "the best receiver I ever saw."

In his debut in the first game of the season, Taylor, nicknamed "Bones" because of his tall, thin frame, caught three touchdowns from Baugh, but Washington lost to Philadelphia 45–42.

"Hugh Taylor had a long stride," teammate Al DeMao said. "After he caught the ball, you could see him open up and spread the distance between him and the defender, running away from them."

Too often in 1947, though, the distance between Redskin defenders and the other team was too great, as the defense fell apart, and the Redskins posted their worst record since moving to Washington, going 4–8, giving up an average of thirty-one points per game.

At the same time, with Baugh and Taylor leading the offense, they scored 295 points over twelve games, and there were a number of memorable moments in Redskin history that season.

One came in the second game of the year, on October 5 against Pittsburgh at Griffith Stadium.

The largest crowd to see a Redskins game yet—36,565—would see a game in which for once, the goalpost would work in favor of Washington.

Pittsburgh opened the scoring first with a field goal, taking the ball down the field after the opening kickoff. But the Redskins came back on the first play of the second quarter when Baugh tossed a fifty-four-yard touchdown pass to Bob Nussbaumer. Pittsburgh recovered a fumble in the second quarter and scored on an eight-yard touchdown pass from Johnny Clement to Steve Lach, and the Steelers took a 10–7 lead into halftime.

Washington got off to a quick start in the third quarter when Dick Todd returned the kickoff fifty yards to the Pittsburgh forty-three yard line.

Two of the premiere passers in the history of the NFL: Washington's Sammy Baugh (right) and the New York Giants' Charlie Conerly. During Conerly's championship seasons in New York, Redskins' fans could only wonder, what if? Conerly had been drafted by Washington in 1945 but decided to return to school. He still signed with the Redskins—in 1948—but by then the Washington brass believed Harry Gilmer was the better prospect; Conerly was dealt to the Giants. (Pro Football Hall of Fame)

Car Trouble

No player captured the hearts of Redskins fans more than Sammy Baugh in the early days of the franchise, and fans showed their appreciation by presenting Baugh with a new car on November 23, 1947, designated as Sammy Baugh Day at Griffith Stadium.

Baugh liked the car so much that that same night, he used it to drive his sister and brother-in-law to Philadelphia. The return trip would prove to be an eventful one.

"My sister and brother-in-law had come to Washington for the day, and I drove them back to Philadelphia that night," Baugh said. "On the way up there, I remembered I was supposed to go to some school back in Washington the next morning. I had been intending to spend the night up in Philadelphia and then come back. But I had this appearance the next morning, so I told them I couldn't stay the night. I turned around and drove back to Washington.

"At that time of night there were hardly any cars on the highway," Baugh said. "I saw the car before it ever got to me. It was coming across the middle of the road too much, I thought. I slowed down a bit, and I thought he would straighten out. But he kept coming toward me.

"I moved over to the right a little bit, but he kept coming toward me, so I had to do something," Baugh said. "I went on the gravel. I thought he was going to hit me head-on. When I hit that gravel, I slid right into a concrete bridge. That guy didn't stop. He just kept going. It destroyed one side of the car."

Baugh was not hurt seriously, though, just "shaken up a bit" and somewhat embarrassed about losing his new car the day after he got it. Like the pro that he was, though, he made his appearance that Monday morning, to crown the queen at a high school homecoming in Virginia.

In 1947, Redskins fans showed their appreciation for Sammy Baugh by presenting him with a new car on Sammy Baugh Day at Griffith Stadium. Teammates vowed to give the quarterback the protection he needed to win that day; they were true to their word: Baugh threw six touchdown passes to defeat the defending league champion Cardinals 45-21. Baugh could have used that protection the next day, when he wrecked the car. Fortunately, he was not injured. (Pro Football Hall of Fame)

Redskins fans have shown consistent loyalty, following their team through good times and bad. These welcome-home luncheons have been a regular tradition for years. (Sid Alpert)

Baugh moved the team down the field and hit Dick Poillon on a short pass for a score. Poillon, who had a streak of thirty straight extra points, missed this point after, and the Redskins took a 13–10 lead.

But the Steelers went back ahead after Baugh was intercepted by Bob Compagno, who ran the ball back sixty-four yards, putting Pittsburgh ahead 17–13. But Baugh bounced back with a thirty-five-yard scoring pass to Taylor, and now it was Washington leading 20–17.

What happens next? Clement hits Bob Sullivan, who gallops fifty yards, putting Pittsburgh back on top 24–20. The Steelers would add two more when, after failing to score on the Redskins just outside the goal line, they turned the ball over to Washington, and Baugh went back into the end zone to apparently punt. But instead of kicking, Baugh tried to pass the ball, and he stepped on the back line of the end zone for a safety.

The Steelers led 26–20 and appeared to be on the verge of making it a 29–20 game, but they missed a forty-yard field goal attempt. With less than ten minutes left in the game, Baugh started a drive from the Redskins' twenty-yard line down to the Pittsburgh goal line, the key play coming on fourth down with eight yards to go on the nine-yard line, when Baugh completed a pass to Sal Rosato on the goal line. Fullback Tom Farmer punched it over for the touchdown, and Poillon connected on this point after to give Washington a 27–26 lead. Redskin fans held their breath as Pittsburgh, with about thirty seconds remaining, tried a field goal from the Washington twenty-three-yard line. As the ball went up it looked as if it might be the winning score, but it hit the left upright and fell down to the field. The Redskins were victorious.

There were not many glorious moments in

Hugh "Bones" Taylor came to the Washington Redskins from Oklahoma City in 1947 and developed into one of Sammy Baugh's favorite targets. He retired in 1954 after two trips to the Pro Bowl and 15 100-yard receiving games over his career, including 212 yards against the Philadelphia Eagles in his rookie year. (Pro Football Hall of Fame)

that 1947 season, but another one came on November 23, at home. It was the day of days for Redskin fans. It was Sammy Baugh Day.

Washington fans paid tribute to their hero by presenting him with a brand new maroon station wagon, with the words, "Slinging Sam—the Redskin Man" on it.

"I think you're the greatest bunch of fans any player ever had the opportunity to play for," Baugh said. "I thank you."

Facing the favored Chicago Cardinals, Baugh returned the gesture by having his greatest day in a Redskin uniform, at least statistically, completing twenty-five of thirty-three passes for 355 yards and six touchdowns, tying the club record for touchdowns in a game that he set against Brooklyn in 1943, as Washington won 45–21.

It was a remarkable win, because Washington's record was 2–6 going into the game, whereas the Cardinals were 7–1, with the NFL's top defense in total yards and passing.

Before the game, Baugh's teammates met and vowed that they would do all they could to keep their quarterback from being sacked that day. "They got together and decided that on that day, I wasn't going to get my pants dirty," Baugh said. "They weren't going to let me get knocked around. That was the easiest game I ever had.

"We weren't supposed to beat them, but we did," Baugh said. "I was proud of them."

Not all days were like that one. Baugh took a lot of punishment as the team struggled, often trying to bring them back from a large deficit.

Though the Redskins would have a poor season that year, it was Baugh's best by the numbers: twenty-five touchdowns, 210 completions on 354 attempts for 2,938 yards.

The youngsters started playing better the following season, and Washington put together a winning record again, going 7–5 in 1948. But it was a blip on the screen of futility that would dominate the franchise for years to come, and a personnel decision made before the season began would be one of many that would prove costly.

The Redskins would select highly touted Alabama quarterback Harry Gilmer in the draft that year. But a 1945 selection they made also joined the team that year. Charlie Conerly had been fighting in the war when his class graduated

Sammy Baugh was joined in 1950 by another future Hall of Famer, running back Bill Dudley (number 35). Dudley's career was winding down by this point, but he nonetheless became a fan favorite in the three seasons he played for the Redskins. He was inducted into the Pro Football Hall of Fame in 1966. (Washington Redskins)

Heads of State, movie stars, war heroes, and other public figures regularly attend Redskins games. General Dwight D. Eisenhower visited in 1945. (Nate Fine)

Redskins Marching Band

George Preston Marshall was a showman as well as a pioneer in the game, and he was ahead of his time in his efforts to bring entertainment other than the game itself to sports fans.

Perhaps the best symbol of his work was the Redskins Marching Band, which started in 1937 and evolved into a tradition that still exists and entertains fans today.

Marshall used a number of promotions to keep fans happy, making halftime into a festive event, including the annual arrival of Santa Claus at halftime in the last home game of the season. Everything from circus animals to the National Symphony Orchestra sometimes would be on hand for Redskins halftime shows.

In fact, Marshall was noted for directing the content of his halftime shows, including song selection, with as much fervor as when he offered his suggestions to coaches.

The highlight in the history of the band took place on June 13, 1947, when it performed at the *Philadelphia Inquirer*'s prestigious Festival of Music alongside Whiteman, Waring, and the Philharmonic.

The Redskins Marching Band best exemplified Marshall's showmanship. The band is one of the league's foremost, in operation in one form or another since 1937. Its popularity has been so immense that in 1947 the band performed at the Philadelphia *Inquirer*'s prestigious Festival of Music. (Nate Fine)

Halftime shows were always special at Redskins games, because owner George Preston Marshall put a premium on entertaining the fans. Sometimes it was a bear walking a tightrope, others it was performing elephants. And in December Santa Claus would visit, often in different vehicles from year to year. Here he comes in a spaceship. (Abbie Rowe)

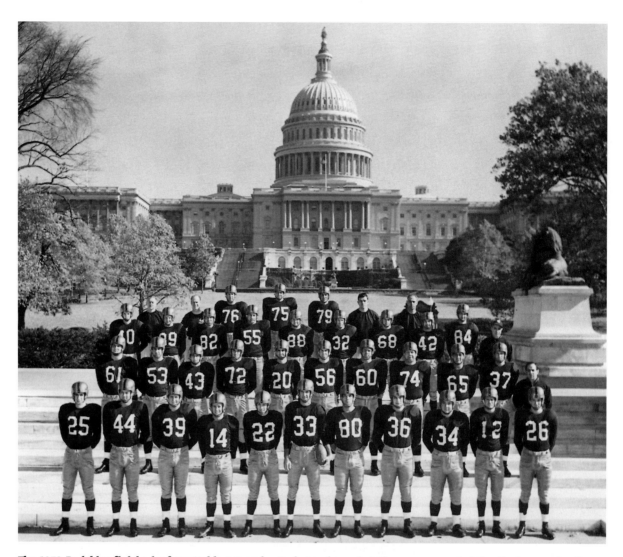

The 1952 Redskins finished a forgettable 4-8 under Curly Lambeau, but the season marked the final campaign for the unforgettable number 33, Sammy Baugh. (Pro Football Hall of Fame)

Not even a legend like ex-Green Bay Packers head coach Curly Lambeau could reverse the fortunes of the Redskins during the fifties. Lambeau posted a 10-13-1 record over two seasons. (Pro Football Hall of Fame)

in 1945, and Washington picked him. He went back and graduated in 1947 and was ready to play for Washington in 1948. But the Redskins believed that Gilmer was the better prospect and traded Conerly to the New York Giants. He would go on to throw 173 touchdowns for the Giants and help them become the "Beasts of the East" in the 1950s, winning an NFL championship.

Gilmer never developed into the quarterback that Marshall believed he would, hurting his leg during his rookie season. And in 1948 there were just six players left from the team that came within one point of winning an NFL title three years earlier.

In Marshall's view, Edwards never became the coach he had hoped for, and, despite the winning season, Marshall moved Edwards into the front office. Marshall nearly hired Paul "Bear" Bryant, the head coach at the University of Kentucky, whom Marshall had met while Bryant had been on the coaching staff at the University of Maryland. But Kentucky did not want to let Bryant go, and Marshall opted instead for someone he believed would bring a measure of discipline that he felt was needed on the team—John Whelchel, a retired admiral who had coached at the U.S. Naval Academy in nearby Annapolis.

"Marshall was always looking for a big name, so he got Admiral Whelchel out of the Navy," Al DeMao said. "But the admiral had been out of football for a while, and the game had changed a lot."

Whelchel's style, though, turned out to clash with that of the forceful Marshall, and he wound up with the shortest tenure of any head coach in Redskins history, lasting just seven games and posting a 3–3–1 record. Strangely enough, he was fired after a 27–14 win at home against Pittsburgh. Then again, when it came to coaches, there were no rules for Marshall. He believed that he had every right to be involved in football decisions on and off the field, and new coaches were faced with the challenge of trying to work with Marshall. "Mr. Marshall was awfully tough on coaches," Baugh said.

Next came Herman Ball, a longtime assistant coach and scout. He won just one game the rest of the season, as Washington finished the year with a record of 4–7–1.

Ball stayed on for the 1950 season and was

Sammy Baugh spent his last season with the team as a player-coach after three or four tentative retirements before that. Often overlooked was Baugh's tremendous ability as a defensive player as well. He once led the league in interceptions as a defensive back. (Pro Football Hall of Fame)

greeted with what appeared to be a solid draft, bringing in running back Charlie "Choo Choo" Justice, center Harry Ulinski, and linebacker Chuck Drazenovich. Marshall also obtained Bill Dudley in a trade with Detroit, but the future Hall of Famer was at the end of his career at the time of the transaction.

Also drafted was a future Redskins star, diminutive quarterback Eddie LeBaron, the five-foot-seven passer from the College of the Pacific. He was seen as the successor to Baugh, who was thirty-five at the time and ready to step down. But LeBaron was called to service in the Korean War and wound up as a decorated war hero in the

Sammy Baugh, being treated for an injury on the field, played 16 seasons, often through pain. He handed the reins over to quarterback Eddie LeBaron (14), who joined the Redskins in Baugh's final season in 1952. (*Lower right*): Baugh, in street clothes on the bench, remains one of the team's—and league's—most popular and luminous figures. (Pro Football Hall of Fame)

Marines, wounded in action. He would not be in a Redskins uniform for two more years.

LeBaron was a good candidate for war hero, because he was a player whose heart was often far bigger than the big men he played against. In Korea he was injured when a mortar shell exploded, and he would up getting a Bronze Star and two Purple Hearts. And on the football field he would often surprise opposing coaches and players with his ability and toughness.

The 1950 season was worse than the previous one, as the Redskins dropped to a record of 3–9, winning just one home game, 38–28 over the Baltimore Colts, one of three teams absorbed into the NFL after the upstart AAFC league folded. The NFL was reorganized into American and National Conferences, rather than East and West divisions.

Despite his record, Ball returned for the 1951 season but wouldn't finish it. After Washington opened up with three straight losses—35–17 to the Lions, 35–14 to the Giants, and a 45–0 beating by the powerful Cleveland Browns—Marshall fired Ball and replaced him with former running back Dick Todd, who turned the team around, posting a 5–4 record and winning his first two games, 7–3 over the Cardinals and 27–23 over the Eagles. But

Marshall Law

Before the season began in 1952, the Redskins showed some signs of the union movement in professional sports in a confrontation with Redskins owner George Preston Marshall. They would not be very successful.

Center Al DeMao recalls the time when the team challenged Marshall on adding an exhibition game to their preseason schedule.

"At the time, we didn't get paid extra for exhibition games," DeMao said. "We knew going out to training camp that we had six exhibition games. But they put in an extra game on us when we got to training camp, which made seven games that we didn't get paid for.

"So one day after lunch we had a players meeting, and everyone decided since the Chicago Bears and the Detroit Lions were getting fifty dollars an exhibition game, we wanted it, too," DeMao said. "So the team nominated Sammy Baugh, Bill Dudley, and myself to see Mr. Marshall about it.

"Sam was the spokesman, and he said we were there to talk to him [Marshall] as a committee," DeMao said. "That was all he got out of his mouth. Mr. Marshall hit the ceiling, saying that he didn't recognize any organizations or unions. He walked out of the back room of his office. Dick McCann was the general manager at the time, and he brought Mr. Marshall back in. Sam then asked for any kind of money. The players said come back with something, even ten dollars. We were agreeable to anything we could get out of them. But Mr. Marshall said no, and as a matter of fact the Bears and Lions aren't getting any money, either. He said he was going to meet with all the players before the afternoon practice.

"He got us all in a circle and told everyone the same thing he had told us in the meeting," DeMao said. "He pointed to the gate and said, 'If you don't like it, there's the gate. Feel free to go.' I don't know what he would have done if we didn't go out to practice. But no one made a move, so we got on with practice and back to where we were."

Marshall wanted the glory days back, and, after two exhibition game losses at the start of the 1952 season, he fired Todd and went for one of the biggest names in the history of the league, a coaching legend—former Green Bay Packers head coach Curly Lambeau. It would not be the last time the Redskins would look to a Packers legend for help.

Lambeau was the founding father of the great Packers franchise, going back to 1919, also playing halfback for the team. He was with the franchise for twenty-nine years, winning six NFL championships, and was one of the inaugural inductees into the Pro Football Hall of Fame when it opened in 1963.

He was every bit Marshall's match in terms of confidence and arrogance, and it was a marriage doomed to fail. Marshall hired Lambeau, who had left the Green Bay franchise in a financial dispute and later coached the Chicago Cardinals, after firing Todd in the 1952 exhibition season.

The results were mixed. Washington went 4–8 under Lambeau in his first season, but that was a difficult year—it was Baugh's last season, and the reins of the club were handed over to LeBaron.

Lambeau led the Redskins to a winning season in 1953, with a record of 6–5–1. But he ran into some problems with the players, particularly LeBaron, because the coach never truly believed that the small quarterback could consistently lead his offense. Then again, according to some players, Lambeau didn't care that much about offense.

"He was a defensive coach and hardly gave any time for offensive practice," said Al DeMao, who played both center and linebacker.

He cared enough to scare LeBaron off, though, as the quarterback went to play in the

Charley "Choo Choo" Justice was a highly-touted running back out of North Carolina in 1950, but he held out his rookie year and did not play until the sixth game of the season. He wound up playing four years for the Redskins, leaving after the 1954 season. (Pro Football Hall of Fame)

Canadian Football League for Calgary.

What was ironic was that if LeBaron had stayed around, Lambeau would not have been his coach. He was fired in the preseason after getting into a shoving match in a Sacramento hotel with Marshall. Marshall had seen several players walking though the hotel carrying beer, and he had a strict rule against players drinking beer in the team locker room or the hotel. Lambeau was with Marshall when the players walked by, and the owner and coach got into a loud argument that broke down into a shoving match.

That was the end of Lambeau's tenure, though his departure may have been helped along by the fact that Marshall was not too pleased about the team losing two straight exhibition games. Another coach would follow.

But before Lambeau left he would have the privilege of being the last Redskins coach to have Sammy Baugh on the roster.

Baugh, thirty-eight, was a player-coach in the 1952 season, his final year. He started the season with a 23–7 win over the Cardinals, but the transition to LeBaron would take place during the season. In the final game of the year, a 27–21 win over Philadelphia at Griffith Stadium, Baugh played for several minutes and received a huge ovation from the hometown crowd of about twenty-two thousand, thanking him for the sixteen years of guts and glory he delivered to them.

Marshall retired Baugh's number, 33, and the legacy of his career numbers include two NFL championships, 186 touchdown passes, 2,995 attempts, 1,693 completions, 21,886 yards, and a punting average of more than forty-five yards. He would be one of seventeen charter members of the

Before the days of jet travel, teams would travel by train. The 1947 Redskins get ready to board "The Columbian" for an away game. (Van Kan)

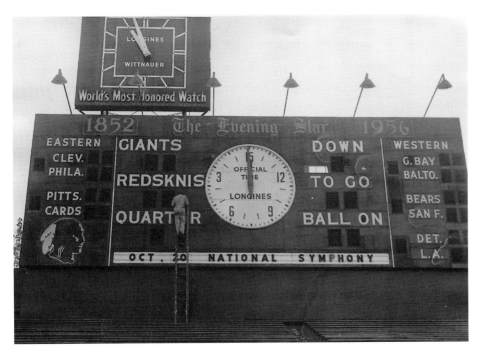

The scoreboard, in need of correction (note the misspelling of "Redskins"), reflects how the team had become an integral part of the nation's capital, with the National Symphony scheduled to perform at a Redskins game. (Pro Football Hall of Fame)

Hall of Fame, inducted in the same year as Lambeau.

The next chosen one to try to turn around the franchise was line coach Joe Kuharich, who would, at least, have the longest tenure since Ray Flaherty. His first-year record was 3–9 in 1954, but that can't be considered as a measure of his success. He took over a team that he did not put together during the preseason.

During the off-season, Kuharich would make the moves to build his team. He talked LeBaron and defensive end Gene Brito, who also left in 1954 to play in Canada, into coming back. He obtained tackle J.D. Kimmel from San Francisco and linebacker Lavern Torgeson from Detroit. Torgeson was a former Pro Bowler who would go on to become a longtime defensive coach in the NFL, with three stints with the Redskins, including defensive line coach for the three Super Bowl Champion squads from 1982 through 1991.

Kuharich's handiwork was on display in the *Times* Charity Game between the Redskins and the Los Angeles Rams during the 1955 preseason. With more than seventy-seven thousand fans filling the coliseum, Washington upset Los Angeles 31–28. And the team showed that that was no fluke when it won 27–17 in the season opener against the defending champion Cleveland Browns on the road.

Washington would go on to put together a record of 7–3 with two games remaining, just a half game behind the conference-leading Browns. But the Redskins would fall to the Giants and onetime Redskin (though briefly) Charlie Conerly 27–20 at Griffith Stadium. They would win the season finale 28–17 over the Steelers at home to finish in second place with an 8–4 mark for the 1955 season.

There was a lot of promise for the Washington Redskins going into the 1956 season. Kuharich had been named NFL Coach of the Year for 1955, and, with the 8–4 record—the most

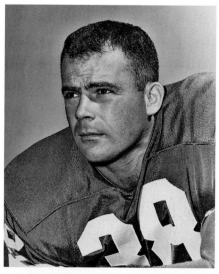

The colorful Sam Baker was an inveterate practical joker—and proficient field goal kicker for the 'Skins in 1953 and 1956-1959. In 1956 he kicked 17 field goals, setting a Redskins record. (Pro Football Hall of Fame)

wins by the team since 1945—Marshall and his troops had every reason to believe they had turned the corner and righted the franchise. But they would be hit by a series of setbacks, one of which was a tragedy that would affect the whole team.

Running back Vic Janowicz was a rising star. In 1955 he scored eighty-eight points, second in the NFL to Doak Walker. One night, while in training camp in Occidental College in California, Janowicz was thrown from a car and wound up in a coma for several days, unable to resume his pro football career.

There were other, less severe problems, but they had a cumulative effect on the team. LeBaron wrenched his knee in one exhibition game and was not able to start the season. What made matters worse was that the team's other thrower, Al Dorow, had a car accident the same week as Janowicz's. But fortunately for Dorow, his injuries would sideline him for only a month.

But with both quarterbacks out, Kuharich was forced to start rookie Fred Wyant in the season opener in Pittsburgh against the Steelers, and the Redskins took a 30–13 beating. Dorow was healthy enough to start the following week, also on the road, this time in Philadelphia, but he wasn't sharp, and Washington fell for the second straight week, 13–9.

Washington's woes continued in the home opener, a 31–3 beating by the Cardinals, and with an 0–3 start, it looked as if the Redskins were on their way to a dismal losing season.

But Kuharich was working new players into the system, and they began to help turn the team's fortunes around, winning five straight and six of their last nine for a respectable 6–6 mark. Sam Baker took over the kicking chores and became a reliable scorer, kicking seventeen field goals that year, a new Redskins record.

Baker was also a colorful character and one of the team's most prolific practical jokers.

The 1956 Redskins, coming off the franchise's most successful season since 1945, fell to 6-6. The 8-4 record the previous year was head coach Joe Kuharich's only winning season at the helm in Washington.
(Pro Football Hall of Fame)

He was a roommate of linebacker Chuck Drazenovich during training camp. Drazenovich was a sharp dresser and liked his suits, according to teammate Dick James, who joined the team in 1956 and took over the running duties. "Drazenovich always talked about how much his suits cost him," James said.

"We came out of the dining hall one time during training camp, and Baker had left earlier. He had gone to their room and took one of Drazenovich's suits. He ran it up the flagpole. We walked out, and there it was fluttering at the top of the flagpole."

The same year, the offensive line was boosted by the arrival of Dick Stanfel in a trade with Detroit. And rookie John Paluck from Pittsburgh began to become a force on the defensive line.

The most memorable moment for that changing squad came against the Lions at Griffith Stadium on November 11. Detroit came into Washington with a 6–0 record and a team of stars like Bobby Layne, Joe Schmidt, and Yale Lary, all of whom would end up in the Pro Football Hall of Fame.

Washington had won two straight, with victories over the Browns and the Cardinals with Dorow at quarterback, so Kuharich stayed with him, even though LeBaron was healthy enough to play. Kuharich was pleased with the way his team had come together with the new faces in the previous two weeks, but he knew that the Detroit game would tell just how far his team had come.

Redskins fans were curious. Attendance had fallen off during some of the lean years, but the Redskins were still a top attraction in town and the focus of much attention, as more than twenty-eight thousand fans showed up for the contest against Detroit.

Washington's defense stopped the Lions, and after taking the ball over and getting a pass interference call, the Redskins scored first with a seventeen-yard field goal. They added a touchdown when they intercepted another Layne pass, and James, on a pitch from Dorow, ran fifty-nine yards for the score. Baker added the point after for a 10–0 lead.

Detroit came back with a twenty-two-yard field goal, but, with the score 10–3, the Redskins offense bogged down, and Kuharich replaced Dorow with LeBaron. He fumbled on the first play from scrimmage, and the Lions recovered.

The Lions would fail to score, though, and before the first half ended, Washington would add another Baker field goal. The Redskins took a 13–3 lead into the locker room.

The good fortune of the Redskins turned on the first play of the second half, though, when Schmidt recovered a Washington fumble on the Redskins' thirteen-yard line. The Lions moved the ball down to the goal line, and on fourth and one Detroit running back Gene Gedman punched the ball over for a touchdown, and the Lions cut Washington's lead to 13–10.

The Redskins held on to their three-point lead going into the fourth quarter and had a chance to increase it early after moving the ball down to the Lions' twenty-nine-yard line. Although the usually reliable Baker missed a field goal, the Redskins had been playing inspired football all day. They came up with a big play on a Baker punt, nailing Lary, who fielded the ball at the seven, down at the Lions' one-yard line. The defense held them, and Lions coach Buddy Parker, who was concerned about being stuck in his own territory during the fourth quarter and risking giving up a touchdown, opted instead for an intentional safety, giving Washington a 15–10 lead. "I

was playing to win," Parker said. "I didn't want a tie."

The Redskins, though, thwarted his plans, as cornerback Art DeCarlo intercepted another Layne pass, and Baker kicked his third field goal for an 18–10 margin. Layne nearly brought his team back with a touchdown pass to Dave Middleton with a little more than one minute remaining in the game. But the Lions failed to convert on an onsides kick, and Washington came away with the upset 18–17 victory.

The Redskins entered the 1957 season again with high hopes, but again those hopes would not materialize into results. And tragedy would hit the team again before the season started, when defensive back Roy Barni was shot to death in a bar he owned in San Francisco.

More new faces would result in some inconsistent play when the season began, as Washington went 2–7 in its first nine games of the year. It would recover, though, winning the last three, including a 10–3 season finale with the Colts. But the 5–6–1 record would be the first in a series of losing seasons that would plague the franchise for nearly thirteen years.

A number of exciting and colorful players would come along during that stretch of losing, and in 1957 three rookie running backs known as the "Lollypops" would capture the imagination of Washington fans—Ed Sutton of North Carolina, Jim Podoley of central Michigan, and Don Bosseler of the University of Miami.

Bosseler led the team in rushing with 673 yards, along with 152 yards in receiving; Podoley had 442 yards rushing and 554 yards receiving, and Sutton ran for 402 yards and also threw for three touchdowns.

One other worthy note about 1957: It is generally recognized as the year that a former player from Whittier College in California began his later well-known devotion as a Redskins fan—Richard Nixon began attending Redskins games as vice president and would be known as one of the team's biggest fans when he took office as president.

Another interesting aspect of that 1957 squad was the number of great football minds that were on the roster. Don Shula, who would go on to become the winningest coach in NFL history, would play cornerback that year for Washington.

Old Friends

The first—and one of the most active—alumni associations in the National Football League was the one established by the Washington Redskins in 1957.

The group has helped sponsor and organize numerous charity events, including an annual golf tournament, a luncheon, and other fundraising activities.

Former Redskins center Al DeMao was one of the organizers of the group. "Dick McCann [Washington general manager] came to me and some others and said we should organize something. We got together and formed the Alumni Association. It's a pretty strong organization."

Al DeMao retired after the 1952 season but remained an important part of the organization and helped form the Redskins Alumni Association. (*above:* Pro Football Hall of Fame; *left:* Nate Fine)

Redskins games drew the attention of the nation's politicians in the 1950s, particularly that of a former Whittier College football player who was now vice president of the country. Richard Nixon, shown here with his wife Pat at a 1957 contest, would become one of the team's best known fans, even offering plays as president to George Allen. (*Center*): He congratulates the team after a win and (*at bottom*) makes a presentation to owner George Preston Marshall of the Helms Athletic Foundation Hall of Fame Award. (*Left, center:* Abbie Rowe; *bottom:* Pro Football Hall of Fame)

Joe Walton, who would go on to be a successful offensive coordinator and later a head coach for the New York Jets, was a rookie end on that squad. Others on that 1957 team who would become NFL coaches were defensive back Norb Hecker, who would later be a head coach of the Atlanta Falcons; Ed Khayat, who would coach in Philadelphia; Dick Stanfel, who would be an assistant coach for a number of teams; and Torgy Torgeson, who would eventually become a successful defensive line coach for Washington.

The "Lollypop" success could not carry the franchise, though. In 1958, Podoley hurt his knee in a season-opening 24–14 win over the Philadelphia Eagles, and Eddie LeBaron was nearing the end of his career. Washington would win only three more games that year, finishing the season with another victory over the Eagles, 20–0, at Griffith Stadium. With few prospects on the horizon to turn the team around, Kuharich, who represented the most

success and stability the franchise had had since the days of Ray Flaherty, opted to get out and left to take the high-profile head coaching job at Notre Dame. It was a surprising move, though, because Kuharich had signed a five-year contract before the start of the 1957 season, and it seemed unlikely that Marshall would let Kuharich out of his contract. But the Redskins owner allowed the coach to leave and turned over the team in 1959 to assistant coach Mike Nixon. Things would not get better.

Redskins fans might have believed that times were better in 1959. After an opening-season 49–21 loss on the road to the Cardinals, Washington came back with a 23–17 win over the Steelers in Pittsburgh. And then, coming home to Griffith Stadium, the Redskins surprised the team that had beat them soundly two weeks earlier, the Cardinals, with a 23–14 victory. But the Redskins would win just one other game the rest of the season, ending with a 3–9 mark. However, that one

The Power of Television

The popularity of professional football has grown with the exposure it has received from television. George Preston Marshall saw the power of the tube long before any of his peers.

In 1950, the Redskins became the first NFL franchise to broadcast their season schedule on television, sponsored by American Oil.

Bernie Nordlinger, Marshall's attorney, said the owner's vision of the power of television would affect the entire league.

"He saw the possibilities of the use of television for football," Nordlinger said. "He grasped it very early. He was responsible for developing the idea of having an amendment to antitrust laws to permit the league to sell television as a group instead of individually.

"The league had a rule where each team sold its television individually," Nordlinger said. "So the Giants would get more money, since they had a big television market, while Green Bay would get little, since it was a small market. The big teams were getting rich, and the little teams were getting poor.

"So they adopted a rule that no team could telecast into another team's area while the game was going on," Nordlinger said. "The government was seeking to get an injunction on the issue of limitation of territory being a violation on its face. The court overruled that, and we won. Marshall was responsible for that."

The 1960 Redskins, under coach Mike Nixon, posted a dismal 1-9-2 record. The team is notable, however, because it was the last one to play at Griffith Stadium. The next year the Redskins moved into their new home, DC Stadium. (Nate Fine)

win would be a special one.

The Colts, the Redskins' backyard rivals from Baltimore, were coming off a championship season that gained the franchise national attention with the game that many believe put the NFL on the map in the television age—the Alan Ameche overtime win over the New York Giants in 1958, and the defending league champions were every bit as strong as they were the year before, heading toward their second title.

At Griffith Stadium on November 8, most people expected Johnny Unitas to have a big day

against a Washington defense that had given up an average of 28.5 points per game. After all, the All-Pro quarterback had already thrown seventeen touchdowns in six games. Marshall publicly made his feelings known about his team's poor defense. "We're lousy on defense, and I'm getting fed up with it," he said. "I can't take much more."

On this day, Washington's defense would prove to bend, but not break, holding the powerful Colts offense to twenty-four points, just enough for the Redskins offense to put twenty-seven points on the board for the upset win.

What Did You Say?

One of the greatest offensive performances by a Washington Redskin came on December 17, 1961, when running back Dick James scored four touchdowns, running for 146 yards, in a 34–24 win over the Dallas Cowboys at Griffith Stadium. But it could have been five touchdowns if rookie quarterback Norm Snead had heard right, according to James.

"I was a yard and a half from the fifth touchdown," James said. "I came into the huddle and said, 'Let's take it in.' So Norm Snead sneaks it in himself. When he was asked after the game why he didn't get the ball to me, since I already had four touchdowns, Snead said, 'I thought he said sneak it in.'"

The sold-out crowd of 32,773 home fans saw its Redskins take a 7–3 lead in the first half, as LeBaron connected on a touchdown pass to Walton, and Baltimore went on the board with Steve Myrha's field goal. In the third quarter, Sam Baker hit a forty-two-yard field goal to extend Washington's lead to 10–3, but Unitas would tie the game on a scoring pass to Jim Mutscheller. But Washington was not intimidated by the defending champions and opened the fourth quarter with an option pass from running back Eddie Sutton to Joe Walton. Baker's point after gave the Redskins a 17–10 lead.

Baltimore answered back quickly after Unitas

Ernie Stautner, talking to a player on the bench, was an assistant coach during the tenure of Coach Bill McPeak. McPeak was one of eight coaches owner George Preston Marshall hired to guide his team during the lean years between 1946 and the mid 1960s. McPeak compiled a 21-46-3 record from 1961 to 1965. He was replaced by Otto Graham in 1966. (Paul Fine)

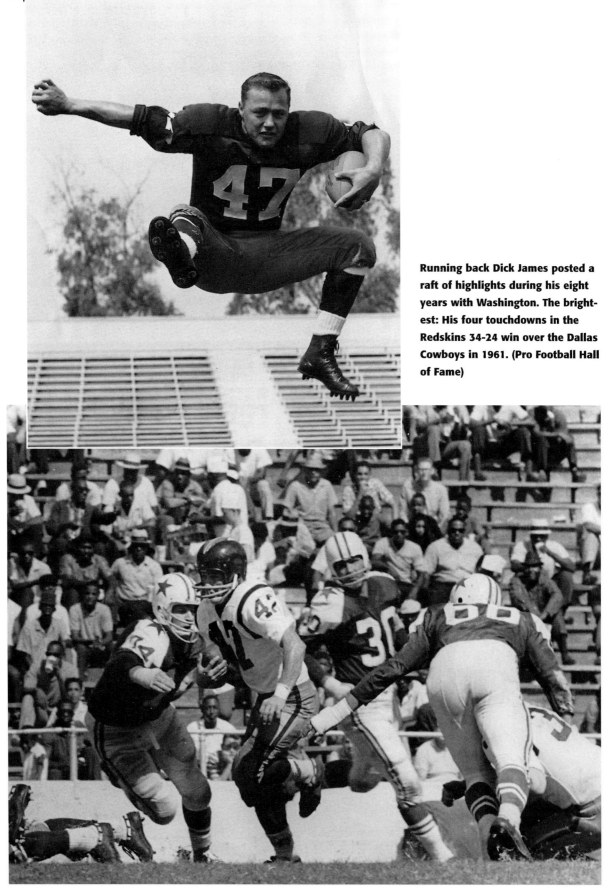

Running back Dick James posted a raft of highlights during his eight years with Washington. The brightest: His four touchdowns in the Redskins 34-24 win over the Dallas Cowboys in 1961. (Pro Football Hall of Fame)

Griffith Stadium served the Washington Redskins well for many years, but by the late 1950s it was at the end of its rope. Thus, ground was broken in 1960 for a new home, originally called D.C. Stadium. Renamed Robert F. Kennedy Stadium in 1970, in honor of the late New York senator, it, like Griffith Stadium, generated many fond memories of its own. The Redskins will now move to yet another brand new facility for the 1997 season. (*left:* Nate Fine; *below:* Pro Football Hall of Fame).

Quarterback Eddie LeBaron, signing autographs for a group of Boy Scouts, may have been small in size, but he was big in the hearts of Redskins fans. The former war hero electrified Griffith Stadium with his helter-skelter style of play. (Pro Football Hall of Fame)

hit Lenny Moore with a short pass that turned into a sixty-five yarder and then connected with Mutscheller again for the touchdown. It was now a 17–17 battle. Yet again, though, Washington played like they were the league champions, taking the lead back, 24–17, on a pass from LeBaron to Bill Anderson. But Unitas wasn't finished, as he led the Colts offense down the field, then called a halfback option pass from Moore to Jerry Richardson to tie the game at 24–24 with about two minutes left.

The Redskins were stopped on offense and had to give the ball back to Unitas—the last thing they wanted to do. But Dick James, who came into the game as an extra defensive back, tipped a pass into the hands of linebacker Tom Braatz, who

intercepted the ball and ran nearly twenty yards to the Baltimore thirty-nine-yard line.

With just a few seconds left on the clock, Baker connected on the game-winning field goal as the Redskins upset the powerful Colts 27–24. There was little else to cheer about that season, but there were reasons to be excited about the future. Griffith Stadium had outlived its usefulness. In fact, Washington Senators owner Clark Griffith was abandoning it, moving his baseball team to Minnesota, though Washington would get a new expansion version of the Senators. Griffith Stadium would be replaced in 1961 by D.C. Stadium, later to be renamed Robert F. Kennedy Stadium in memory of the former attorney general and New York senator after he was shot and killed during the 1968 presidential campaign.

Washington players had mixed feelings about leaving the old ballpark. It was home, but it had its share of quirks. "We had some good times at Griffith Stadium," Dick James said. "But the field was shot. If you stood down on what was left field (the goal line) and looked at the other goal line, it was three or four feet higher. They sodded the infield and built it up. It sure looked high if you were running in that direction."

The Redskins' final year at the ballpark that

had seen so many good and bad times turned out to be more bad times. Eddie LeBaron was gone, his distinguished career with the Redskins over. He would wind up with, of all things, the expansion Dallas Cowboys. Mike Nixon's team would manage to win just one game in 1960, and that would be against the Cowboys, a 26–14 win, giving the Redskins a record of 1–9–2 (they had two straight ties in the third and fourth games of the season, 24–24 against the New York Giants and 27–27 against the Pittsburgh Steelers).

Of course, winning just one game would try

The 1963 Redskins stumbled to an all-too-familiar dreadful record, 3-11, prompting another series of changes, which this time actually worked. The team traded for Sonny Jurgensen and Sam Huff and nabbed Charley Taylor in the draft. For the first time in years, the Redskins were poised for a return to respectability. (Nate Fine)

Bobby Mitchell was the first African-American to play with the Redskins, coming to Washington in a trade with the Cleveland Browns in December 1961. Mitchell would go on to become one of the greatest offensive players in the history of the franchise. He scored 55 touchdowns over seven seasons and caught 393 passes for 6,491 yards. Mitchell was inducted into the Pro Football Hall of Fame in 1983. (Pro Football Hall of Fame)

the patience of Marshall, and he would not go into the new stadium with the same coach. Nixon was fired and replaced with Bill McPeak, a former NFL defensive end and a coach from Nixon's staff. McPeak worked to rebuild the team, starting eight rookies, including their promising young quarterback, Norm Snead, drafted out of Wake Forest.

Another change was to come before the start of the 1961 season. On January 11, 1961, Redskins stockholder Milton King sold some of his holdings to a Toronto minor league baseball owner, a man named Jack Kent Cooke. Washington fans had little idea of what the impact of that transaction would be on the future of the franchise.

Redskin fans were excited about moving into the new stadium, and the franchise sold more than twenty thousand season tickets. What would have made 1961 a storybook season would have been any sort of success on the field. But the team opened on the road with two straight losses, then came home for the opening of D.C. Stadium.

With a crowd of more than thirty-seven thousand, at the time the largest ever to see a Redskins home game, Washington played the New York Giants tough but wound up losing 24–21. The Redskins would lose their next ten games until facing the Cowboys in the final game of the year at home.

Again, the one game Washington would win—on December 17, 1961, the first win in the new stadium—was a memorable one. Halfback Dick James would score a club-record four touchdowns, leading the Redskins to a 34–24 victory.

The game also nearly became memorable for another reason—the great chicken caper. Dallas fans tried to sneak about ten pounds of chicken feed and some chickens into the stadium. Their plans were to spread the feed on the field and let the chickens go at halftime, when Santa Claus was scheduled to make his annual appearance at a Redskins game. Police stopped the fans and took into custody about one hundred chickens.

That same month, a historic event occurred in the franchise—the team got its first black player. Marshall had refused to use black players—his supporters argued that it was for business reasons, because the Redskins were considered the team of the South—but many accused the Washington owner of racism, and he was taken to task by the federal government, which threatened to try to move the Redskins out of their new stadium if they didn't integrate.

So on December 4, 1961, Washington drafted its first black player, Syracuse's gifted running back Ernie Davis. But McPeak, who would return despite his team's dismal 1961 record, heard that the Cleveland Browns were looking to trade running back Bobby Mitchell, so Washington traded Davis for Mitchell and a future number-one draft choice. It would turn out to be a huge move for the Redskins. Mitchell would go on to be a star and a Hall of Fame player. Davis, tragically, would never play for the Browns. He was diagnosed with leukemia and died in 1963. Washington would draft two more black players, running back Leroy Jackson from Illinois Central and fullback Ron Hatcher from Michigan State, in the eighth round. Also, guard John Nisby, another black player, would arrive in 1962 by trade.

Jackson flopped as a number-one pick, but Mitchell was another story, turning out to be one of the finest moves the Redskins ever made. He had a huge impact on the 1962 squad, setting Redskins records with seventy-two receptions, 1,384 yards, and eleven touchdowns. He also led the team in scoring with seventy-two points.

It appeared as if the franchise was turning around. The Redskins opened the season with a 35–35 tie in Dallas against the Cowboys. Then Mitchell got his payback against the Browns in Cleveland on September 23. Washington was a sixteen-point underdog against the Browns, led by Brown, the NFL's greatest running back.

With Cleveland leading 16–10 with less than two minutes in the game, Mitchell took a short pass over the middle from Norm Snead on a third and four, with the ball at midfield. Mitchell dodged and leaped tacklers for a fifty-yard touchdown, as the Redskins took a 17–16 lead. The defense rose to the occasion in the final seconds of the game, as it blocked not one, but two field goal attempts by the Browns to seal the victory.

Washington would go on to win three of its next four games, and the team had a record of 4–0–2 after six games. But the Redskins lost two straight, then managed another win over the Browns, 17–9, but would lose their last five games to finish with a record of 5–7–2—another season of disappointment.

More changes were coming in 1963, though, at least geographically. The Redskins moved their training camp from Occidental College in California to Carlisle, Pennsylvania, a small town near Pennsylvania Dutch country and home of Dickinson College. Carlisle would give Redskins fans a chance to drive two hours from Washington to see their team in a training camp atmosphere.

The change didn't do much for the play of the team, though. McPeak's charges would be even worse, managing just a 3–11 record. But the players still have fond memories of those years, even with those losing marks, thanks to their teammates and the Washington fans who still supported them.

"We won a championship with the [Philadelphia] Eagles [1960], but I had more fun playing for the Redskins," said linebacker Bob Pellegrini, who came to Washington in a trade in 1962. "We didn't have a lot of talent, but we had a lot of unity. We played hard, and the fans were great. They backed us when we tried our best."

The end of the 1963 season would also see the end of an era. George Preston Marshall had led the Redskins from the days in Boston, when pro football was a novelty to that city, to the days when the team was the passion of the nation's capital. From the championship years after the team first arrived in Washington to the losing seasons of late, Marshall had presided over both the good and the bad times. Like him or not, it was Marshall's team. But he was experiencing failing health and had to turn over the operation of the team to three of his board members—Milton King, Leo De Orsey, and famed trial attorney Edward Bennett Williams, who would come to the forefront as the decision-maker for the franchise, starting in 1964, with some big off-field moves that marked the start of a new age in Washington—the age of Sonny and Sam.

Four

Sonny and Sam Arrive

Dick James was a good player for the Washington Redskins. He had set the club record with four touchdowns, rushing for 146 yards, against the Dallas Cowboys in a game in 1961. And he was popular with the fans. Sportswriter Mo Siegel once wrote of James after a particularly difficult Redskins loss, "The boobirds were out again at D.C. Stadium, and, to a man, everyone was booed, with one exception. That was Dickie James, and nobody, but nobody, boos Dickie James in D.C. Stadium."

The fans' affection, though, wasn't shared by Washington coach Bill McPeak. "I got in the doghouse with McPeak one time [in 1963] after a sportswriter was in the dressing room following a game and went around asking players what they thought about stories in the paper saying that McPeak was on his way out," James said. "The other players pumped McPeak up, but I told it like it was. 'I get paid to play football. I love the Washington Redskins and the fans. There are none better. But I get paid to play football and do the very best I can, and I will play the best I can regardless of who the head coach is.'"

It was hardly a glowing endorsement of McPeak, and the next week James was benched. A

few months later, on April 10, 1964, he was traded to the New York Giants, along with end Andy Stynchulka and a number-five draft choice in 1965, for rookie defensive lineman George Seals and the most recognized defensive player in the game, All-Pro linebacker Sam Huff.

James wasn't surprised to be traded, but it was the biggest shock of Huff's career. The West Virginia middle linebacker was an integral part of those great New York Giant defenses, and his stature leaguewide grew with the CBS football documentary, "The Violent World of Sam Huff."

"Sure, I was surprised," Huff said. "I was twenty-nine years old and felt like I was on top of the world. We had just finished playing in the World Championship Game in January, and we lost 14–10, with seven turnovers. But we were still able to hold the Chicago Bears to fourteen points.

"I was feeling pretty good at the time," Huff said. "I was working for the J.P. Stevens Company in New York and doing a lot of other things, like radio and television. And all of a sudden the rug is pulled out from under you. You're traded to the Redskins, a team you competed against and beat on a regular basis. I was surprised and depressed."

He had company. On April 11, another All-Pro player had been traded to Washington in

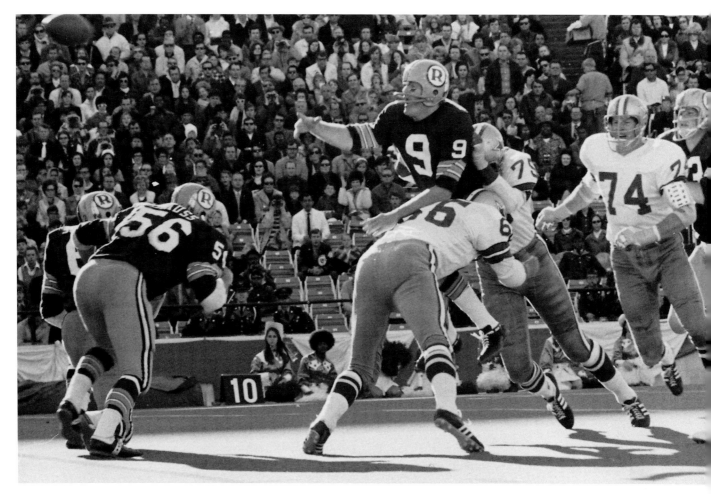

The Redskins rivalry with the Dallas Cowboys began soon after the Cowboys entered the league, but really took off during the Sonny Jurgensen era. One of Jurgensen's most memorable days was when he led Washington back from a 21-0 deficit to defeat Dallas 34-31 in a November 1965 contest. (Pro Football Hall of Fame)

another startling move—quarterback Sonny Jurgensen, dealt from the Philadelphia Eagles in exchange for Redskins quarterback Norm Snead.

Jurgensen, too, was surprised. "I had just had a lengthy meeting in Philadelphia with the coach [former Redskins coach Joe Kuharich] about what we were going to do," Jurgensen said. "I left the office with the understanding that I would be playing there in Philadelphia. I went to have some lunch, and some people told me they heard I was traded to the Redskins. I said, 'Don't tell me that. I just left the coach.' It was April Fools' Day, and I thought they were just kidding me. But that wasn't the case.

"It was a shock, especially after that meeting," said Jurgensen. The teams also swapped

defensive backs—Claude Crabb going to Philadelphia and Jimmie Carr coming to Washington.

It was easier for Jurgensen than it was for Huff. He wasn't as established a presence in Philadelphia as Huff was in New York. "And I was from the South, and what little pro football we had down there was the Washington Redskins," Jurgensen said.

It was a much harder adjustment for the older Huff. "It changed my whole perspective on the game," Huff said. "You realize that these moves have been made for you. As an athlete, you have very little to say in what goes on. You're a performer. These moves were made by people in front offices. My only salvation, at the age of twenty-

Sonny Jurgensen was shocked when he was traded in 1964 from the Philadelphia Eagles to the Washington Redskins. He had just met with new Eagles coach (and former Redskins coach) Joe Kuharich to discuss plans for the season when he learned from friends that he had been traded to the Redskins. "I thought they were just kidding me," he said. (Nate Fine)

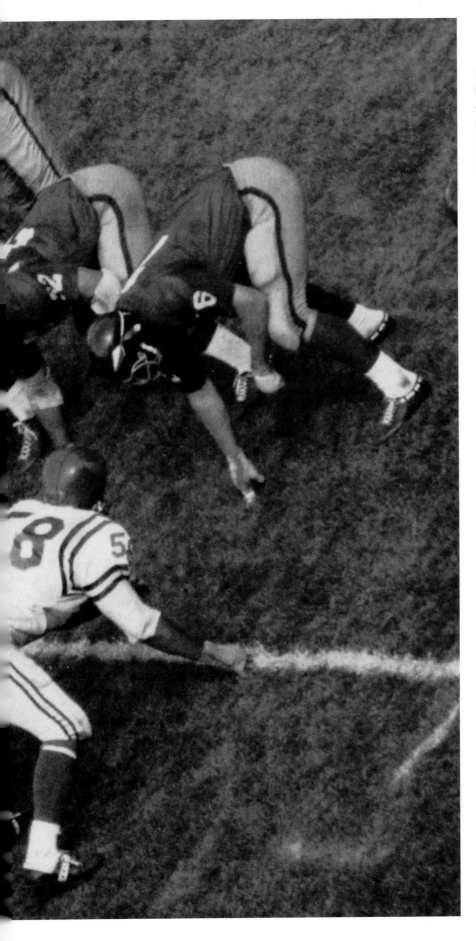

Sonny Jurgensen handed out a little payback against his old team by outdueling the quarterback he was traded for, Norm Snead. He tossed four touchdown passes in a 35-20 win over the Eagles in his first game at D.C. Stadium against his old mates. (Nate Fine)

Huff's Call

There were more than a few bizarre moments in the Redskins' 72–41 win over the New York Giants on November 27, 1966. But perhaps the most bizarre came when, with the score 69–41 and seven seconds left, the Redskins sent in placekicker Charlie Gogolak for a field goal, adding three points to a twenty-eight-point lead.

Why? When asked that question, Redskins coach Otto Graham answered, "Gogolak needed the work."

What Graham didn't tell reporters, though, is that he wasn't the one who sent Gogolak into the game. Linebacker Sam Huff made that call.

Huff was still carrying a grudge against the Giants and coach Allie Sherman for trading him in 1964. "I had taken an oath that I would never quit until Allie Sherman got fired," Huff said. "I carried a chip on my shoulder for thirty years about that man."

So when the Redskins had the ball down near the Giants' end zone with seconds left and fourth down, and Graham did not motion for the field goal team, Huff yelled from the sideline, "Field goal," and the field goal team went into the game to put the final nail in the Giants' coffin.

"I'll never forget looking across the field at the guy who changed my life and traded me after the game," Huff said. "I looked up at the sky and said, 'Justice is done.'"

Though he found a home in Washington, linebacker Sam Huff never forgave Giants coach Allie Sherman for trading him. After watching films of the Giants before the Redskins' Nov. 27, 1966, contest against them, Huff told Sonny Jurgensen that the New York defense was ripe for picking. He was right; the Redskins romped to a 72-41 win over the Giants, scoring the most points in a single regular season game in league history. The crowning blow for Huff was when Charlie Gogolak kicked a field goal for Washington with seven seconds left to set the record. Huff was the one who called the field goal team in for the kick. (Nate Fine)

Former Cleveland star quarterback Otto Graham took over the head coaching job for Washington in 1966. He inherited a number of talented players, among them Charley Taylor, Chris Hanburger, Sonny Jurgensen, and Jerry Smith. (Nate Fine)

nine, was 'Do I want out of the game, or do I want to play?' I came to the realization that I'm a football player, and now I've been traded to the Redskins, and if I want to play, I'll have to play in Washington."

The two of them shared mutual shock, enjoyed mutual respect, and would become roommates. "We came there together," Jurgensen said. "He came here for the defense, and I came for the offense. It was natural that we would get along."

They were joined by some talented young players, like rookie defensive back Paul Krause and the Redskins' number-one draft choice that year, Arizona State running back Charley Taylor.

Taylor was one of the building blocks of what turned out to be a powerful offense. He gained 755

yards rushing and would catch fifty-three passes for 805 yards. But he would make his mark in Redskins and NFL history as a wide receiver, switching to full-time two years later. He would retire in 1977 with 649 receptions, at the time a league record, seventy-nine of the them for touchdowns. He also gained 9,140 yards receiving over his illustrious career.

This high-powered offense didn't get off to a rousing start, though. They scored a total of fifty-eight points in their first four games of the season—all losses. But they defeated the Philadelphia Eagles at D.C. Stadium 35–20 for their first win of the season, as Jurgensen out-dueled the man he was traded for, Norm Snead, by tossing four touchdown passes.

Though they were both great quarterbacks, Sonny Jurgensen was not on the same wavelength with Redskins coach Otto Graham, who sought to change Jurgensen's game. (Nate Fine)

After another loss to the Cardinals, the Redskins would win their next two—27–20 over the Bears and 21–10 over the Eagles, completing Jurgensen's revenge over his old team with two straight wins.

They would lose the next week, 34–24, to the Cleveland Browns, then bust out with three straight high-scoring wins, starting with a 30–0 victory over Pittsburgh and winning the next two at home—28–16 over the Dallas Cowboys and 36–21 over the New York Giants. Huff, too, got a measure of revenge in that win, but it would be nothing compared to the sweet payback against his old team that he would dish out two years later.

The Redskins lost the last two games, 14–7 to

the Steelers and 45–17 to the Colts, but wound up with a 6–8 record, three wins better than the year before. They also scored 307 points, twenty-eight more than the previous season and the most they had ever scored as a team.

There were other reasons to believe that good times were ahead, such as Taylor's strong rookie season and Jurgensen's performance. The red-headed thrower completed 207 passes, only the second quarterback in the history of the franchise to complete more than 200 passes (Baugh completed 210 in 1947), passing for 2,934 yards and twenty-four touchdowns.

The defense also showed some improvement, surrendering 305 points, 93 less that the year before and the least given up since 1958, when they allowed 268 points, but in a twelve-game schedule.

McPeak added Huff and talented rookie free safety, Paul Krause, to a squad that had some good individual players, like defensive end John Paluck and defensive back Johnny Sample.

"They built the defense around me because of my success in New York, and it came together real quick," Huff said. "In fact, the defense came together before the offense did. We had a few players who could play. We had a decent defense at the time. But it didn't hold up because they started drafting all offensive ballplayers."

But in 1965, Washington did manage to draft what turned out to be a pretty good defensive player in the eighteenth round—linebacker Chris Hanburger, who went on to help anchor the defense until retiring in 1978.

But, like Huff said, the Redskins did concentrate on offense and picked a pretty good player, Jerry Smith, who had played with Taylor at Arizona State, on the ninth round.

The year turned out to be a disaster, though. The Redskins matched their 1964 record of 6–8, but the expectations were greater than that. Those expectations took a brutal beating in the first half of the season, as McPeak's team opened with a 17–7 loss to the Cleveland Browns and would go on to lose four more. They would score a total of just thirty-seven points in the first five games before finally getting their first victory of the season, on October 24, in St. Louis, a 24–21 win over the Cardinals.

Two more wins would come, 23–21 over the

Eagles and 23–7 over the Giants, followed by another loss, 21–14 to Philadelphia. The offense exploded for thirty-one points in a 31–3 beating of the Steelers in Pittsburgh, then came back to D.C. Stadium to face the Dallas Cowboys, a franchise that was in the early stage of developing into one of the strongest in the league, with players like Don Meredith, Bob Hayes, Don Perkins, and other future All-Pro players.

More than fifty thousand people were on hand that day, and they sat in frustrated shock as they watched their Redskins fall apart early. In the first quarter, Jurgensen threw two interceptions and fumbled. Charley Taylor fumbled twice in his first three carries, and the Cowboys lead 14–0 by the end of the quarter.

The game continued to take on a life of its own, all against the Redskins. Cowboys safety Mike Gaechter blocked a field goal attempt by Bob Jencks, picked up the ball, and ran sixty yards for a touchdown. The point after gave Dallas a 21–0 lead.

Just before the end of the half, Jurgensen managed to rally the team on an eighty-yard drive, hooking up with Charley Taylor for a twenty-six-yard scoring pass to finally put Washington on the board, 21–6, as the Redskins missed the extra point.

Halftime didn't seem to offer any answers at first. Shortly after taking the field for the third quarter, the Cowboys took the ball downfield and scored again on a twenty-nine-yard field goal by Danny Villanueva, giving the Cowboys a seemingly insurmountable 24–6 lead, made all the worse when Jurgensen had to take the ball at the Washington ten-yard line.

But Jurgensen got hot and eventually moved the ball eighty-nine yards to the one-yard line, where he took it over himself. With the point after, Dallas's lead was now 24–13 at the end of the third quarter.

Jurgensen began finding receivers with ease, hitting Taylor and Smith, ending with a touchdown run by Danny Lewis, and the extra point made it a 24–20 ballgame, a far cry from the twenty-one-point lead the Cowboys had in the second quarter.

Chris Hanburger, with coach Otto Graham, was rare, a defensive player who starred during the Redskins offensive-minded era of the mid and late 1960s. The linebacker from North Carolina, an 18th-round selection in 1965, went on to become a nine-time Pro Bowler. (Washington Redskins)

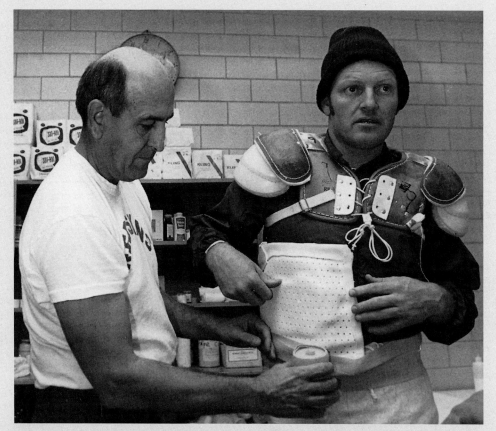

(*Opposite*): Sonny Jurgensen's scrambling style of play endeared him to Redskins fans. The fearless field leader also did his share of scrambling off the field. "I did enjoy my life, but I played hard, and they (fans) knew that, too," Jurgensen said. (*Above*): The quarterback is wrapped up by Redskins trainer Joe Kuczo in preparation for battle. (Pro Football Hall of Fame)

Sonny's Style

S onny Jurgensen is a Hall of Fame quarterback and one of the best of his time. But part of what made the red-headed quarterback a fan favorite was his persona off the field. He was a swashbuckler type who enjoyed himself.

"They [the fans] knew that I did enjoy my life," Jurgensen said. "But I played hard, and they knew that, too."

It was Jurgensen's style, as well as his talent, that made him such a Washington personality. Center Len Hauss remembers one time when Jurgensen was going to share the stage at a dinner with one of the top stars in show business.

"The Washington Touchdown Club had chosen Sonny as the Most Valuable Player in football one year, and Tom Jones, the singer, was chosen Most Valuable Performer," Hauss said. "We were at the function, Sonny, myself, Tom Jones, one of the biggest entertainers in the business, and some other people. One of the Washington reporters asked Sonny, 'What does it feel like to be in the presence of a real star?' And Sonny answered, "Why don't you ask him?'"

Jurgensen's charisma extended from Washington to the Redskins training camp in the quiet, small town of Carlisle, Pennsylvania. The surroundings didn't put a crimp in his style.

"We had fun in Carlisle," Jurgensen said. "I had different methods for getting out, and one night I went out to this place called the Walnut Bottom. It was one of our watering holes.

"I was playing shuffleboard with a young man, and I get a call saying they had double-checked on bed check," Jurgensen said. "I had to come back, and when Otto was there, you had to go to the coach's room and let him know when you got back in, and that's when you were fined accordingly.

"So I knock on Otto's door, and he is in his pajamas," Jurgensen said. "He said, 'What do you want?' I said, 'I was told to come to you because I was out after bed check.' He said, 'What do you do that for? Who were you with?' Right next to me behind to the door was his son, Dewey. I said, 'I was with your boy, Dewey.' He was so mad that he kicked Dewey out of training camp.

"Dewey had just been sitting outside when I came out the back door to go out that night," Jurgensen said. "I asked him, 'You want to go?' He said, 'Sure,' and he went out with me. There were a lot of nights of getting caught out."

What also endeared Jurgensen to football fans everywhere was his physique, with the little paunch his signature feature. "I didn't have a good tailor in my day, so I always had this little roll in front of me," Jurgensen said. "People could sit at home and say, 'I want to watch football,' and the wife would say, 'You're just sitting around here drinking beer. Get in shape.' But they could point to the television and say, 'Wait a minute. Look at this guy. If he can play, I can play.'"

Linebacker Sam Huff was devastated when he was traded in 1964 from the New York Giants to the Washington Redskins. But the All-Pro linebacker from Farmington, W. Va., enjoyed some fine years with the Redskins, and still remains very much a part of the scene, teaming up with Sonny Jurgensen for many years to broadcast Redskins games on the radio. (*above, opposite:* Pro Football Hall of Fame; *right:* Associated Press)

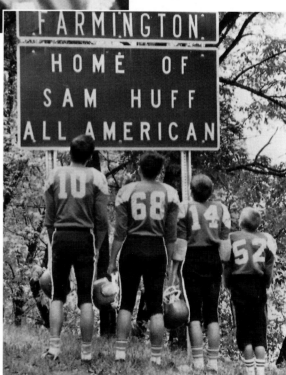

Sam Huff, in front of his locker (*opposite*), often was frustrated by the team's defensive woes. Huff noted that when he first arrived in Washington, they had a good defense. "But it didn't hold up because they started drafting all offensive players." So he unleashed his frustrations on opponents, such as the man across from him on the line of scrimmage (*above*), former Washington quarterback Norm Snead, traded to the Eagles for Jurgensen. (Nate Fine)

Tight end Jerry Smith was a key member of the Redskins' powerful, Sonny Jurgensen-led offense. The former Arizona State star was drafted in the ninth round in 1965 and would catch 421 passes for Washington over 13 years. Sixty of those receptions went for touchdowns. (Nate Fine)

But Dallas was not about to lie down. With Jurgensen firing away often, linebacker Dave Edwards picked off a pass, and the Cowboys turned the game back around in their favor when Don Meredith hit end Frank Clarke on a short pass that turned into a fifty-three-yard score, extending Dallas's lead to 31–20.

Time was running out—less than six minutes remained in game. Jurgensen, though, was up to the task, connecting on three straight passes, including a ten-yard touchdown to Bobby Mitchell, and the point after brought the Redskins to within four of the Cowboys, 31–27.

With a little more than three minutes left, Dallas nearly turned the game back around again when Mel Renfro had a fifty-six-yard kickoff

return to the Washington forty-one. But the defense stopped Dallas there, and Villanueva missed a field goal attempt. With 1:41 left, Jurgensen got the ball again at his own twenty-yard line.

Then, disaster, or so it seemed. Jurgensen went back to pass, but he fumbled. However, he managed to get the ball back and wound up turning the play into a nine-yard gain, running the ball out. A pass interference call and a twenty-two-yard completion to Jerry Smith moved the Redskins down to the Dallas forty yard line. Then Jurgensen found Mitchell and connected with him on a thirty-five-yarder down to the Dallas five-yard line, with 1:14 left.

With the deafening roar of the crowd at D.C.

Sold Out

In 1966, a streak began that continues to this day: consecutive sellouts of Redskins home games.

Redskins tickets have become among the hardest to get in all of sports and entertainment. Season tickets are handed down from one generation to the next. Divorce settlements are hung up over who gets the Redskins tickets.

The length of the waiting list for season tickets is legendary, with some fans waiting more than twenty years for their name to come up on the list to get the golden ducats.

Fans will get some relief with the new stadium, which should result in twenty-two thousand more tickets being available for what had become the most important weekly social event in the nation's capital—Washington Redskins home games.

Stadium nearly drowning out their words, Jurgensen called a time-out—Washington's last—and went to the sideline to talk to Redskin coaches about what would be the biggest play of the season. He came back and tossed a pass over the heads of Dallas defenders, finding end Angelo Coia in the end zone. The stadium rocked with joy and disbelief as Washington now had a 34–31 lead.

But the Cowboys had their own fearless gunslinger, Don Meredith, and with thirty-seven seconds left, they still had enough time to make a move. Despite getting sacked twice, Meredith got Dallas to the Washington thirty-seven-yard line. Villanueva entered the game to attempt the tying field goal with seven seconds remaining. The crowd tensed up when the ball was snapped. Then Lonnie Williams brought everyone in the stadium to their feet when he rushed in and blocked the kick. Jim Steffen recovered, and the greatest comeback in Redskins history was in the books on November 28, 1965.

Sam Huff was probably the National Football League's first defensive star, thanks in part to the CBS documentary, "The Violent World of Sam Huff." The All-Pro linebacker was inducted into the Pro Football Hall of Fame in 1982. (Pro Football Hall of Fame)

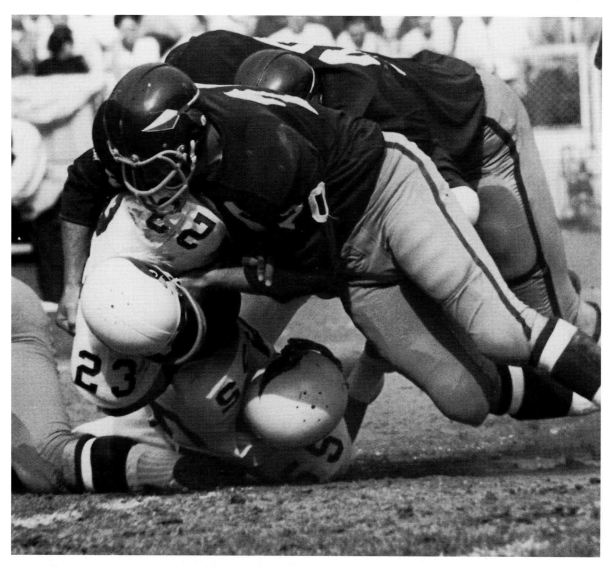

Sam Huff was still a defensive force at the end of his playing career. Huff retired after the 1967 season, but after sitting out one season, returned for one more year when Vince Lombardi took over in 1969. (Nate Fine)

"The Cowboys had the game won, but they got conservative," Huff said. "As a matter of fact, Cowboys owner Clint Murchinson left at halftime. He got on his plane to go back to Dallas, thinking he had a win. When he landed he found out things had changed."

The win elevated Jurgensen to legendary status in the city, as fans now believed that there was always a chance to win as long as he was taking snaps behind center. He wound up completing twenty-six of forty-two passes for 411 yards and three touchdowns.

"We kept plugging and plugging," Jurgensen said. "We were a quick-striking team, and we had that capability. The kind of offense we were, you may stop us three or four times, but then we are going to hit one on you."

There would be many wins—and losses—over the next few years, with scores, if not events, similar to that 34–31 game.

"We weren't blessed with the most talent in the league, but we were still a team," Jurgensen said. "In some of those years we had good years and put up some big numbers offensively. But we

Missed Signals

S am Huff was one of the best middle linebackers of his time. He was with the New York Giants during their winning days of the late 1950s and early 1960s, helping the Giants win one world championship and five division titles before being traded to the Redskins in 1964.

He was proud of his accomplishments and still believed he was better than most toward the end of his playing days. Certainly he didn't think he should have been dismissed like he was by Dallas Cowboys receiver Pete Gent one night on a television show in 1967.

"I'm watching television in my hotel room in Dallas the night before the game, and Pete Gent is on with his own show," Huff said. "He gives a scouting report on the Redskins, and he gets to me. He says, 'Number 70 in the middle, eleven or twelve years in the league, no longer the great star that he was. He should have retired a few years ago.'

"I nearly tore up that television, I was so mad," Huff said. "I wanted to get to this guy, but I didn't know how. He plays wide receiver, and he doesn't come over the middle. But I'm going to get a shot at this guy. I didn't sleep all night. That's how mad I was.

"I figured the only way I could get Gent was to make a deal with Don Meredith," Huff said. "So when we go out before the game to flip the coin, I say to Don, who is one of the Cowboy captains, 'Dandy, I need a favor today.' He said, 'What do you need, Sam?' I said, 'Pete Gent doesn't think I can play this game. Bring that guy across the middle on a pass pattern. I want to hang him out to dry. I'll show him who can play this game.'

"Don said, 'Okay. I told him to keep his mouth shut.' I said, 'Just bring him across the middle.'"

It didn't work out the way they planned, though. "We didn't develop a signal for when he was going to send him [Gent] across the middle," Huff said. "Now we're leading 14–0, and I'm happy we're leading, and I've forgotten about Pete Gent. I told Chris Hanburger that we were going to blitz in, a double blitz. 'I'll go up the middle, and you go from the outside. We're going to get Dandy.'

"I go up the middle, and nobody blocks me," Huff said. "They blocked Chris, because they expected him to be blitzing, but I come up the middle. Dandy is standing there with the ball, and I hit him in the chest and knock him unconscious. This turned out to be the very play that he had Pete Gent go across the middle. This was the guy who was trying to help me get Gent, the guy I made the deal with, and I knock him out."

Craig Morton would then come in and throw two touchdown passes to tie the game at 14–14. "Everybody's mad at me now because I knocked Meredith out of the game and let Morton come in, who got them going," Huff said. Washington would go on to win the game 27–20, and Gent would go on to write the acclaimed football novel, *North Dallas Forty*.

Sonny Jurgesen is all business in Carlisle, site of the Redskins' training camp. In Jurgensen's time, training camp lasted longer; players worked in jobs during the off-season and used camp to get into playing shape. (Nate Fine)

didn't always win because we had to outscore people. We would lose games 31–30 or 34–31. We had to put up points."

The comeback win was not inspiring enough to propel the team for the rest of the season, though, as Washington lost two of its final three games, finishing again with a 6–8 record. Offensive numbers were down, from 307 to 257 points, and the defense was only slightly improved, from 305 to 301 points surrendered.

Those were enough reasons for Edward Bennett Williams, who now called the shots as club president after the passing of Leo De Orsey, to fire McPeak, who was Marshall's choice. Williams was one of the most high-profile attorneys in the country, and he wanted the Redskins to have a high-profile coach. So he hired former NFL quarterback great Otto Graham, who had led the Cleveland Browns to title after title during his reign as quarterback in the 1950s. He had been coaching at the Coast Guard Academy and claimed that he was not

looking to become an NFL coach.

But Williams's ten-year, $500,000 contract offer was too good to turn down, and Graham accepted the job. It turned out to be a case of a great player not being able to make the transition and to find the same success coaching. He lasted just three seasons, his best year coming in 1966 when the team finished at .500, with a 7–7 record. He was fired after the 1968 season—a disappointing 5–9 campaign—with a three-year mark of 17–22–3.

Graham and Jurgensen did not hit it off, as Graham tried to change Jurgensen's styles and methods. "He wanted Sonny to change the way he threw," Huff said. "It was one thing after another, and it doesn't take much for a coach to lose the respect of his players."

But Graham certainly didn't take away from

Charley Taylor joined the Redskins in 1964 as a running back out of Arizona State and gained 755 yards rushing. But he would make his mark in Redskins and NFL history as a wide receiver; he displayed his skills immediately by catching 53 passes for 805 yards in his first season as a receiver. (Pro Football Hall of Fame)

Joe Don Looney

There may have been no more enigmatic player in football in the 1960s than running back Joe Don Looney, a big, talented athlete who marched to a far different drummer than anyone else in the game.

Looney made the rounds around the NFL during his tumultuous career. He was drafted by the New York Giants in the first round, but lasted only a month before he was dealt to the Baltimore Colts, who later traded him to Detroit. It was the Lions who convinced the Redskins to take Looney off their hands in 1966. He would last just two seasons in Washington, but he was unforgettable—for all the wrong reasons.

"Joe Don Looney was potential talent that nobody could ever tap," Sam Huff said. "Otto Graham called Sonny and myself down to his office and said they had a chance to get Looney. He asked us what we thought. Sonny and I agreed. 'We have enough problems here holding the players together as it is,' we told Otto. 'None of the other teams could control him. And he's going to come here?' We both voted against it, and the next morning, Joe Don was in uniform."

Then, of all things, Graham asks Huff to be Looney's roommate to try and straighten him out. "They offered me a bonus if I would room with Joe Don to keep him out of trouble," Huff said. "I said I would, but it was one of the toughest things I ever did. I didn't trust him. I didn't know whether he was going to try to beat me up or what. I never slept much before a game."

Huff's fears turned out to be well grounded. The two did get into a fight once, but it wasn't until Looney's second year with the Redskins, during practice.

"It was before the opening game in Philadelphia," Huff said. "We were out in full pads on a Friday before the Sunday game, and it was hot and miserable. Looney is running the Philadelphia plays for our defense. They run a toss to the fullback, and Looney runs around the end.

"I go in pursuit and kind of take it easy," Huff said. "Joe Don lowers his shoulder and runs over me. Then he taunts me with the ball. Hell, this is just practice. I'm trying to save myself for the Philadelphia Eagles on Sunday.

"I'm down on the ground, and he sticks the ball in my face and says, 'How do you like that, big guy? I knocked the hell out of you.' I looked up at him and said, 'You crazy so-and-so, you picked the right guy this time. You're going to get yours.'

"So they come out of the huddle for the next play, and I know what the play is," Huff said. "Looney said to me, 'All right, big guy, here I come again.' I'm gritting my teeth. I'm going to nail this guy. When he got the ball, I came off the ground with my fist and hit him dead on the chin as hard as I could. He shook his head, his knees buckled, but he didn't go down. I gave him the best shot I could ever give him. Then we got into a hell of a fight. They couldn't get us apart. Then Otto says, 'I don't think you guys better room together this week.'"

Joe Don Looney was one of the strangest players ever to put on a football uniform. He was full of talent, a strong, fast running back, but was a rebel without a cause, bouncing from team to team, including the Redskins, who brought him to Washington in a trade in 1966. He wound up rooming with Sam Huff, who got paid extra for putting up with him. (Pro Football Hall of Fame)

In 1967, Sonny Jurgensen set new Redskins and NFL passing records for attempts, completions, and yards. Additionally, receivers Charley Taylor, Jerry Smith, and Bobby Mitchell finished first, second, and fourth in the league in receiving, the highest finish ever by a group of receivers on the same team. (Nate Fine)

Jurgensen's performance in his first year as coach. Washington showed some slight improvement in 1966, posting a 7–7 record. The offense exploded for 351 points. Jurgensen led the league with 3,209 yards passing and 254 completions, also throwing for twenty-eight touchdowns. Charley Taylor lead the league with seventy-two receptions, tying the record set in 1962 by Bobby Mitchell, who himself caught fifty-eight passes for 905 yards in 1966, and Jerry Smith, who brought in fifty-four passes for 686 yards.

However, the Redskins also gave up 355 points on defense, continuing their frustrating pattern of explosiveness on offense and futility on defense that would continue under Graham. "We had such a strong offense, I don't think there was anybody in the league that could compete with us

offensively," Taylor said. "It was just that we couldn't stop anybody. Our defense wasn't that bad. We just had some holes we couldn't shore up. We had some great defensive players."

Huff was one of those great players, but he also carried a great grudge against the team that traded him, the Giants—even though he acknowledges that the trade was probably the best thing that happened to him—and against the man who traded him, Coach Allie Sherman. At the time, Huff still thirsted for fulfilling revenge. Washington had gone 2–2 against the Giants since Huff arrived in 1964 but lost in their first game in New York in 1966 by a score of 13–10. That game offered no clue to what would happen the next time the two teams met that season, on November 27 at D.C. Stadium.

The Giants had fallen apart that year, with their win over the Redskins the only one they had, and New York had gotten even worse since then. Huff saw just that as he watched the game films before their second game that season. "I looked at the Giants offense and defense this time," he said. "Normally, I just looked at the offense. But it was one of the worst teams I had ever seen. It might have been the worst defensive team in the history of the NFL.

"I just knew we were going to beat them, because they were just awful," Huff said. "Kyle Rote, who was playing for the Giants at the time and was a good friend of mine, was doing a radio show and had me on as guest. He asked me, 'What do you think about today's game?' And I said, 'This is one of the worst teams the Giants have ever fielded. They're terrible on offense and terrible on defense.' I told him, 'We will score sixty points today.'" Huff was close. The Redskins wound up scoring seventy-two in one of the most lopsided games in the history of the league, setting a record for most total points scored in a game in a 72–41 Redskins victory before more than fifty thousand fans.

Jurgensen got Washington on the board first with a short touchdown pass to A.D. Whitfield, who scored again later in the first quarter on a sixty-three-yard run to give the Redskins a 13–0 lead.

Washington quickly scored again when Brig Owens recovered a Giants fumble and ran sixty-two yards for another touchdown. New York got on the board to make it a 20–7 game, but the Redskins marched down the field at will on their next two possessions, each ending with touchdown runs by A.D. Whitfield and Joe Don Looney. The Giants scored before the end of the half, but by then Washington had a 34–14 lead and was on its way to a big win.

The Giants would hang tough for a while, matching the Redskins with fourteen points for each team in the third quarter, and Jurgensen was frustrated by the Giants' refusal to roll over. Huff said, "At one point I was running on the field with the defense, and Sonny was coming off, and he said, 'Damn it, Sam, how many do I have to get?' I said, 'Sonny, don't let up,' and he didn't." Washington would score twenty-four points in

the fourth quarter for the 72–41 win.

It should have been even more. "It should have been seventy-nine," Charley Taylor said. "I dropped a sure touchdown. I felt this guy on my shoulder as I dropped the ball, and after the ball had fallen to the ground, I looked over and it was the official running along with me. It sort of distracted me."

The Redskins also split two showdowns with the Cowboys that year, the first a 31–30 loss at D.C. Stadium and the second a 34–31 win in Texas. In that first loss, the Redskins led 30–28, with the go-ahead score an eighteen-yard touchdown pass from Jurgensen to Taylor with about five minutes remaining.

But Don Meredith moved the Cowboys,

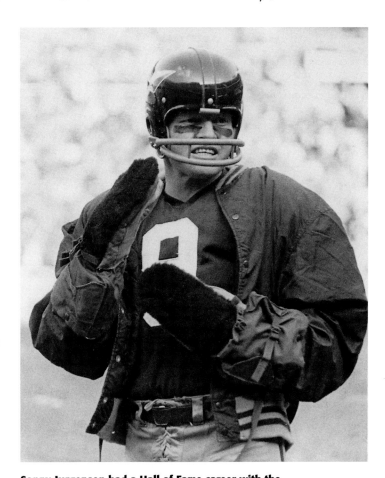

Sonny Jurgensen had a Hall of Fame career with the Redskins. He was inducted into Canton in 1983, one year after his friend and former teammate Sam Huff. During his 11 seasons with Washington, he threw 179 touchdown passes, including a stretch of 23 games from 1966 to 1968 in which he notched a TD pass. (Nate Fine)

starting from their own three-yard line, down to the Washington twenty-yard line with less than a minute remaining. Danny Villanueva nailed a field goal with about twenty seconds left to give a 31–30 victory to Dallas and heartache to more than fifty thousand on hand that day in Washington.

In the rematch, though, the Redskins came out slightly better, in this case, *three* better, than the Cowboys. At one point, the score was tied 24–24 in the fourth quarter when Don Perkins scored on a six-yard-run for a 31–24 lead. But Jurgensen was never put off by catching up, which always kept the Redskins in any game. "We always knew we had a guy with a great arm and no fear," Taylor said.

On a broken play, Taylor got open, and Jurgensen hit him on a sixty-five-yard touchdown pass to tie the game again at 31–31. The Redskins got the ball back with less than two minutes on their own forty-six-yard line. Washington moved the ball down to the Cowboys twenty-two. With eight seconds left, Charlie Gogolak hit the winning field goal for a 34–31 win.

It was an exciting season, with some important developments off the field as well, as minority owner Jack Kent Cooke gained more stock, a move that would eventually lead the team to the winning tradition it developed. But at the time, a 7–7 record itself was cause for optimism.

The optimism carried over at the start of the 1967 season. After an opening-game 35–24 loss to the Philadelphia Eagles, the Redskins won two in a row, 30–10 over the New Orleans Saints and 38–24 in the home opener in Washington over the New York Giants. But they wouldn't win again for six more weeks, losing three and tying two before coming out on top on November 12 against the San Francisco 49ers 31–28 at home. They would defeat Dallas 27–20 in Texas but would win only one of their final four games, losing two and tying another,

and finishing with a disappointing record of 5–6–3.

What made it all the more frustrating was the fact that the Redskins had some of the best offensive players in the league. Jurgensen set NFL records for attempts, completions, and yardage, throwing 508 passes, completing 288 for 3,747 yards and thirty-one touchdowns. That figure is still the best ever for a Redskins quarterback. Charley Taylor, Jerry Smith, and Bobby Mitchell finished first, second, and fourth in the league in receiving, as Taylor caught seventy passes for 990 yards, Smith brought in sixty-seven passes for 849 yards, and Mitchell had sixty receptions for 866 yards.

If 1967 was frustrating, 1968 was marked by futility. The sidelining of Jurgensen with injuries, the retirement of Sam Huff, and the misguided trade of safety Paul Krause to Minnesota all contributed to a 5–9 season, with the offense scoring just 249 points, its lowest total since 1961.

Washington opened with a 38–28 win over the Chicago Bears on the road, then lost their next two to the Giants and the Saints. They finally got back home to D.C. Stadium, where familiar surroundings resulted in two close wins, 17–14 over Philadelphia and 16–13 over Pittsburgh. Things were looking up, with a 3–2 record after five games.

But they would win only two more the rest of the season—16–10 over the Eagles and, in the final game of the season, 14–3 over the Detroit Lions in Washington—and would take some bad beatings in the process, including a 41–14 thumping by the Cardinals. The defense allowed 358 points, the most since the team went 3–11 in 1963.

That spelled the end of the Graham regime. "At times, Otto sort of lost control of the direction we were going," Charley Taylor said.

Soon the Redskins would have all the direction they needed. A block of granite was coming to town.

Five

LOMBARDI

Vince Lombardi had no more dragons to slay. He was ruler over all he saw, having lead the Green Bay Packers to six conferences titles, five NFL championships, and two Super Bowl victories.

But after the 1967 Super Bowl win over the Oakland Raiders, Lombardi stepped down as coach, staying in his general manager role. His place in history was assured as one of the most successful coaches in all of football, a legend who was as much a part of the history of American society as of football. He was the ultimate warrior leader.

When he stopped coaching at Green Bay, he was exhausted physically and mentally, and at the time there appeared to be little left to accomplish. He turned the coaching duties over to Phil Bengston, his defensive coordinator, and moved to the front office.

It turned out to be a big mistake. He was a fish out of water and missed the action back on the field.

"He just had to go back to coaching again," said Tony Canadeo, a former Packer who later became a team broadcaster and who was a friend of Lombardi's. "He felt lost up in that press box. He was the type of general who couldn't fight a

war from his desk."

No, Vince Lombardi needed to be on the field, where he had always been, from the time he was one of the "Seven Blocks of Granite" at Fordham University during the mid-1930s. He went on to coach from 1938 to 1946 at St. Cecilia's High School in New Jersey, winning thirty-six straight games over one stretch. He went back to Fordham as an assistant coach for two years and then moved to West Point to work on the staff of Colonel Earl "Red" Blaik. In 1954, he broke into professional football as an assistant coach with the New York Giants, and five years later he was chosen to turn around the once-proud Packers franchise, which had fallen on hard times, with an 8–27–1 record over the previous three seasons. Lombardi guided the Packers to a 7–5 record his first year, and they never looked back.

Now Lombardi realized he had made a mistake by leaving the sidelines, and he wanted to come back badly. But he couldn't return to the field in Green Bay. How could he kick Bengston out of a job just because he wanted to be a coach again? No, he would have to leave the Packers if he wanted to lead a team again.

That prospect had come up before while Lombardi was coaching Green Bay. In fact, it was

Sonny and Vince

The player who seemed to gain the most from his devotion to Vince Lombardi was quarterback Sonny Jurgensen. He thrived under Lombardi's tough style and developed a special relationship with the legendary coach.

"It was so much fun, the times with him," Jurgensen said. "In our first practice up at Georgetown University, he told me I was throwing the ball too quickly. I said, 'I've had to throw the ball very quickly to get rid of it.' He said, 'We'll give you the best pass protection you've ever had.'

"We had good year offensively, and after the year he was congratulating me for the season in front of the other coaches," Jurgensen said. "He said, 'I appreciate how hard you've worked, and the kind of year you had, and next year you'll complete seventy percent of the passes because you didn't even know the system.'

"I said, 'By the way, you said I was going to get the best pass protection I ever had. Look at how many times I got sacked.' He said, 'Yeah, but you knew the personnel better than I did.' And he just walked out. But if he had been here the next year, we would have completed seventy percent of our passes."

Sonny Jurgensen calls the season he played under Vince Lombardi the best of his career. "It was unfair to have him all the time," Jurgensen said. "What an advantage you had. He turned the franchise around." (Nate Fine)

Vince Lombardi had retired in 1967 from a successful coaching career with the Green Bay Packers, having led them to five NFL championships and two Super Bowl victories. But after serving as the team's general manager in 1968, Lombardi pined for a return to the sidelines. He persuaded Redskins owner Edward Bennett Williams to hand him the coaching reins in Washington. The move electrified the city. Lombardi told reporters he would demand of his team "a commitment to excellence and to victory." Shown here with Williams at the press conference and leaving the team's downtown offices, Lombardi kidded, "In spite of what you've heard, I can't walk on water. Not even when the Potomac is frozen." (Nate Fine)

Pat Fischer was a hard-nosed cornerback who arrived from the St. Louis Cardinals as a free agent in 1968 and played 10 seasons with the Redskins, under Otto Graham, Vince Lombardi, and George Allen. Though Lombardi was with the Redskins only one season, the legendary coach had the respect of the team before he arrived, Fischer said. "Lombardi was preceded by his reputation," said Fischer, also shown here stopping Walt Garrison in a 1969 loss to the Cowboys. (*left:* Pro Football Hall of Fame; *below:* Nate Fine)

The 1969 Redskins were the first and only Redskins team coached by Vince Lombardi, who passed away from cancer in 1970. It was a pivotal year. Washington's 7-5-2 record represented the franchise's first winning season in 14 years and set the tone for the raging success that followed. (Pro Football Hall of Fame)

the Redskins who tried to woo Lombardi from the Packers before. Leo De Orsey tried unsuccessfully to get Lombardi to coach the Redskins in 1963, and Edward Bennett Williams made a run at the legendary coach in 1966 before Otto Graham was hired.

When word spread that Lombardi wanted to return to coaching, teams lined up for his services. Atlanta, New Orleans, Philadelphia, and even the Boston Patriots in the American Football League all sought Lombardi. But they were competing against the likes of Williams, the nation's top trial attorney, a man who perhaps had the best persua-

sion skills in the country. Those skills, along with a stock deal for part ownership of the team, an annual salary of $100,000, and other perks, convinced Lombardi to come to Washington. It was big news in the big city.

"In spite of what you've heard, I can't walk on water," Lombardi told reporters at a news conference on February 7, 1969. "Not even when the Potomac is frozen."

Despite the humor, Lombardi was very serious when he outlined his plans for his new team. "I will demand a commitment to excellence and to victory. . . I would like to have a winner my first

Lombardi promised change, and it started with a much tougher training camp at Carlisle. The first time Lombardi met with the team, he cut a player, fullback Ray McDonald, for being five minutes late for a meeting. (Nate Fine)

year, if possible," he said.

That was a bold goal. The Washington Redskins had not had a winning season since 1955.

But Lombardi was different from the host of coaches who came and failed in Washington. He had mastered the concept of winning to the point that it became his aura, and it rubbed off on other people.

Also, his reputation as a tough taskmaster was well documented. "There was a lot of fear when Lombardi got here," defensive back Brig Owens said. "He was a legendary coach. When a coach of that stature comes in, you know there is going to be some house cleaning, so you worry about whether or not you're going to have a job."

Some survived, others didn't. Owens was one of the survivors. "He [Lombardi] was everything that I expected," Owens said. "He had his way of

testing everybody. He felt if you could withstand his pressure, the games would be easy. And he was right."

Lombardi enlisted the help of the two leaders of the Redskins over the past few years, Jurgensen and Huff. That wasn't easy for Huff, who, after all, wasn't on the team anymore. He had retired at the end of the 1967 season. But a chance to play for Lombardi would bring Huff back.

"I had retired because I just couldn't take it anymore, what I saw was happening to the team," Huff said, citing his frustration with the team's play and work under Graham. "I didn't want to be part of that.

"I met Lombardi on the airplane going to the Super Bowl [January, 1969]," Huff said. "He and Marie [Lombardi's wife] were on the plane, and we started talking."

Sam Huff was coaxed out
of retirement by Lombardi
to serve as player-coach.
Huff credits Lombardi for
the franchise's turnaround.
"He changed the mental
attitude of the Washington
Redskins," Huff said.
(Nate Fine)

Lombardi was close to his deal with the Redskins, and he and Huff were talking about the team. "I said to him, 'You know, I'd still like to play.' He said, 'You think you can still play?' I said, 'I think I can,' and he said, 'I need you.' At the time, I wanted to be a coach, so we struck a deal that I would be a player-coach. It was hard work, but it was quite an experience for me to sit in the meeting rooms with Lombardi and learn all about the man. I wasn't afraid of him. Most people were scared to death of him.

"There's two ways of motivation," Huff said. "One is through fear, and the other is through group motivation. Lombardi motivated through fear. That's the quickest way. He was all business."

Huff was a tough veteran not easily impressed, but he quickly became a Lombardi devotee. In fact, many of the players who played on that Redskins team credit Lombardi with changing the fortunes of the Redskins franchise, from a losing team for the most part since the championship game in 1945 to the team that would win three Super Bowls over ten seasons.

"He turned this team around," Huff said.

"He changed the mental attitude of the Washington Redskins."

Charley Taylor was another quick convert. "He [Lombardi] taught us how to win," Taylor said. "He would get the most out of every athlete he had. He knew their limits, he knew how far to push them. He had a great feel for his talent and his people."

That may have been Lombardi's greatest talent—to have the respect of the players he would be so tough on. "He had the respect of the players right from the start," Huff said.

One of the players who respected him the most was Jurgensen. Some thought the free-spirited quarterback would resent Lombardi's Draconian methods, but the opposite occurred. Jurgensen became Lombardi's biggest supporter.

"I played for nine different head coaches but didn't have a chance to get on the field with all nine because some were fired before we ever got on the field," Jurgensen said. "[Norm] Van Brockline in Philadelphia, they let him go while we were having meetings. [Joe] Kuharich traded me before we ever got on the field.

Lombardi Time

The Redskins learned very quickly that there was regular time, and then there was Lombardi time. To stay on the coach's good side, it was best to show up any place you were supposed to be five minutes early. To keep your job, it was important to show up on time, as players learned in their first team meeting at training camp in Carlisle, according to cornerback Pat Fischer.

"Ray McDonald [the team's fullback the season before] came in late for the meeting," Fischer said. "There were two swinging doors in the back of the auditorium. McDonald came through after about four or five minutes of Coach Lombardi presenting himself and the program for the night.

"When those two doors opened up, Lombardi stopped and yelled, 'What is your name?' Ray said, 'Ray McDonald.' Lombardi announced right there that Ray was released from the team. Once he realized it was Ray McDonald, Lombardi said, 'Get your helmet and equipment.' He wanted Ray to report to a semipro team the Redskins had a relationship with in Virginia Beach. He never did come back to the team.

"We didn't have anyone come late to a meeting after that," Fischer said.

The Redskins got off to a rocky start under Lombardi in the exhibition season. In the pouring summer rain, Washington defeated the Chicago Bears 13-7 in the team's first preseason game, but they finished a shaky 2-4. Lombardi and his assistants knew they faced a stiff challenge. (Nate Fine)

Famed trial attorney Edward Bennett Williams was determined to change the fortunes of the Redskins when he became the controlling partner of the franchise. First he brought in Otto Graham to coach, and when that failed, he helped Jack Kent Cooke lure Lombardi to Washington. (Pro Football Hall of Fame)

"Nobody, though, was close to this guy [Lombardi]," Jurgensen said. "It was unfair to have him all the time. What an advantage you had. He turned the franchise around."

Jurgensen remembers vividly his first meeting with Lombardi. "I sat down across from him, and he said, 'I've heard some good things and some bad things about you, and I'm sure you've heard some good things and some bad things about me. All I ask is that you be yourself. I don't want you to try to emulate anyone else and be something you're not, and we'll get along fine. If you do anything that reflects on the Redskins in a derogatory manner, I'll call you in and talk to you about it privately. Any questions?' That was it," Jurgensen said.

"I played eighteen years, and that was by far the highlight of my career, having the chance to play for him," Jurgensen said. "It was easily understandable why Green Bay was so successful. He had very simple concepts, easily understandable, and great preparation. He was going to make us a winner. He said that."

A Lombardi training camp was like no other that these players had been through, with an intense summer in Carlisle. Lombardi needed to weed out the players who didn't meet his standards, so he put even more pressure on during camp that he had during his days in Green Bay, when he knew what sort of team he had.

His style had its admirers, like Jurgensen, but it was tough to deal with for other players—not just the ones who couldn't handle it, but the ones who were self-motivated, who already pushed themselves and didn't need the Lombardi-style pressure to perform. Center Len Hauss was one of those players.

"That year with Lombardi was my toughest year in football," Hauss said. "I didn't appreciate the type of coaching that Lombardi did. I'm not saying he wasn't a great coach. He was. But I did not particularly care for his methods.

"One day after practice, Sonny and I were talking, and Sonny said to me, 'Isn't this great? Lombardi is the greatest coach I've ever seen. He kicks you in the butt and makes you give 100 percent. That's what we need.' I said, 'Sonny, you need that, but he's kicking me in the butt, and I'm giving 110 percent anyway. I don't need that.'" Hauss had a case. He was one of the all-time gamers for the Redskins, holding the franchise record for consecutive games played, appearing in 196 straight games from 1964 to 1977.

The results during Lombardi's preseason were mixed. The team went 2–4 in six exhibition games, but the coach was working on changing the whole philosophy of Redskins football, which had been throwing bombs and putting up points and catching up to the other team, with the defense offering little resistance. This team would learn how to execute Lombardi-style drives—perhaps not as effectively as the Packers had in Green Bay, with Jerry Kramer leading the way for Jim Taylor, but certainly better than what had passed for a running game in Washington.

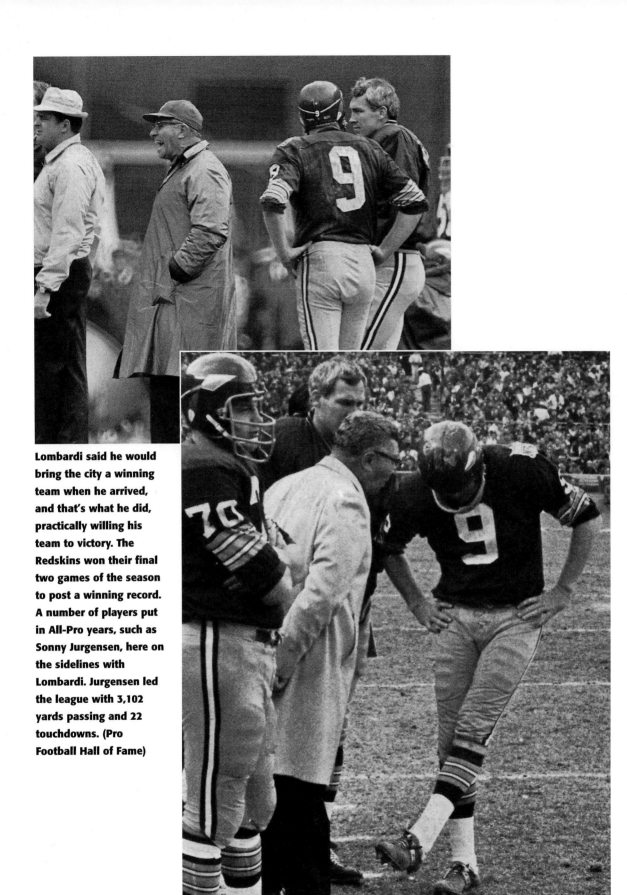

Lombardi said he would bring the city a winning team when he arrived, and that's what he did, practically willing his team to victory. The Redskins won their final two games of the season to post a winning record. A number of players put in All-Pro years, such as Sonny Jurgensen, here on the sidelines with Lombardi. Jurgensen led the league with 3,102 yards passing and 22 touchdowns. (Pro Football Hall of Fame)

The city of Washington and the entire football community was devastated by the death of Vince Lombardi, who passed away on Sept. 3, 1970, of cancer. At his funeral in Washington, Edward Bennett Williams told mourners that Lombardi "had a covenant with greatness, more than any man I've ever known." (Nate Fine)

The man who would lead that running game would be an eighth-round draft choice from Kansas City, Larry Brown. Not much was expected from him, and he didn't start out changing those expectations, until Lombardi noticed something about Brown during training camp. He saw that Brown was moving a little differently off the ball than he should. Brown was moving when he saw the ball snapped, not when he heard the quarterback's voice. He couldn't hear it sometimes, or hear it well, it turned out, because he had hearing problems. Lombardi provided Brown with a hearing aid for his helmet, and the unheralded rookie wound up being a Hall of Fame running back,

rushing for 888 yards in that rookie season and retiring after 1976 with 5,875 yards rushing.

Before the season began, though, the club would be faced with the end of an era. George Preston Marshall, who had been out of the operation since 1964, passed away on August 9, 1969, after a long illness. He had been one of the most influential men in the history of professional football, and he left the team in the hands of men who would take care of the franchise he had molded.

Lombardi's Redskins opened the season on the road in New Orleans against the Saints before a crowd of more that seventy-three thousand fans at Tulane Stadium. Jurgensen would be dueling against a quarterback who would someday be his rival on the Redskins, Billy Kilmer.

Kilmer put the Saints up 7–0 early in the game by finding Ray Poage in the end zone. And Washington hardly looked like a Lombardi-coached team, as fullback Henry Dyer fumbled at the start of the second quarter on the Washington twelve-yard line. That led to a Tom Dempsey field goal and a 10–0 New Orleans lead.

Lombardi didn't waste any time. Dyer and Gerry Allen had been the starting backfield. They were replaced in the second quarter by what would be the signature Redskins backfield for years to come, Brown and fullback Charlie Harraway. They would help kick-start the Washington offense, which got on the board with a ten-yard touchdown pass from Jurgensen to Charley Taylor. Then Mike Bass recovered a New Orleans fumble, and Jurgensen would find Jerry Smith in the end zone for a 14–10 lead, which the Redskins would take into the locker room at halftime.

The Saints would cut the lead to 14–13 in the third quarter on another Dempsey field goal, but Jurgensen connected with Taylor on another scoring pass, this one for fifty-one yards, and Curt Knight's point after would make it a 21–13 contest. The Saints answered back and came to within one again, 21–20, but the Redskins would pull away on a field goal by Knight, and they added to it for a 26–20 final when the Saints gambled and took an intentional safety on fourth down rather than risk punting deep in their own end zone, to get better field position. New Orleans would manage to get just to midfield before time ran out, though, sealing Lombardi's first professional win as a head coach with a team other than the Packers.

The following week, the Redskins would face the Browns in Cleveland and play well, despite coming up short in a 27–23 loss. For the third straight week, the Redskins would be on the road, this time in San Francisco against the 49ers. They wouldn't win, coming away with a tie, but nearly pulled it out with two seconds left on a free kick by Knight from fifty-six yards out, but it passed to the left of the crossbars, and the game ended in a tie.

With a 1–1–1 record, the Redskins came home for the first time that season, to Robert F. Kennedy Stadium this time. D.C. Stadium had been renamed in June in memory of Kennedy, who was assassinated while campaigning for president the year before.

Going against the St. Louis Cardinals before an excited home crowd of more than fifty thousand, Jurgensen threw for 239 yards and two touchdowns to lead Washington to a 33–17 win. It was a big victory for the Redskins, because the Cardinals, with a 2–1 record, were a good offensive team lead by quarterback Jim Hart and running back Johnny Roland. The Washington defense harassed Hart all day, holding him to thirteen completions and intercepting five passes.

The Redskins would go on to win their next two games, 20–14 over the New York Giants and 14–7 over the Pittsburgh Steelers, putting together an impressive 4–1–1 record and experiencing a feeling that a Redskins team hadn't felt for quite some time—a winning feeling.

"Players here were used to losing, and that's what Lombardi turned around," Jurgensen said. "It was a different feeling. If you were going to be satisfied with losing, you weren't going to be here."

However, the high hopes were brought down to earth the following week, when the Redskins faced the defending league champion Baltimore Colts at Memorial Stadium. The Colts, led by their young coach Don Shula, blasted Washington 41–17. Jurgensen threw three interceptions. And a blocked punt by Baltimore's Tom Mitchell in the second quarter, when the score was Colts 13, Redskins 10, was the key play in the game. Mistakes lost the game for Washington, because the Redskins' offense nearly matched Baltimore's, as the Redskins' offense gained 357 points and the Colts, 359 yards.

The Redskins came back home to play the Eagles, and again, a mistake cost them a win. Defensive back Mike Bass was called for a pass interference play on, of all plays, a fourth and twenty-five. With Washington leading 28–21 and less than a minute remaining in the game, the penalty put the ball on the Redskins' one-yard line, and the Eagles punched it over for the touchdown, with the extra point tying the game at 28–28. When a similar play wasn't called by officials with seconds left on a Redskins drive as the clock ran out, Lombardi had his share to say to the officials. He later called it "one of our most disappointing games." Players would later tell reporters that after

The Habit of Winning

Vince Lombardi was a student of winning and understood that to preach it, he needed to create a code, something to reduce the intangibles of victory into words. In one way, he did this through his essay, "The Habit of Winning":

"Winning is not a sometime thing. You don't win once in a while. You don't do things right once in a while. You do them right all the time.

"Winning is a habit. Unfortunately, so is losing. There is no room for second place. There is only one place in my game, and that is first place. I have finished second twice in my time at Green Bay and I don't ever want to finish second again. There is second place bowl game, but it is a game for losers played by losers. It is and always has been an American zeal to be first in anything we do, and to win, and to win, and to win.

"Every time a football player goes out to play, he's got to play from the ground up. From the soles of his feet right up to his head. Every inch of him has to play. Some guys play with their heads. That's okay—you've got to be smart to be number one in any business, but more important, you've got to play with your heart. With every fiber of your body. If you are lucky enough to find a guy with a lot of head and a lot of heart, he's never going to come off the field second.

"Running a football team is no different from running any other kind of organization—an army, a political party, a business. The problems are the same. The objective is to win. To beat the other guy. Maybe that sounds hard or cruel. I don't think it is.

"It is a reality of life that men are competitive and the most competitive games draw the most competitive men. That's why they're here—to compete. They know the rules and the objectives when they get in the game. The objective is to win—fairly, squarely, decently, by the rules—but to win. And in truth, I have never known a man worth his salt who in the long run, deep down in his heart, did not appreciate the grind—the discipline. There is something in good men that really yearns for . . . needs . . . discipline and the harsh reality of head-to-head combat.

"I don't say these things because I believe in the 'brute' nature of man, or that men must be brutalized to be combative. I believe in God and I believe in human decency. But I firmly believe that any man's finest hour, his greatest fulfillment to all he holds dear, is the moment when he has worked his heart out in a good cause and lies exhausted on the field of battle victorious."

the game Lombardi was as angry as they had ever seen him so far in Washington.

It wouldn't get better the next week. The Dallas Cowboys were coming to town, and they were far tougher than the Eagles. Though the Redskins-Cowboys rivalry would reach new heights under George Allen, it was already intense by this point, fueled by a combination of some bitterly close games the two teams had played and the fact that a number of Texas players on the Washington roster didn't like the idea of going home to hear the jokes about their Redskins team.

The Redskins had the added pressure of having the nation's number one football fan at RFK Stadium that day. President Richard M. Nixon would attend this game, the first time that a president came to see a pro football game in Washington. Nixon would later become known as one of the Redskins' most ardent fans, becoming friends with George Allen, and even offering play and strategy suggestions.

Dallas, with a running game led by brilliant rookie Calvin Hill (he would beat out Larry Brown for Rookie of the Year honors that season), took a 3–0 lead, but Washington answered back quickly with a drive that ended on a twenty-seven-yard touchdown pass from Jurgensen to Jerry Smith. The point after gave the Redskins a 7–3 lead. It was short-lived.

Craig Morton hit Lance Rentzel on a sixty-five-yard touchdown pass halfway through the first quarter. And then came another mistake, this one an interception of a Jurgensen pass and touchdown return by Larry Cole. Suddenly the Cowboys had a 17–7 lead by the end of the quarter. It quickly became 24–7 early in the second quarter when Bob Hayes returned a punt to the Washington three-yard line, and Hill took it in for another score. It looked as if the Redskins were falling apart.

But they hung tough, sparked by an eighty-eight-yard touchdown pass from Jurgensen to Taylor in the second quarter, for a 24–14 game. Dallas added a field goal for a 27–14 lead, but the Redskins came back with a scoring pass to Jerry Smith to come close, 27–21, when the half ended.

In the third quarter, it appeared that Washington was ready to take the lead when Rickie Harris returned a Dallas punt eighty-three yards for an apparent touchdown. But Chris Hanburger was called for clipping on the play, a disputed call, but it changed the face of the game. The Cowboys would get the ball back and then score on a five-yard run by Hill for a 34–21 Dallas lead. The Redskins would come back on Smith's third touchdown catch of the game, but Dallas would hold the Redskins off and score again with about a minute left for a 41–28 victory.

Things got easier for the Redskins the following week, when the Atlanta Falcons, with a 3–6 record, came to Washington. Jurgensen was nearly perfect in a 27–20 win as he completed twenty-six of thirty-two passes for 300 yards, and Larry Brown rushed for 102 yards. Washington now had a 5–3–2 record. The breather didn't last long, though, as the undefeated Los Angeles Rams (10–0), with head coach George Allen, were next in the Redskins' fourth straight home game.

Vince Lombardi would have likely been a leader in any field he entered. He understood the concepts of victory and motivation, and even wrote an essay titled, "The Habit of Winning," which declared, "There is only one place in my game, and that is first place." (Pro Football Hall of Fame)

It was a cold day, the thirtieth of November, and the weather helped the Redskins stay close, putting a crimp in the Rams offense. Washington scored first on a Curt Knight field goal for a 3–0 lead on their first drive of the game, but the Rams came back with their own drive of the game, but the Rams came back with own drive and field goal, tying the game at 3–3. Los Angeles took a 10–3 lead in the second quarter, and just before the half Knight hit another field goal, and the Rams now had a 10–6 lead. They made it 17–6 on a pass from Roman Gabriel to Billy Truax in the third quarter, then Washington scored again to cut the lead to 17–13. But the Rams put the game away with a fourth-quarter touchdown for a 24–13 victory.

The next game would be an important one for the Redskins. With a win over Philadelphia, Washington would clinch second place in the Capital Division. For a team that had little to brag about in terms of finishes in the recent past, it was a small but significant accomplishment, and the Redskins were up to the task with a 34–29 win at Franklin Field, with Larry Brown rushing for 136 yards. The victory, their sixth of the season, also assured the Redskins of a winning season, something that nearly a generation of Washington fans had never seen. And the team would treat Redskins fans to a win in the final home game of the season, a 17–14 triumph over the Saints, which meant that the worst this team could do would be 7–5–2. And that's how it would end in the last week of the season with a 20–10 win over the Redskins.

This was what Lombardi had said he would do when he came to Washington—bring the city a winner. Fans were more than pleased with the results and were enthusiastic about the future. So were the players, who saw the personality of the franchise change in just one year. "Lombardi brought a sense of organization to the club, hard work and a no-nonsense approach to the game," Brig Owens said.

A number of players prospered under Lombardi. Jurgensen led the league in passing with 3,102 yards, 274 completions, and twenty-two touchdowns. Charley Taylor caught seventy-one passes for 883 yards, Brown rushed for 888 yards, and six Redskins went to the Pro Bowl: Jurgensen, Larry Brown, Jerry Smith, Pat Fischer, Len Hauss, and Chris Hanburger.

All the promise, though, was crushed in June, 1970, when Lombardi learned he had colon cancer. He was too sick to run training camp, so his assistant, Bill Austin, took over. On September 3, at the age of fifty-seven, Lombardi passed away.

The progress made the year before disappeared, as did the spirit of the team after the man who was showing them the way to a championship suddenly was gone. Austin had a difficult task, and it showed. The Redskins would fall back into their losing ways, going 6–8 in 1970, though Larry Brown would become the first Redskin to win an NFL rushing title and to run for 1,000 yards, with 1,125 yards rushing on 237 carries.

In one year, Lombardi had touched the lives of many people in a way they would never forget. "When he died, it was like your father passed away," Huff said.

Edward Bennett Williams, the man who brought Lombardi to Washington, said in a eulogy: "He had a covenant with greatness, more than any man I've ever known. He was committed to excellence in everything he attempted. Our country has lost one of its great men. The world of sports has lost its first citizen. The Redskins have lost their leader. I personally have lost a beloved friend."

Williams did not want to start the losing again. Events three thousand miles away would help put the team back on track, thanks to the help of one of his fellow owners, Jack Kent Cooke, who was a big fan of George Allen's work with the Rams. When Los Angeles owner Dan Reeves fired Allen at the end of the 1970 season, Cooke recommended that the club quickly make a move for him. On January 6, 1971, the future became now.

The Future Is Now

The future didn't look very good for the Washington Redskins on January 5, 1971. The team was coming off a 6–8 season, had fired its head coach, Bill Austin, and was still reeling from the effects of the untimely death of the man credited with bringing winning to the franchise, Vince Lombardi.

The next day, the future looked a lot better. In the words of the new coach of the Washington Redskins, "The future is now."

George Allen, the winningest coach in the National Football Conference, was hired as the head coach and general manager of the Redskins on January 6, 1971. "We have had a losing syndrome for fifteen years with one exception," Edward Bennett Williams said in the announcement of the hiring of Allen. "I think we have an obligation to get the best possible coach and personnel. I think we have taken a dramatic step in signing George Allen."

Washington took that step thanks to a feud between Allen and Los Angeles Rams owner Dan Reeves, who fired Allen in December, 1970, despite the fact that Allen had a record of 49–17–4 during his tenure with Los Angeles, including eleven straight victories in 1969. Allen had angered Reeves

with some of his personnel decisions, and they also clashed over the aggressive way that Allen did business.

He was not out of work long. Washington minority owner Jack Kent Cooke was familiar with Allen's work and accomplishments in Los Angeles and had eyed him as a coaching candidate once before, back in 1968, when Reeves fired Allen the first time. Reeves would bring Allen back, but this time Cooke and Williams had already developed a good relationship with Allen, and they convinced him that the Washington job was the best opportunity for him.

Williams and Cooke, extremely successful men away from football, were secure and intelligent enough to let Allen run the team without interference, so he did not encounter the problems he had with Reeves in Los Angeles. In fact, Williams joked about Allen's style. "When Coach Allen came to Washington, we agreed he had an unlimited budget," Williams said. "He's already exceeded it."

Allen was forty-nine when he took the Redskins job, and his route to the job was one of small stepping-stones. He was born on April 29, 1922, near Detroit. He was a star athlete in football, basketball, and track in high school. He joined the

U.S. Navy during World War II and also attended several schools under a special program in the service before finishing college at Michigan after the war. His first coaching job was at tiny Morningside College in Sioux City, Iowa. He would later coach at Whittier College—the alma mater of the Redskins' best-known fan, Richard Nixon—in California, and from there he got his start in the pro game as an assistant coach on Sid Gillman's staff on the Rams in 1957, and he would later move to work with George Halas and the Chicago Bears. He was the defensive coordinator of the Bears when they won the 1963 championship and became head coach of the Rams in 1966, but not without a legal battle from the Bears to prevent him from leaving.

Along the way, Allen developed a tunnel-visioned style of coaching that would serve him well. Football came first, second, and last for Allen, with little in between. "George was so committed, you could not talk to George at anytime and not talk about football," Pat Fischer said.

When he was hired, Allen made a brief statement that would define the personality of the Washington Redskins while he was coach. "The team that makes the fewest mistakes wins," he said.

Billy Kilmer was a favorite of George Allen, who brought the field general to Washington to help direct Allen's ball-control offense. Though Kilmer w as not the pure passer that Sonny Jurgensen was, he found ways to win. (NFL Properties)

George Allen and Billy Kilmer will forever be linked as symbols of the Allen years—two warriors tenaciously dedicated to winning. (Pro Football Hall of Fame)

"Our system will stress execution, with defense aimed to get better field position for the offense."

Right then and there, it was clear that Allen would place a premium on defense. And, given the defensive holes in the team he inherited, that would mean changes. But nobody expected what was about to come.

Allen used Redskin draft choices like money burning a hole in his pocket. He brought the core of his old Rams defense to Washington, trading for linebackers Jack Pardee, Myron Pottios, and Maxie

Baughan, defensive tackle Diron Talbert, defensive back Richie Petitbon, guard John Wilbur, and special teamer Jeff Jordan for linebacker Marlin McKeever and seven draft picks. He also brought assistant coaches and any staff he could convince to leave Los Angeles whom he wanted in Washington.

The group from Los Angeles would be known as the "Ramskins," but Allen wouldn't stop there. He traded for quarterback Billy Kilmer from New Orleans, signed defensive end Verlon Biggs, and traded for the other end on the defensive line, Ron McDole, obtained from the Buffalo Bills. And before the season would begin, Allen would also deal for wide receiver Roy Jefferson.

"He had given up all those draft choices, but he wanted a team that was ready to play right away," Talbert said.

It was a big change for the players who were there already, and it took some getting used to. "Those of us who were on the team didn't know what to expect," Fischer said. "But a lot of guys were players that we already knew. And it was reassuring to the older players, because many times when you have a change in coaching, there is usually a movement to start with youth. That's not the

philosophy that George Allen had."

No, it wasn't. Allen took a totally different approach, picking up veterans who may not have fit in to the plans of their existing teams, molding what became known as the "Over the Hill Gang."

"The Over the Hill Gang gave us an identity, and it also stimulated us," Fischer said. "We're too old? If we had been with any other team, we probably would not have been on the team."

Probably no coach could have pulled it off except Allen, who was a master at molding all these different men into a team. "George was able to bring all the cliques together to play as a team, all working together for the same cause," Talbert said.

Sonny Jurgensen did not work well under George Allen's conservative offensive style, and he was also plagued by a series of injuries in his final seasons in Washington. "His (Allen's) idea of offense was don't make any mistakes, and we'll win it defensively." Jurgensen said. "That didn't sit well with me, and it was frustrating." (Tony Tomsic)

One of the biggest controversies in all of professional sports in the 1970s was who would play quarterback for the Washington Redskins—Sonny Jurgensen or Billy Kilmer. Both quarterbacks managed to stay friends despite the frenzy generated by the debate in Washington. Fans made their feelings known one way or another, as this banner illustrates. (Nate Fine)

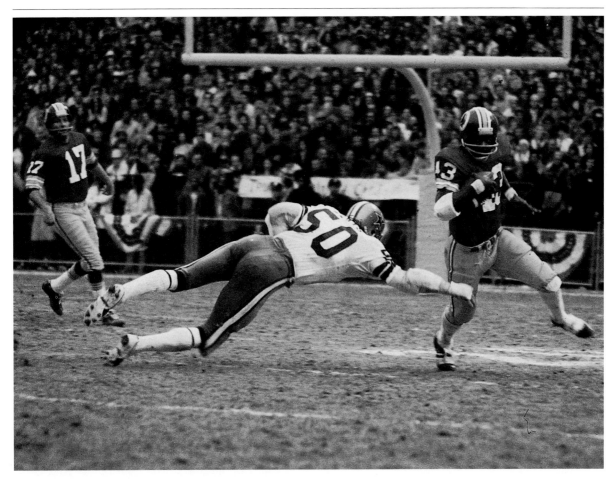

Washington's 26-3 victory over rival Dallas in the NFC title game Dec. 31, 1972, at RFK Stadium capped off a deliriously successful year for fans and players alike. Larry Brown gave Washington the running game it needed that day,
rushing for 104 yards. (NFL Properties)

"I don't think anyone else could have pulled off what he did with all these different players," Ron McDole said.

Allen knew the type of players he wanted, and he knew everything that anyone possibly could about a player before he brought him to a team. In player personnel decisions, as in everything else, Allen was as thorough a man as there was in the game.

"George did a lot of research," McDole said. "When George would lock in on somebody he wanted, he would really research them. He kept a chart in his office of players and how many winning teams they had played on. His feeling was that those players know how to win and were used to winning and would demand more of themselves. He had that knack of knowing everything about you that he could."

His research on players—including those he would be facing—was legendary. "With George, no stone was left unturned," Brig Owens said. "He would research a guy's background all the way back to junior high school and find out how he did in big games. Did he fumble in big games? George would find those kind of things out and try to use it against him."

If his research found that a player had a trou-blemaker reputation, that didn't necessarily mean that Allen didn't want him. "George enjoyed a challenge," Owens said. "He felt that he could change a person who had problems. He always felt a person needed a second chance. This was during a time, if a person became a player representative, he was either blackballed or traded. Well, we had about seven or eight player reps on our team at one point. George would pick them up because

Rivals Forever

One of the passions of Washington Redskin fans over the years has been the rivalry between Washington and the Dallas Cowboys. And what has fueled this legendary rivalry has been the fact that the players have felt it more than anyone else. This is no media invention.

Ever since the Cowboys turned into a winning team in the 1960s, the rivalry has been hot and heavy. It grew in intensity during the George Allen years, continued through the Joe Gibbs era, and has not subsided yet.

It came about for a number of reasons, one of which was the fact that so many Redskins were from Texas, which was a hotbed for football products.

Charley Taylor was from Grand Prairie, a suburb of Dallas. "The Redskin-Cowboy rivalry was down to the bone, down the marrow," Taylor said. "My mother would get threatening phone calls down in Texas. All the guys from Texas felt they had to produce because we had to live down there in the off-season."

Allen took the rivalry to new heights. Diron Talbert, a Texan, remembers Allen's theatrics before one Dallas Thanksgiving game: "We had played on Sunday, and we had to go right back to work on Monday because we played on Thursday, so we didn't get a day off," Talbert said. "We came to practice on Monday, and we were all beat up.

"George came into the meeting room," Talbert said. "He said he was going to leave the team at home and fly down to Dallas on his own. He said, 'We're beat up, they're beat up. I'm just going to take me a Lear jet and fly to Dallas the day before the game. We're not going to tell anybody. We're going to let the fans come out to the game, the press, everybody. Then I'm going to walk out on the sideline representing the Washington Redskins. Then Tom Landry is going to walk out on the other sideline by himself and leave his team at home. We're going to walk out to the middle of the field, and then the fight will be on, winner take all.'

"He [Allen] went through the motions of how he was going to fight him," Talbert said. "You never heard forty-five men scream and laugh so hard. George said, 'I'll chop him in the groin, and I'll knee him in the face.'"

No other player stoked the fires of the rivalry more than Talbert, the defensive tackle who played college football at the University of Texas. One of this more memorable moments came during that Dallas Thanksgiving game in 1974, when he declared before the game that the Redskins were going to knock Roger Staubach out of the game. They did, as linebacker Dave Robinson knocked Staubach out with Washington leading 16–3.

In came Clint Longley, a player whom the Redskins knew very little about. "We didn't have Longley on our depth chart," Ron McDole said.

The Redskins and the whole football world knew after that game. Longley connected on his first two passes, the second a touchdown to Billy Joe Dupree. As the Cowboys came back, the Redskins held them off and had a 23–17 lead in the fourth quarter. But, with less than a minute remaining, Longley connected on a fifty-yard pass to Drew Pearson for a touchdown, and the point after gave the Cowboys a 24–23 victory and forever sealed Clint Longley's place in history as the "Mad Bomber."

Talbert was at his finest, though, after the game. "My locker was next to Talbert, " McDole said. "The press came in after the game, and they couldn't wait to get to him. Someone asked him, 'What do you think of Clint Longley?' Talbert answered, 'Who the hell is Clint Longley?'"

From Clint Longley to memories of "We want Dallas" roaring through the RFK Stadium during the playoff run in January, 1983, the Cowboys have always held a special place in the hearts of Redskins players and fans.

Charley Taylor became one of the game's greatest receivers. From 1964 to 1977, he caught 649 passes. He broke the NFL record for all-time receptions with his 634th on Dec. 21, 1975, against the Philadelphia Eagles in the final game of the season. (Nate Fine)

they were leaders. With all these leaders on the team, he didn't have to do a whole lot to get players to perform."

That is why Allen would take a chance on players like Duane Thomas, the troubled Dallas running back who was with Washington for two years. "George would try to coach these guys because he thought the nucleus of older players would be strong enough to influence and enroll these players in the program," Fischer said. "His idea was that you come in and be welcomed. You want to line up with us and go off to war? This is your last chance. You may have to modify a little bit, but that doesn't mean you have to give up your identity. You just have to be with us. Don't be

against us. George did a pretty good job with that."

Allen's approach was simple—not to lose sight of his ultimate goal, to win football games, and to treat players like men. "I treat them like I hope I would be treated," Allen said.

In his first year, he would run his operation from a new state-of-the-art facility known as Redskin Park, near Dulles Airport. The team had previously practiced at RFK and other sites in and around Washington before that, but now they would have one of the first permanent training facilities in pro football.

Allen would have his work cut out for him at the start of the season. The biggest challenge appeared to be quarterback. In a preseason game

George Allen relied so heavily on veteran players, often cast away by their former teams, that his Redskins became know as "The Over the Hill Gang," which, said cornerback Pat Fischer, "Gave us an identity, and...also stimulated us." (Nate Fine)

against Miami, Sonny Jurgensen had tried to tackle Dick Anderson, who had just intercepted a Jurgensen pass, and broke a bone in his left shoulder, missing much of the season.

That would put the team in the hands of Kilmer. He didn't have the skills of Jurgensen as a passer, with a body busted up from a car accident that nearly killed him, but he did have tremendous leadership skills and a will to win. It would also set up one of the hottest quarterback controversies for several years—Sonny or Billy?

With Kilmer at the helm, the Redskins would start the season with three games on the road, opening with a victory in St. Louis. It was the defense, of course, that ruled the game, causing seven Cardinal turnovers.

The following week they would go to New York to play the Giants. Allen particularly enjoyed beating the Giants and getting the New York media in the process. "George loved going to New York and beating the Giants and beating the New York press," Brig Owens said. "If we won, they wouldn't have much to say, so he enjoyed that. After a win, George would say, 'Let's see what the New York press has to say now.'" The press had little to say, because the Redskins pounded the Giants 30–3.

The rival Cowboys were next in Dallas. Allen, along with some of his players, would fan the flames of the Redskins-Cowboys rivalry during his tenure as coach. Allen knew the Cowboys well from his days in Los Angeles. "We [the Rams] used to play Dallas every year in the [Los Angeles] Times Charity Game," Talbert said. "Then we practiced against them. We were at Fullerton; they were at Thousand Oaks. So we used to have a three-ring circus with them, drills, scrimmages. We knew them real well when we got to Washington."

Again, it was the defense who led the way, complemented by key offensive plays. After the Redskins stopped the Cowboys on their first possession, Washington took the ball, and Charlie Harraway ran fifty-seven yards for a touchdown, and Curt Knight's point after put Washington on top 7–0.

Dallas would come back with a field goal to make it a 7–3 game, but in the second quarter, Kilmer found Roy Jefferson for a fifty-yard scoring pass. The Redskins now led 14–3.

In previous years, a Dallas scoring drive would have usually resulted in a touchdown, and Redskin-Cowboy contests would be high-scoring affairs. But not with a George Allen defense. The Cowboys would get just a field goal again with five minutes left in the half, cutting the Washington lead to 14–6. And they would add one more field goal for a 14–9 score going into halftime.

In the third quarter, Washington would add two more field goals for a 20–9 lead and hang on as the Cowboys finally found the end zone for what would turn out to be the final score of 20–16 for the Redskins' third straight win—all three coming on the road.

When the Redskins came home, they got a greeting normally reserved for a championship team when more than five thousand fans showed

Running back Larry Brown found his game under Vince Lombardi and continued to flourish under George Allen's ball-control offense. In 1972, Brown set a team rushing record with 1,216 yards and was named NFL Player of the Year. (*below*: NFL Properties; *right*: Nate Fine)

Diron Talbert was a fan favorite in Washington for his outspokenness, particularly when it came to the rivalry with the Cowboys. Once, after the mad bomber, Clint Longley, led the Cowboys to a come-from-behind win on Thanksgiving, Talbert, when asked about Longley's performance, mockingly asked, "Who's Clint Longley?" (Pro Football Hall of Fame)

up at the airport cheering their undefeated heroes. That enthusiasm only grew with two straight wins at RFK, 22–13 over the Houston Oilers and a shutout, 20–0, over the Cardinals, for a 5–0 record. When the team went to Kansas City and lost its first game of the season, 27–20, it was evident that Redskins fever had captured the city like never before, as a crowd of about twenty thousand fans came to Dulles Airport to show their support.

The city simply went crazy over the Redskins. Politicians and celebrities all wanted tickets now for Redskins games. Television and newspaper coverage was all-consuming, from the editorial pages to the sports pages to advertisements as local businesses began taking out ads to congratulate the Redskins.

"We of the Giant Food Family know that we echo the sentiment of every family in Washington, in suburban Maryland, and Virginia when we say . . . Redskins, you are beautiful and we love each and every blooming one of you!"

Not even the chief executive was immune to Redskins fever. After the loss to the Chiefs, Richard Nixon wrote Allen a note, saying, "A truly great team must prove that it can be great in defeat as well as in victory. The Redskins proved they were a great team yesterday."

The Redskins showed their appreciation with a 24–14 win over the New Orleans Saints before a frenzied crowd of more than fifty-three thousand fans. RFK Stadium had become an asset to the home team. That was no accident, as Allen made a point of enlisting the fans to be part of the team.

"George Allen was the first coach in the game that really challenged fans to back their home team, to really use the fans against the opponents," Brig Owens said. "Sure, you had fans in

Ron McDole was another veteran George Allen brought in. The former Buffalo defensive end went on to play eight seasons for the Redskins, retiring after the 1978 season. "Everyone fit in," McDole said. "It was a good time, a lot of fun." (Pro Football Hall of Fame)

other cities that supported their teams, but George said, 'This is your team, and when we come out, we want a standing ovation when the team is introduced.'

"We had teams come in and players would ask, 'How come these fans give you guys standing ovations?' We became the team where players wanted to come and play, and we also became the place where other teams didn't want to come to play," Owens said. "We would go on the road, and our goal was to turn the fans against their own team and cheer us for our play. That was the fun of it."

But it wasn't much fun the following week at RFK. Although the sold-out ballpark was still raucous and wild about the Redskins, they managed to squeeze out only a 7–7 tie to the underdog Philadelphia Eagles. The offense had hit a brick wall with seven turnovers, Kilmer struggling, and running back Larry Brown was slowed with leg injuries. Those factors combined for two straight losses, 16–15 to the Bears in Chicago and, most troubling, a 13–0 shutout by the Cowboys at RFK.

Jurgensen had been activated before the Philadelphia game but saw no action. His presence, though, in light of the team's offensive problems, fueled the Sonny-Billy debate to a fever pitch. People began putting bumper stickers on their cars reading either "I love Sonny" or "I love Billy." And the *Washington Daily News* even conducted a poll, which Jurgensen won, 1,225 to 594. And Jurgensen saw some brief playing time in the Chicago game in the final two minutes. So when it came time for the Dallas game, the pressure mounted to start Jurgensen, and it continued into the game, when, with Dallas leading 13–0 in the third quarter,

Field Inspection

I n 1971, the Redskins moved into their new practice facility, Redskin Park, near Dulles Airport. With practice fields, a weight room, and other amenities, it was a state-of-the-art headquarters, but it was not without a few "holes" when it first opened.

"We had just come back from training camp in Carlisle, and we were staying over at the Dulles Marriott. We were going to drive over to the new place, but, no, George brought two buses over. He wanted to take us all over so he could see how impressed everyone was. And everyone was impressed. It was really nice.

"But we got on the grass field, and George said, 'This grass field has some holes in it. I want everybody to get on the goal line.' We still had a bunch of players who hadn't been cut yet, so there were a lot of us there. So we all stood on the goal line, enough to go all the way across the field. He gave us a bunch of tongue depressors and those long cotton swabs.

"He said, 'We're going to walk down this field and every time you feel a hole, stick one of those into the ground.' Well, he was talking to the craziest group in the world. By the time we got to the fifty-yard line, we ran out of the tongue depressors, so they got some more. By the time we got to the other end of the field, there must have been two thousand of those things stuck in the field. It was the funniest thing you'd ever seen. We stuck them everywhere we could. We got to the end, and George said, laughing, 'I should have known I couldn't count on you guys.'"

Redskins Park was a state-of-the-art practice facility, the first of its kind. When it opened near Dulles Airport in 1971, however, it had a few "holes" in it, including some on one of the practice fields. When Allen lined up his players from one side to the other with tongue depressors to locate the holes, the results were humorous. (Washington Redskins)

the crowd chanted, "We want Sonny." They didn't get him that day.

The quarterback rivalry was between Jurgensen and Kilmer, but the two wound up being friends and handled it well. Jurgensen's problems were more with Allen than with Kilmer, as Jurgensen disagreed with Allen's conservative offensive style.

"His idea of offense was don't make any mistakes, and we'll win it defensively," Jurgensen said. "That didn't set with me, and it was frustrating. We'd never done anything like that. We had all this talent. We could score. But it became three yards and a cloud of dust.

"We clashed over the system," Jurgensen said. "Believe me, he was a heck of defensive coach. But we didn't do anything with the offense."

Jurgensen got his chance to start again against the Eagles in Philadelphia the week after the Dallas loss. It couldn't have turned out much worse.

With the score 0–0 in the second quarter, Jurgensen hurt his shoulder again while running the ball. There would be no more Sonny-Billy debate that year. Jurgensen was done for the season.

Kilmer came in and led the Redskins to a 20–13 win. The following week, at home against the Giants, Washington prevailed again, 23–7, for a record of 8–3–1 going into a big game on the West Coast—Allen's homecoming to Los Angeles to face his old team.

It would have been enough of a distraction just to make the trip out west, let alone with all the hype that would accompany Allen as he faced off against the team that fired him. He didn't need any more to deal with, but Kilmer would give him plenty.

On December 6, early in the morning—about 2:00 A.M.—the day after the Giants game, Kilmer was arrested and charged with being drunk in public after getting into an argument with a waitress at the Toddle House in Arlington, Virginia.

Kilmer, who denied that he was drunk, had gone to pay for his $4 breakfast with the smallest bill he said he had—a $100 bill. The way the story goes is that the waitress didn't like having to give change for a $100 bill, and Kilmer had some words

George Allen confers here with one of the "Ramskins," defensive tackle Diron Talbert, while assistant coach Ted Marchibroda, who would go on to become a head coach of note in his own right, listens. (Nate Fine)

with her. An off-duty policeman at the restaurant tried to get Kilmer to calm down, but the argument led to his arrest. He was out of jail in a few hours, and it was front page news in the Washington papers. Kilmer took it in stride. "Pete Rozelle will probably put that whole chain of coffee houses off limits," he said.

That incident was quickly set aside, though, with the Ramskins heading back to Los Angeles to face the Rams in a game that could clinch a playoff spot for Washington.

There was bad blood between the Rams and Allen, and it spilled over to the papers, where Rams defensive end Deacon Jones was quoted as saying, "The Rams will blow the Redskins out of the Coliseum." And Allen got into a battle with his replacement, Tommy Prothro, when Allen called the Rams "a great gadget team."

With more than eighty thousand on hand and a Monday night television audience watching the grudge match, the Rams drew first blood when Kermit Alexander intercepted a Kilmer pass and ran eighty-two yards for a touchdown. But Kilmer

Richie Petitbon was one of the players brought to Washington by George Allen to form the "Ramskins," a group of players who had been on Allen's Rams team in Los Angeles. Petitbon was a star safety who went on to become the architect of the Washington defenses during the Super Bowl years to come in the 1980s and '90s. (Pro Football Hall of Fame)

came back with a scoring pass to Roy Jefferson, and the Redskins tied the game at 7–7. After the teams traded field goals for a 10–10 tie, Kilmer found Clifton McNeil for a thirty-two-yard scoring pass to give Washington a 17–10 lead. Washington then made it 24–10 on a short run by Charlie Harraway before the half.

The Redskins offense didn't let up, opening up a 31–10 lead in the third quarter on Kilmer's third touchdown pass, a short toss to Jefferson. Los

Angeles would come back to within seven, at 31–24, but Speedy Duncan intercepted a pass from Roman Gabriel and ran forty-six yards for a score, putting the final tally of Allen and the Ramskins' revenge at 38–24, clinching Washington's first playoff spot since 1945. It was Kilmer's finest game, as he completed fourteen of nineteen for 246 yards and three touchdowns.

The Redskins suffered a letdown in the final game of the season at home, losing 20–13 to Cleveland as Washington turned the ball over four times—not the Allen offensive plan. But with a regular-season mark of 9–4–1 and a playoff game coming against San Francisco, for Washington the loss to the Browns was an afterthought, lost in the excitement of the team's greatest success in twenty-six years.

It seemed as if the storybook season would continue for Washington on that day after Christmas, 1971 at Candlestick Park. The Redskins blocked a Steve Spurrier punt, and Kilmer quickly hit Jerry Smith on a five-yard touchdown pass to put Washington up 7–0.

In the second quarter, each team added three to the score on field goals for a 10–3 game. Right before the half, it appeared that Washington was ready to jump out to a big lead when Speedy Duncan returned a 49ers punt forty-seven yards, giving Washington the ball on the San Francisco twelve-yard line with thirty seconds left.

But the offense faltered, and a field goal attempt by Curt Knight was blocked, so the Redskins had to be happy with their 10–3 lead at halftime.

In the third quarter, Allen did something very un-Allen-like—he went for fourth and inches on the 49ers eleven-yard line—instead of attempting what seemed like a sure field goal. Washington's one-thousand-yard rusher, Larry Brown, didn't make it, though, and soon after, John Brodie found Gene Washington for a seventy-eight yard touchdown pass to tie the game at 10–10. The 49ers made it 17–10 when Kilmer threw an interception and Brodie tossed a scoring pass to tight end Bob Windsor. Knight brought the Redskins closer with a field goal, but, with the score 17–13, a missed snap on a Mike Bragg punt resulted in a recovery in the Washington end zone by the 49ers, opening up a 24–13 lead. The

No Stone Unturned

George Allen was known for his obsession for preparation, leaving no stone unturned to find a little edge over his opponent. That was never more evident than the day before Super Bowl VII.

"For the Super Bowl, we had all the game films of the Miami Dolphins, including when we had beaten them in the exhibition season." Ron McDole said. "So it came down to the day before the game, and we had seen all the films. We went over to the stadium and figured we wouldn't have to watch any films, since we had seen them all.

"But George had this big reel ready to run," McDole said. "Turns out it was Bob Griese [the Miami Dolphins quarterback] playing against Ohio State when he played for Purdue, in a game in the mud. George said, 'We can get something out of this.' Well, there was so much mud we couldn't even tell which one he was."

Allen was a New Age kind of coach, using all sorts of psychological ploys to motivate his guys. Here, with Larry Brown, he carves a cake with St. Louis quarterback Jim Hart's name on it. (Nate Fine)

George leads his team in prayer, then incites them to a fever pitch. (Nate Fine)

Redskins did add a touchdown on a sixteen-yard pass from Kilmer to Brown, but it would fall short, along with the Redskins' hope of an NFL championship.

It was a remarkable season, though, in so many ways—the winning record, the playoff appearance, the recognition of Washington's success, as Allen was named Coach of the Year by numerous organizations—but two accomplishments may have been the most significant.

The Redskins brought the people of a city together in a common goal at a time when there was tension in the streets of America. D.C. Mayor Walter Washington told Allen that the team's play had helped bring some needed civic pride to the city. "There was tremendous support for us at a time when the community was going through tough times," Pat Fischer said. "Players were going out and talking to kids in the schools, and it gave people something in common to rally around."

It also allowed Vince Lombardi's work to continue. Winning and excellence would replace losing and mediocrity as Redskin trademarks.

Obviously Washington had high hopes for the 1972 season, and Allen laid out his goals—to win a minimum of ten regular season games and to win the Super Bowl. The road to the big game, though, would have to go through Dallas, who defeated the Miami Dolphins 24–3 to win Super Bowl VI.

The Redskins showed that the 1971 season was no fluke when, in the fifth preseason game of 1972, they defeated Miami 27–24. "I remember Jim Kiick and I saying to each other, 'See you at the Super Bowl,'" Brig Owens said. It turned out to be a pretty good prediction.

Washington opened the 1972 season on a Monday night in Minnesota. Allen's decision to go with Kilmer as the starter for the season drew a lot of criticism. Jurgensen was thirty-eight but healthy, and many fans couldn't understand why Allen wouldn't use one of the best passers in the history of the game instead of a quarterback with a shaky arm. Kilmer was simply Allen's man, though, the guy he believed was perfect for his low-key, mistake-free offensive goals. "If I had stayed in Los Angeles, I made up my mind that I wanted Kilmer there," Allen said in defending his decision. "He has a fierce determination to win."

It was the special teams who set the tone for a 24–21 win over the Vikings. When Minnesota was forced to punt on their first possession, Bill Malinchak, a special teams star under Allen, rushed in to block the punt by Mike Eischeid. Malinchak managed to pick the ball up and run it in for the score, and the extra point gave the Redskins a 7–0 lead. Washington held on to a 10–7 lead at halftime but lost it in the third quarter when Karl Kassulke intercepted a Kilmer pass and Fran Tarkenton hit John Gilliam for an eleven-yard touchdown pass to put the Vikings on top 14–10.

Washington, though, would answer with two touchdowns, one a Larry Brown run and the other a Charlie Harraway score, to open up a 24–14 lead with about nine minutes left in the game. The Vikings would make it close with a touchdown toss from Tarkenton to Bill Brown, but a last-second onside kick by Fred Cox was smothered by another special teams star, Rusty Tillman, and Washington came away with a 24–21 opening-game victory.

Washington followed that with another win, 24–10, in the home opener before more than fifty-three thousand fans, as Kilmer threw two touchdown passes. Then came a bizarre contest in Foxboro against the New England Patriots, a losing team playing in a new stadium, with sixty thousand fans showing up to see Allen's team.

After a scoreless first quarter, Kilmer connected with Charlie Taylor for a thirty-yard touchdown, with the point after by Knight putting Washington on top 7–0. The pair connected soon after for another score, and, with a 14–0 lead over the hapless Patriots, a win seemed like a lock.

Nobody told Patriots quarterback Jim Plunkett, though. He moved his team methodically down the field with a mixture of passing and running plays that ended with a touchdown by halfback John Ashton, cutting the Redskins' lead to 14–7 just before the first half ended.

New England kept the pressure on coming out of the locker room for the third quarter with an eleven-yard scoring pass from Plunkett to Reggie Rucker, tying the score at 14–14.

But the Redskins seemed to turn the momentum back in their favor early in the third quarter when Mike Bass intercepted an option pass. But the Patriots stopped a Washington drive by inter-

Defense was the name of the game under George Allen. The Redskins defense huddles together, with linebacker Jack Pardee calling the formations. (Pro Football Hall of Fame)

cepting Kilmer at the goal line.

Plunkett continued to take apart the vaunted Redskins defense, and New England took a 17–14 lead on a forty-two-yard field goal as the third quarter ended. Washington hardly fell apart, answering with a ten-yard touchdown pass from Kilmer to Jerry Smith, taking back the game 21–17.

But this was Plunkett's day. He threw another touchdown, this one twenty-four yards to Ashton, giving New England the lead, 24–21, with just minutes remaining in the game.

It appeared that Washington had pulled the game out, though, when, with about two minutes left, Kilmer hit Roy Jefferson in the end zone, but he was called out of bounds after being knocked out by a New England defender. Curt Knight connected on a thirty-three-yard field goal, but a roughing the kicker call gave the Redskins the option of taking the three points and tying the game at 24–24 or taking the penalty and trying to win the game with a touchdown. Allen opted for

the win—a gamble that failed. Washington would not be able to move the ball, and this time Knight's field goal attempt from the twenty-seven-yard line missed.

Remarkably, the Redskins nearly won the game again when Bill Malinchak blocked a Patriots punt and had the ball as he slid out of the end zone. But it was ruled a safety instead of a touchdown as officials determined that Malinchak did not have control of the ball before sliding out of the end zone. The game would end with a 24–23 New England win as Knight missed another field goal, this one from fifty yards, as time ran out.

The shock of the bitter loss moved Allen to make a change, and Jurgensen got the start the following week against Philadelphia at RFK Stadium. He was very rusty, throwing three interceptions in the first half, which ended 0–0, but recovering to toss one touchdown pass in the second half as Washington got back on the winning track with a 14–0 victory. Jurgensen was better the following

The 1972 Redskins were the first championship team for the franchise since 1942–and probably one of its best of all time, posting an 11-3 record. George Allen, seated between two playes in the center, possessed some odd beliefs about team photos, though. Because his 1973 Redskins failed to make the conference title game, he refused to allow a team photo for that year. (Washington Redskins)

week, completing thirteen of eighteen for 203 yards in a 33–3 beating of St. Louis, and he would get another starting assignment in the biggest game of the early season—against the Cowboys at RFK Stadium.

It was a typical Dallas game, with the city whipped up into a frenzy the entire week in anticipation of a chance at its mortal enemies, the Cowboys. But the RFK crowd nearly was taken out the game early when, with the Cowboys leading 3–0 after getting a field goal on their first possession, Charley Taylor fumbled, Dallas recovered, and Craig Morton hit Ron Sellers on a thirty-nine-yard touchdown pass for a 10–0 Dallas lead in the first quarter.

The Cowboys added another field goal at the start of the second quarter for a 13–0 lead, but Jurgensen got his team back in the game on a nineteen-yard scoring pass to Larry Brown, cutting the Dallas lead to 13–7 at the end of the first half.

Dallas roared through the Washington defense at the beginning of the third quarter, resulting in another touchdown and a 20–7 lead. Jurgensen, though, led a comeback drive that

ended with a Larry Brown scoring run, making it a 20–14 game. And, at the end of the third quarter, Curt Knight hit a field goal to come within three, 20–17.

In the fourth quarter, Washington put its stamp not only on the game, but also on the season. The defense held off the Cowboys, while Charlie Harraway put his team ahead to stay with a thirteen-yard touchdown run for a 24–20 Redskins win. Allen credited the deafening home crowd, particularly in the fourth quarter, when, Allen said, the field itself seemed to shake.

The Redskins were the unstoppable force in the league after that, winning six straight and taking an 11–1 record into the final two games of the season. Allen had accomplished his first goal of at least ten victories. But the Redskins would be without their new leader on the field, Jurgensen, who tore an Achilles tendon the week after the Dallas win in a 23–16 win over the Giants in New York. Kilmer returned to start the rest of the year, leading the team on its six-game run before suffering a letdown at the end, with a 34–24 loss to the Cowboys in Dallas and 24–17 home loss to the

Buffalo Bills in the season finale.

Washington had home field advantage in the playoffs, with their 11–3 regular-season record, and they faced the Green Bay Packers, who were returning to the playoffs under Dan Devine. They had a powerful running game, led by John Brockington, but the Redskins defense held the Packers to just seventy-eight yards rushing, and the offense was a textbook Allen performance—a touchdown from Kilmer to Jefferson and three Knight field goals—as Washington prevailed 16–3, moving on to the conference title game to face the team everyone knew all along they would have to beat to get to the Super Bowl—the Dallas Cowboys.

With the RFK crowd reaching new heights of intensity, the Redskins were fired up when they hit the field and never looked back. The Cowboys looked unnerved and out of sync.

Both teams had trouble moving the ball early until Curt Knight hit an eighteen-yard field goal in the second quarter for a 3–0 lead. Kilmer would find Charley Taylor on another second-quarter drive for a fifteen-yard field goal, and Dallas would finally get on the board with three points for a 10–3 game going into the second half.

Those three points would be all the Cowboys would have to show for the day. Both teams would battle again in the third quarter, but the Redskins exploded for sixteen points on another scoring pass to Taylor and three field goals by Knight for a 26–3 victory and the NFC championship.

For Taylor, who caught seven passes for 146 yards and two touchdowns, it was one of his finest days as a pro. "Everything was so easy for me that day," Taylor said. "It was so smooth."

Center Len Hauss has a vivid memory of the first touchdown pass from Kilmer to Taylor, the sort of moment that an offensive lineman toiling in the ditches can appreciate. "We had worked on a play, a little thing where one of the Dallas safeties would blitz and all our blocking had to be slide blocking," he said. "So often you practice things like that and you never use them. But Kilmer thinks the safeties are going to blitz, and he calls the audible for that play.

"I call the line blocking, and I notice the same thing he [Kilmer] does, and we call the slide play," Hauss said. "All of our blockers slide to the right, and they blitz their safety to the right. Billy dumps the ball over, and we get a touchdown. It was one of the easiest things you ever saw. It was one of those instances where everything you worked on happened, and it happened just like it was supposed to, like it was drawn on paper and run one thousand times in practice."

Right in front of the Redskins then, was the other goal that Allen had laid out when the season started—winning the Super Bowl. But they would go against a team that had an even better season—the Miami Dolphins, with a 16–0 record and a chance to go the entire season undefeated.

The Dolphins, having been through the Super Bowl hoopla before in their 24–3 loss to the Cowboys, were ready for the pressure and distractions that filled the two weeks prior to the game. The Redskins were not.

The Dolphins figured they could play the same game the Redskins did—conservative, mistake-free offense—and do it better, with Bob Griese as quarterback rather than Kilmer. They shut off Washington's running game, leaving Kilmer to shoulder the burden of the offense.

It made for an anticlimactic contest before a record crowd of more than ninety thousand at the Coliseum in Los Angeles. Toward the end of the first quarter, Griese moved the Dolphins down the field on the ground, with the running game of Larry Csonka, Jim Kiick, and Mercury Morris grinding out the yards. Griese connected with Howard Twilley on a twenty-eight-yard touchdown pass, and Garo Yepremian's point after gave Miami a 7–0 lead.

In the mistake waiting game, Washington broke first when Kilmer threw an interception to linebacker Nick Buoniconti, and Miami took over on the Redskins' twenty-seven-yard line. Soon after, Kiick took the ball over, and Miami led 14–0 at halftime.

The Dolphins would continue to hold Washington in check in the second half, but in the fourth quarter it seemed as if the Redskins might have a shot at coming back, moving the ball down to the Miami ten-yard line. But Kilmer threw another interception, this time to safety Jake Scott—who would come to the Redskins in 1976. Scott returned the ball to the Washington forty-eight-yard line. Several plays later, Yepremian

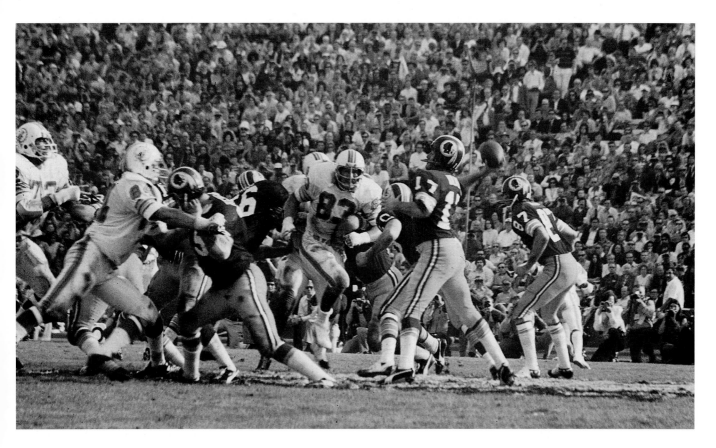

The 1972 season was a jewel. It seemingly wiped away all the years of frustration between championship seasons. Allen led the team to an NFC championship and a trip to the Super Bowl. The final chapter to the storybook year ended on a down note, however, a 14-7 loss to the Miami Dolphins. Many Redskins players believe pregame practice was too tough, wearing them down to the point where they left their best game on the practice field.

(*Left*): The indelible image from the game was Garo Yepremian's attempt to pass the ball after his field goal attempt was blocked. Mike Bass scooped up the ball and ran it back for a touchdown, Washington's only score of the game. (NFL Properties)

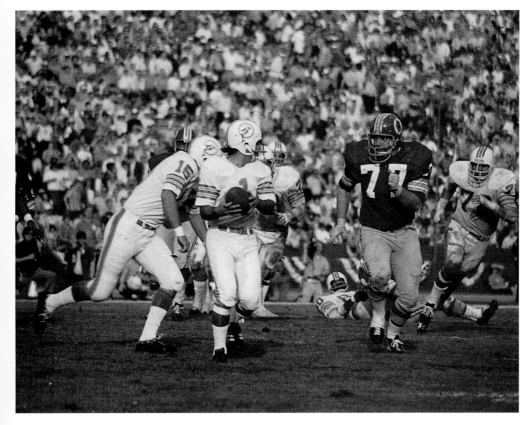

would come in to attempt a forty-two-yard field goal in what turned out to be the most memorable play of Super Bowl VII.

Yepremian's kick was blocked, and the diminutive kicker picked up the bouncing ball, and, of all things, tried to throw it. His desperate lob was probably the worst pass in Super Bowl history, because it landed in cornerback Mike Bass's hands. Bass ran forty-nine yards for a touchdown, putting Washington on the board 14–7, the final score of the game.

There were missed opportunities—a Kilmer pass to a wide-open Jerry Smith hit the goalpost, a pass to Taylor that would have gone for a score was knocked away at the last minute—but many players believed they lost that game in the time leading up to it.

"We didn't know how to manage our time," Fischer said. "We practiced hard for two weeks, the same schedule. We were kind of an exhausted team. We had never experienced anything like that, even though we were a veteran team. We mismanaged ourselves."

Taylor agrees that the best they had to offer had been left on the practice field. "I think we lost that game on Thursday," he said. "We practiced so strong and so hard and had that plan down so pat, we went out Thursday and executed it perfectly, and I think we left it there."

It was one time when Allen's obsession for preparation may have backfired. "George was so worried about us staying in California, especially with the kind of guys we had, who liked to roam a little bit, that he kept us in a lot of long meetings and kept us in practice too long," Brig Owens said. "Once we got to the game, we were flat."

Still, it was the most successful season many Redskins fans had ever been a part of, and the team received a hero's welcome back in Washington. George Allen had been named Coach of the Year for the second straight season, and Larry Brown was named NFL Player of the Year, setting a new Redskins rushing record with 1,216 yards. It was a year to celebrate.

Seven

The Quest to Win

Although the 1972 season ended with the disappointing loss to Miami in the Super Bowl, there was still enormous pride in what the team had accomplished and optimism about the future. Allen had given Redskins fans the confidence that the franchise would continue its winning ways.

Allen continued to bring veterans onto his quad and to trade draft choices. Safety Ken Houston, linebacker Dave Robinson, tight end Allen Reed, and running back Duane Thomas all came to Washington that year. Thomas, the talented but troubled former Dallas back, didn't even play in 1972. He had been dealt to the San Diego Chargers but refused to report, and Allen was willing to take a chance on him, obtaining Thomas for several draft picks. It was a trade that would not work out, as Thomas never showed the skills he'd had in Dallas.

Washington showed signs of making another championship run in the season opener, a 38–0 win over San Diego before a crowd of more than fifty-three thousand at RFK Stadium. But the season would not be as smooth as in 1972. The battle between Sonny and Billy would still go on after Kilmer had a poor game in the second game of the

year, a 34–27 loss to St. Louis.

But the thirty-nine-year-old Jurgensen had a tough time staying healthy with bad knees, and he saw limited playing time after the fifth game of the season. Kilmer had his own physical problems, bothered by a stomach disorder.

Jurgensen took target practice on his old team, the Eagles, in a 28–7 win in Philadelphia. Then came the first Dallas game, this one at RFK. It would prove as memorable as any of the classic contests.

The Cowboys were 3–0. The Redskins were 2–1. Early in the season, it was already a big game with playoff ramifications. And to add to the excitement, it was on "Monday Night Football."

The game opened with Redskins style. Dallas had to punt after being stopped the first time they had the ball, and special teamer Bill Malinchak blocked a punt by Marv Bateman at the Dallas thirty-eight-yard line. However, the Redskins would fail to capitalize.

It was that sort of game, full of big defensive plays. The Cowboys finally broke through in the second quarter on a fifteen-yard touchdown pass from Roger Staubach to Otto Stowe, and the point after gave Dallas the lead 7–0, which was the score going into halftime.

Though they fell short of winning Super Bowl VII, George Allen's attitude–and constant exhortations–gave Redskins players and fans alike the confidence that the franchise would continue its winning ways.
(Pro Football Hall of Fame)

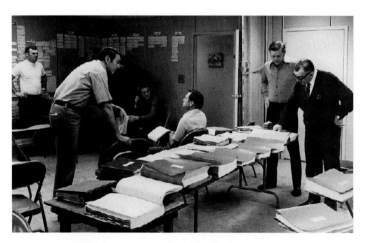

Allen, in the "War Room" before the 1973 draft, used these opportunities to trade draft picks for veteran players. He was relentless in his research of players. "He would research a guy's background all the way back to junior high school," Brig Owens said.
(Nate Fine)

In the second half, the Cowboys hung on to their 7–0 lead, stopping the Redskins offense, once on a crucial fourth-and-one play. But Washington would get a break later in the fourth quarter on a pass interference call, putting the ball on the Cowboys' one-yard line. Soon after, Charley Taylor caught a pass in the corner of the end zone, and Curt Knight's extra point tied the game at 7–7, with a little more than three minutes left.

Dallas got the ball back, this time with Craig Morton at quarterback. On third down at his own twenty-yard line, Morton tried to hit Billy Joe Dupree, but Brig Owens cut in front of Dupree for the interception, racing twenty-six yards for the go-ahead touchdown, putting Washington on top 14–7.

"I dreamed that interception, played it in my mind a number of times, and there it was," Owens said.

But the best was yet to come. With about two minutes remaining, Dallas got the ball back but was unable to move it, and they punted. But when the ball bounced as it landed, it hit a Redskins blocker, and the Cowboys recovered on the Washington thirty-two-yard line. Morton moved the team down to the Washington four-yard line for first and goal, but Dallas couldn't get the ball in on three pass attempts by Morton. On fourth down, with twenty-four seconds left, Morton threw a short pass to fullback Walt Garrison right on the goal line. Garrison was as hard a runner as you would find in the league. But safety Ken Houston made perhaps the most famous tackle in Redskins history, sticking his shoulder into Garrison, grabbing him, and throwing him back away from the goal line. Garrison tried to lateral the ball as he was being tackled, but it bounced around and was recovered by the Redskins, sealing the 14–7 win.

Houston would later say, "It was the biggest tackle of my career," and it is forever seared in the memory of all who were in the stands and on the field that day at RFK. "It was the most exciting memory for me," Pat Fischer said. "I can still see the scoreboard, fourth quarter and fourth down, with seconds to go."

It seemed that the tackle would propel the Redskins to another conference championship, as they won their next two, 21–3 over the Giants and

A determined George Allen leads his team out of the RFK dugout and into battle. (Nate Fine)

31–13 over St. Louis. But with a 5–1 record, the team suddenly had a letdown, losing to the Saints, a three-touchdown underdog, 19–3 in New Orleans, and 21–16 to the Pittsburgh Steelers, before recovering to win four straight, including a comeback 27–24 win over the New York Giants before a frenzied crowd at RFK. Down 24–13 in the fourth quarter, Jurgensen relieved an injured Kilmer and led the team back to victory, completing twelve of fifteen passes for 135 yards and one touchdown, even though he was still suffering from knee problems.

Washington left its best performance in the Giants game, though, as they were beaten decisively 27–7 in Dallas by the Cowboys the following week in a game that decided that division title. But they would recover to win the final game of the season, 38–20, over the Eagles, for a 10–4 mark and a wild card berth.

They would face the Minnesota Vikings the following week, three days before Christmas, in frigid Bloomington. The Vikings, with a record of 12–2, were led by Fran Tarkenton and the Purple People Eaters defensive line of Alan Page, Carl Eller, Gary Larsen, and Jim Marshall.

This game would not be a repeat of the Redskins' playoff success of 1972, though. Curt Knight missed a field goal after the Redskins' first drive, and the Vikings connected on a Fred Cox kick to take a 3–0 lead. But Washington's special teams would put the Redskins back on top as they recovered a fumbled punt in the second quarter on the Vikings' twenty-one-yard line. Kilmer managed to move the ball down to the three-yard line, where Larry Brown took it in to give the Redskins a 7–3 lead going into halftime.

Minnesota roared out in the third quarter, moving seventy-nine yards for a score and a 10–7

Iron Man

Len Hauss began playing center in 1964 for Bill McPeak. He finished his career in 1977 playing for George Allen.

In between, he never—*never*—missed a game, playing in 196 consecutive games over fourteen seasons. To be an iron man in a game so physically punishing is a remarkable achievement, but Hauss said he didn't know any other way to play the game.

"You've got to be lucky to some degree to play in that many ball games," Hauss said. "But you also have to have a work ethic that is a little bit different. I came up thinking that I was supposed to play every down of every game. When I watched Cal Ripken, Jr. break Lou Gehrig's record, I almost stood up at home watching it on television. I got a lump in my throat because I can imagine what type of guy he must be.

"For someone to be able to do what this guy has done, he must have a work ethic, a mentality, like the way I thought about it," he said. "You're supposed to play. That's your job, and you're supposed to do your job.

"I had five knee operations over my career, and I was able to put them all off until after the season," Hauss said. "You can play with cartilage or joint damage, whatever it took to do the job. But there were times when I had injured my back, or my knees were bothering me or one thing or another that made it very difficult to play. And I think there were a few times I was ill or something other than a football injury, the kind when you stay up all night and you can't keep anything down and have a temperature. I had a few of those where maybe I thought I wouldn't be able to play, but things just fell into place. But you've got to expect to play. My attitude was that I've got to go out there and play. There was no option."

Hauss showed his teammates his intense attitude right from the start. "When Len Hauss was a rookie, nobody knew him," Sam Huff said. "We had this nutcracker drill, where you put two blocking dummies down, and it's one on one. The offensive lineman has to block the defensive lineman, and the quarterback would hand the ball to a back. It's almost like a split-T play, where the back has to break on the lineman's block, in between the two blocking dummies.

"In training camp, when we were doing the drill once, since I was the middle linebacker, my guy was the offensive center," Huff said. "So Number 56 comes up there, and I don't know who he is. He's some rookie from Georgia. On the snap of the ball, I popped him and knocked the stuffing out of him. I'm feeling pretty good about the play, and I get back on the defensive line. Hauss goes back and gets in the offensive line. My turn comes up, and he's there again. I didn't think much about it. He went on a different count, snapped the ball, and, boom, knocked the daylights out of me. I said, 'What's his name? I think he's going to be around here for a while.' He was a great center. He had heart and never quit."

Diron Talbert (72) and Bill Brundige (77), with assistant coach Lavern "Torgy" Torgeson, were two of the stalwarts on the Redskins' defensive line during the Allen years. (Nate Fine)

lead. Knight would move Washington back ahead with two field goals, but Tarkenton would connect on two touchdowns, and the Vikings would eventually prevail 27–20, ending the Redskins' season and hopes for a return to the Super Bowl.

In 1974, a significant event would dictate the future of the team and continues to do so today. Minority owner Jack Kent Cooke acquired enough stock to become majority owner, which meant the winning style that had come to be associated with the franchise would continue.

Allen made a notable personnel acquisition that year. He traded his 1976 first-round draft choice to Miami for the rights to quarterback Joe Theismann, the former Notre Dame star quarterback who had been playing in Canada for the past three seasons.

Theismann presented another quarterback controversy for the Redskins. He wanted to play and let his feelings be known. He even offered to field punts as a way to get into games, an offer that Allen took him up on.

But his aggressive style added an interesting twist to the perennial "Sonny or Billy" argument—it gave the two veterans a common enemy. "He [Theismann] came in and said if he couldn't play in front of these two old guys, that something was wrong," Jurgensen said. "That bonded us [Jurgensen and Kilmer] together more than anything else. We figured we may be two old guys, but we'll keep him on the bench. One of us will be out there playing. It seems to me he was returning punts before he got on the field."

Theismann would eventually get his turn,

(*Above*): George Allen, reviewing defensive plays with Brig Owens, Richie Petitbon, Jack Pardee, and Chris Hanburger, took his share of criticism in his final years as the Redskins head coach for his "The Future is Now" philosophy, which left the team with few draft choices. Allen, though, put his faith in veteran players, who often delivered for him. (Nate Fine)

(*Left*): Linebacker Harold McLinton (53) and wide receiver Roy Jefferson (80) were two of the veteran players who George Allen relied on to play mistake-free offense and to create turnovers on defense. (Nate Fine)

though, and would prove to be an able leader and a championship quarterback, throwing 160 touchdowns over his career and leading Washington to its first Super Bowl win.

For now, though, it remained Kilmer and Jurgensen. The team got off to a rocky start, barely defeating the Giants 13–10 in New York and then losing the home opener to St. Louis 17–10. They would win three of their next four games before facing the Cardinals again, this time in St. Louis. But the Cardinals, under head coach Don Coryell, had become a much improved team, an offensive force, and beat Washington again 23–20. Part of the reason for St. Louis's success was the coaching staff Coryell had assembled. It included a little-known offensive backfield coach named Joe Gibbs.

The Redskins had a 4–3 record, and that sec-

ond Cardinals loss seemed to wake them up as they went on a four-game winning streak, including a 28–21 victory over the Cowboys at RFK before losing, this time in Dallas on Thanksgiving Day, when the "Mad Bomber," Clint Longley, became part of Redskins lore by relieving Roger Staubach, who was knocked out of the game by the Redskins linebacker Dave Robinson. Longley led the Cowboys from a 16–3 deficit to the one-point win.

It may be a good story now, but the loss devastated Allen. "I think that was the worst loss George ever suffered with the Redskins," Ron McDole said. "I don't think he ever recovered from that loss. It was hard on him, because we had the game pretty well wrapped up, and it got away from us."

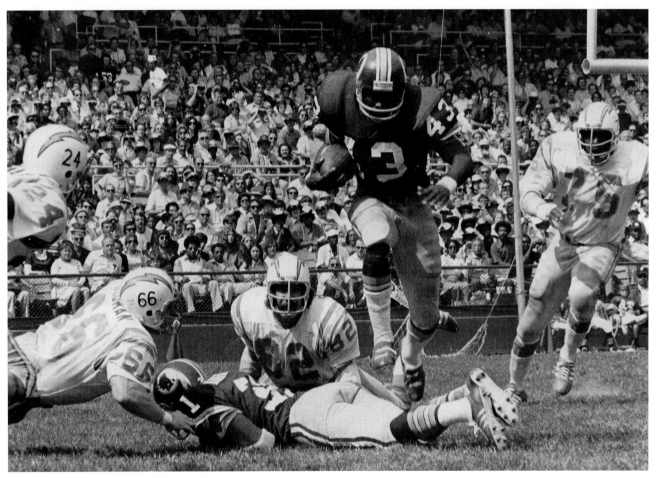

Larry Brown retired after the 1976 season, having set at the time nearly all the team's rushing records, with 5,875 career yards rushing (1,216 in one season, 1972), 21 games with 100 yards or more and 35 career rushing touchdowns. (Nate Fine)

Special Teams

Geaorge Allen was the first NFL coach to truly realize the value of special teams, hiring a coach just for that unit and picking players whose talents fit the play of special teams.

From special teams coach Marv Levy (who would go on to coach the AFC champion Buffalo Bills and face the Redskins in the 1992 Super Bowl) under Allen, to Wayne Sevier with Joe Gibbs's staff to Pete Rodriguez today under Norv Turner, special teams have always been a Washington Redskins strength.

And those teams have produced unique stars who became fan favorites, from Bill Malinchak to Otis Wonsley.

"George was the first coach to introduce the special teams before a game on national television," Brig Owens said. "It was on a 'Monday Night Football' game, and the league went bananas. George said, 'We're going to introduce the special teams. They're doing great things for us, and they deserve to be introduced.' That was a combination of us going against the establishment, and also the fact that we were very proud of our special teams.

"I remember when he brought back Bill Malinchak," Owens said. "Bill had retired, but we were getting ready to go into the playoffs [December, 1976]. George said he was going to bring him back because he can block at least two field goals or punts that's going to help us in the playoff. The next day Bill Malinchak was in a practice uniform." Two weeks later, Malinchak blocked a Danny White punt against Dallas that lead to a Redskins touchdown in a 27–14 win in Texas.

But they finished with two straight wins, including a 23–17 victory over the Rams in Los Angeles, for another 10–4 season, the third consecutive season of double-digit wins. Allen had built a solid house with a philosophy of winning. "Good coaches do that, build a philosophy," Pat Fischer said. "They enroll you in a set of beliefs. Lombardi did that, and so did George Allen. Eventually you have to reduce everything down to some slogans, a few words that excite, that kind of reflects immediately all the hours. Somehow you have to justify all the time you spend by winning. And that's the only way you can justify it—by winning."

In the first round of the playoffs in Los Angeles, the Redskins would face the Rams, the team they had beaten two weeks earlier. It wasn't the same Redskin team who showed up in the playoff game, though. They were the antithesis of a George Allen team, turning the ball over six times, three on fumbles and three on interceptions, as the Rams won 19–10. Individually, it was a down year for Washington's offensive stars, such as Larry Brown, who rushed for just 430 yards in an injury-filled season.

Before the 1975 season began, one of the most popular players in the history of the franchise would call it quits. On May 1, 1975, Sonny Jurgensen retired after playing eighteen seasons in the NFL, eleven with the Redskins. Those last eleven, even with the battle over the starting quarterback job in his last few years, were the most rewarding for him.

"Washington was a special place to play," said Jurgensen, who would later be inducted into the

Pro Football Hall of Fame. "You couldn't ask for a better place to play."

The 1975 team had a changing of the guard in the backfield, with rookie Mike Thomas becoming the team's primary rusher, gaining 919 yards that season, with Larry Brown at the end of his career, gaining just 352 yards. Brown would gain 5,875 career yards before retiring the following year as one of the greatest running backs in the history of the franchise.

With Kilmer relatively unchallenged now at

quarterback, Washington opened the season with two offensive explosions at RFK, 41–3 over the New Orleans Saints and 49–13 over the New York Giants. But they then went on a roller-coaster season, losing 26–10 to Philadelphia, beating St. Louis 27–17, losing 13–10 to Houston, and defeating Cleveland 23–7. Then, with a 4–2 record, the Redskins took on the Cowboys at RFK for what proved to be another Washington-Dallas game for the books.

Regulation time wasn't long enough to decide

George Allen began using Joe Theismann as a punt returner, but the spunky quarterback eventually split time with Billy Kilmer in 1976 and 1977. When Jack Pardee took over in 1978, Theismann became the starting quarterback. (Nate Fine)

The 1977 Redskins, who went 9-5, were George Allen's last team in Washington. Appropriately, Allen's final win was a 17-14 victory over his old team, the Los Angeles Rams, before more than 54,000 fans at RFK Stadium. (Washington Redskins)

this contest, as after four quarters the score was 24–24. It wouldn't end in a tie, though, because the league now allowed an extra quarter of sudden death in regular-season games. Dallas had first possession, which often means victory in overtime games. But Ken Houston intercepted a Roger Staubach pass and returned it to midfield. An unsportsmanlike conduct penalty against Staubach for punching Pat Fischer moved the ball to the Dallas thirty-five. Kilmer connected on two passes to Charley Taylor, moving the ball down to the eleven-yard line. After runs by Thomas and Brown, the ball was on the one-yard line. Kilmer took it in for the score and a 30–24 victory.

Washington would play .500 ball for the next six games, going 3–3, with an 8–5 season mark and no chance for a playoff spot. The final game of the season was a disappointing 26–3 loss to the Eagles. However, that December 21 game at RFK against Philadelphia had one significant moment for Redskin fans—Charley Taylor passed Don Maynard and became the NFL's all-time reception leader with his 634th catch.

It was a bright moment on a dreary day. "After I caught the pass to set the record, every-

body left the stands," Taylor said. "We still had about ten minutes to play. It was a rainy day, and we were getting beat bad, but people hung around until I made that catch, and I appreciated that."

One sad note would start off 1976—Milton King, vice president and treasurer of the Redskins, passed away on January 23, at the age of eighty-five.

Before everyone went their separate ways at the end of the 1975 season, Allen promised Redskin fans that the team would return to the playoffs in 1976. "The Redskins will be back," he said.

He appeared to be right. Washington won its first three games, including an overtime 20–17 win over the Eagles. But then they lost four of their next seven games. But they saved the season with three straight wins over St. Louis, Philadelphia, and the New York Jets, taking a 9–4 record into Dallas for the season finale.

The Redskins scored first when Bill Malinchak blocked a Dallas punt, and Mark Moseley followed with a twenty-five-yard field goal for a 3–0 Washington lead. But Dallas went ahead on a twelve-yard run by Doug Dennison.

Jean Fugett, the former Dallas tight end now

with the Redskins, struck back at his old team with a touchdown catch in the second quarter to put the Redskins back in front 10–7 going into the locker room.

In the third quarter, Roger Staubach connected with Butch Johnson on a forty-four-yard scoring pass for a 14–10 Dallas lead, but Washington drew closer on a Mosely field goal for a 14–13 game.

In the fourth quarter, another former Cowboy, Calvin Hill, gave the Redskins a 20–14 lead with a fifteen-yard dash into the end zone. The Redskins defense then delivered when Diron Talbert tipped a Staubach pass at the Dallas twelve-yard line, and it was recovered by the Redskins on the Cowboys' three-yard line. John Riggins took the ball in to give Washington a comfortable 27–14 lead. That was the final score of the game, and it gave Washington a 10–4 mark and a return to the playoffs.

Washington squared off against the Vikings in Minnesota, but the Redskins' playoff woes continued as they were beaten 35–20. And it was far from that close—at one point the Vikings had a 35–6 lead.

Again, there was much to look back on with a feeling of accomplishment, as Allen was named NFC Coach of the Year. But the playoff losses brought out their share of people who criticized the Redskins for failing to win those big games.

Mike Thomas continued to excel, finishing the season with 1,101 yards. And John Riggins, in his first year with Washington after signing as a free agent, rushed for 572 yards, though he was used primarily as a blocker for Thomas.

The next year, 1977, would see a number of changes, beginnings, and ends. Theismann would see much more playing time at quarterback, splitting time with Kilmer. Charley Taylor retired, and injuries to Chris Hanburger and Pat Fischer suddenly made the "Over the Hill Gang" a point of controversy. It was an old Redskins team, and, with Allen having traded all of their draft choices, few ways were available to rejuvenate the squad with youth.

The season started off rough with a 20–17 loss to the New York Giants. The Redskins won three straight, though, before losing again, this time 34–16 to the Cowboys. With a 3–2 record, they

faced the Giants again, this time at RFK, and suffered another loss, this time 17–6.

Charley Casserly, a former Massachusetts high school coach who came to work for free under Allen—one of the all-time success stories, because he would rise through the organization to become general manager—remembers how Allen reacted to the loss to the Giants.

"We had lost twice to the Giants, and they weren't a very good football team," Casserly said. "The following morning, on Monday, he called the whole organization together—coaches, scouts, secretaries, and staff. He walked into the room and looked like he hadn't slept all night. He gave everyone a lecture. 'We win together, we lose together,' he said. 'This is the lowest we've ever been, and we're going to find a way to come out of this thing.' He made everyone feel like it was everyone's fault that we lost the game. And when we won, he had a way of making everyone feel like they were part of the win."

The speech must have worked, at least for one week, as the Redskins defeated Philadelphia 23–17 the following game. But they would lose 10–3 to Baltimore, win two straight, and then lose again to Dallas, this time 14–7, leaving Washington with a 6–5 mark and in danger of having their first losing season under Allen. The team would come back strong, though, with three straight wins, including a season-ending 17–14 victory over the Los Angeles Rams at RFK before a crowd of fifty-four thousand who would be seeing Allen's last game as the Redskins' head coach.

Washington finished 9–5 but failed to make the playoffs. Tension between Allen and the club management grew, and Allen's status became an off-season soap opera as he was considering either staying on in Washington or possibly taking his old job with the Rams. The tension ended when Allen was fired.

It was the end of the most successful tenure of a Redskins coach since Ray Flaherty forty years before. Allen left with a record of 67–30–1 and one NFC championship and had helped make the Redskins the number-one passion of the Washington area—a passion that continues today. "George Allen did a great deal for establishing a legacy and tradition of winning," Pat Fischer said.

One of Allen's protégés, Jack Pardee, would

take his place, as the former "Ramskin" was hired on January 24, 1978. Pardee had been grooming for this job, first as an assistant coach under Allen. He then joined the World Football League as a head coach before being hired to coach the Chicago Bears in 1975. Pardee turned the Bears from a losing squad into a 9–5 playoff team in 1977, being named Coach of the Year in the process. But he wanted the Washington job when it became open. The Bears made it easy for him by firing him when he asked for permission to talk to the Redskins about their coaching vacancy.

After hiring their sixteenth head coach, Washington made another significant move, hiring its first truly independent general manager. Until then, the head coach acted as the GM, but in February Washington hired Bobby Beathard, the director of player personnel for the Miami Dolphins, as their general manager.

Beathard, a former quarterback, found his true calling in evaluating talent and putting together a football team. He had worked as a scout with the Kansas City Chiefs and the Atlanta Falcons before being named Miami director of player personnel in 1972. The Dolphins would win the following two Super Bowls, and Beathard would be called upon to bring his skills to Washington.

It would be the challenge of his career. In Allen's quest to win, he had traded nearly all of the team's future draft choices while acquiring veteran players. The team was the oldest in the league now, and the "Over the Hill Gang" simply could no longer play at a championship level.

During his eleven years in Washington, Beathard would have just three first-round draft choices. But by using free agent picks and having a savvy scouting staff who included Casserly, Beathard would build championship squads.

The first year of Pardee was transitional, and it showed on the field as the Redskins failed to have a winning season for the first time since Allen had been hired. Washington went 8–8 in 1978.

It was two different seasons in one. The Redskins opened the season with a 16–14 win over New England and would go on to win six straight, with their 6–0 record putting them on top of the NFL East. One of those victories was a 9–5 win at RFK over the defending Super Bowl champions. But the Redskins would win just two of their final

ten games while losing five straight at the end of the year.

Pardee had made the change at quarterback that year, moving Kilmer out and giving Joe Theismann his shot. Theismann had an erratic season, completing 187 of 395 passes for 2,593 yards, thirteen touchdowns, and eighteen interceptions. But Pardee also made John Riggins his man in the backfield, using him as the primary ball carrier, and the fullback responded by rushing for 1,014 yards.

Hopes were much higher in 1979, when Pardee's squad showed marked improvement, posting a 10–6 mark. Beathard began finding his diamond in the rough, bringing young players like Don Warren, Monte Coleman, and Neal Olkewiwicz into the fold.

As it turned out, the Redskins had a chance to make the playoffs going into the final game of the season if they won in combination with the outcomes of other games going on in a logjam for the final playoff spot.

Playing in Texas, Washington opened up a quick 10–0 lead in the first quarter on a Mark Moseley field goal and a Dallas fumble that lead to a scoring run by Theismann.

The Redskins seemed to be on their way to a big win when Theismann hit halfback Benny Malone on a fifty-five-yard touchdown pass, and the Moseley point after meant Washington now led 17–0 in the second quarter.

Everything, though, fell apart as quickly as it had risen. The Cowboys scored twice to come within three, 17–14, at halftime and on their first possession in the third quarter, drove fifty-two yards for another score to go ahead 21–14. The Redskins had blown a seventeen-point lead, but they didn't panic. Moseley hit a short field goal to make it a 21–20 game, and then an interception by Mark Murphy of a Roger Staubach pass put the ball at the Cowboys' twenty-five-yard line. A pass interference call against Cliff Harris put the ball on the one-yard line, and Riggins went over to give Washington the lead again 27–21.

Remarkably, the Redskins would seem to have the game in hand for the second time when Riggins took off on a sixty-six-yard touchdown run, burying the Cowboys 34–21 in the fourth quarter with less than eight minutes remaining.

A Biggs Man

Verlon Biggs was a talented defensive end who played on the 1969 Super Bowl champion New York Jets. He was also one of the many players George Allen brought to Washington as part of the "Over the Hill Gang", playing for Allen from 1971 to 1975.

Biggs has since passed away, but he left a legacy of smiles among his teammates as one of the most entertaining players in the history of the franchise.

"One time we went to play in New York, and they had an offensive tackle named Joe Young," Ron McDole said. "We used to call him Mighty Joe Young. On this day, Verlon was going against him.

"Verlon asked me for a copy of the game program, and he was cutting out Joe Young's picture," McDole said. "He had two of them, and he was taping them on his shoes. I said, 'What are you doing?' After all, the one thing you don't want to do is get the other guy mad you're playing against.

"We play the first half, and the score is 7–3 or something like that when we come into the locker room," McDole said. "Normally, when you're rushing the passer and you're playing end, you kind of run into each other once in a while.

"Verlon was sitting in front of his locker with his head in his hands," McDole said. "I said, 'Verlon, I haven't seen you the whole first half.' He said, 'He's [Joe Young] pissed. I can't get off the line of scrimmage.' I said, 'I wonder why. You went out with his picture pasted on your shoes.'"

Verlon Biggs was one of the many players George Allen brought in to quickly build a veteran squad. The big defensive end, who played on the 1969 New York Jets Super Bowl team, was a defensive standout and also a favorite of his teammates for his quirky behavior. Here he relaxes in Biggs' style in the locker room before a 1973 preseason game. (Nate Fine)

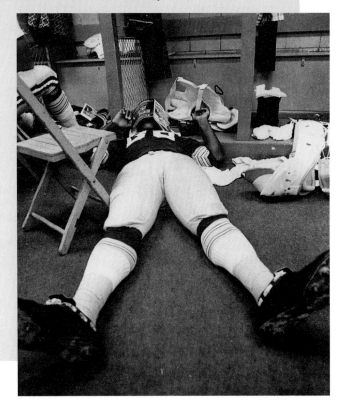

Not a Kodak Moment

If you're a Redskins fan who perhaps has been searching for one particular team photo—1973—to complete your collection, you can stop. There is no 1973 team photo.
It turns out that George Allen felt that because his team did not make it to the NFC championship game that season—going 10–4 before losing 27–20 to the Minnesota Vikings in the first round of the playoffs—there would be no team photo.
"If the team doesn't make it to the NFC championship game, it doesn't deserve its picture taken," Allen said.
He changed that rule, though, because there are team photos for the remaining years of Allen's tenure, though his team never made it to the title game in those seasons.

Staubach, though, was not called Mr. Comeback for nothing. He moved his team quickly down the field, getting on the board and coming within six points, 34–28, when he hit Ron Springs on a twenty-six-yard touchdown pass. Dallas held the Redskins offense in check and got the ball back with less than two minutes remaining. Staubach picked the Washington secondary apart quickly and, with about forty seconds left, connected with Tony Hill for the go-ahead score and a 35–34 lead. It was the final score of the game and the end of the Redskins season, as the loss stopped them from making the playoffs.

Riggins came through the season with his second one-thousand-yard campaign for Washington, rushing for 1,153 yards. And Theismann had his breakout year, completing 233 of 395 passes for 2,797 yards and twenty touchdowns.

Also, Moseley became the club's all-time scoring leader, compiling a six-year career mark of 546 points and leading the league for the third time in four years in field goals, connecting on eighteen.

Pardee seemed to be on his way to continuing the legacy started by Lombardi and built up by Allen. His 10–6 mark earned him Coach of the Year honors. But that was before his meal ticket decided to take a year off.

To say that John Riggins marched to the beat of his own drummer would be an All-Pro understatement. He marched to the tune of a band that few people could even hear. He had been known for his outrageous statements and mohawk haircut in his early years with the New York Jets, and he continued to be a maverick with the Redskins, a talented maverick, signing as free agent in 1976.

But after 1980, Riggins felt he wasn't getting paid what he was worth. He sought a new contract, but the Redskins wouldn't budge, and Riggins did the unusual and unexpected—he sat out the entire season.

Diron Talbert remembers talking to Riggins in his last night in training camp before he left. "It was early in the morning, and Riggo was knocking on my door, 'Talbee, let me in. These guys ain't giving me no money.' He kept beating on the door, so we let him in. We did some talking, and he came to the conclusion, 'They're not going to give me the money I want. I'm going home,' I said, 'Well, get on out of here and go home.' So he left.

"The next morning I went to practice, and someone asked, 'Did you hear about Riggo?' I said, 'No, what?' They said, 'He's in Washington at the Dulles Marriott, fixing to get on a plane to go back to Kansas.' The next time I talked to him was two days later, and he was in Kansas. 'I told you I was going home,' he said. The next time I saw him was next year at training camp."

Without Riggins, the offense would suffer, although they would find a star in Art Monk, the rookie from Syracuse who caught fifty-eight passes for 797 yards. It was the beginning of one of the greatest pass-receiving careers in the history of the NFL.

But Washington would lose five of its first six games and would end the season with a 6–10 mark. Winning had become the tradition of the Redskins franchise, particularly under owner Jack Kent Cooke, who sought to make a change for the future, investing in an untested but highly recommended assistant coach. The Redskins had a string of high-profile names leading them over recent years—Lombardi, Allen, and Pardee—but few fans had ever heard of the man Cooke would bring aboard to take the Redskins into the 1980s—Joe Gibbs.

Eight

The Glory of Gibbs

Jack Kent Cooke has always been a superior judge of talent, and one has to look no further than the man he hired to coach the Redskins in 1981—Joe Gibbs. When the two men met, Cooke's instincts told him that Gibbs had the inner strength to handle the job. "I was satisfied that he had an inner intensity that matched any man I'd run into in the coaching ranks," Cooke said.

Gibbs had a long coaching career, well known within the game but obscure to the public. He started as a graduate assistant in 1964 at his alma mater, San Diego State, under the man who would help mold Gibbs's career, Don Coryell. After several years coaching the Aztecs' offensive line, he moved to Florida State, again as an offensive line coach.

Gibbs continued to work with the top college programs in the country, spending two seasons with John McKay at USC and two more with Frank Broyles at Arkansas before getting his crack at the pros. Coryell would bring Gibbs on as offensive backfield coach for the St. Louis Cardinals. He would move up to be an offensive coordinator for McKay at Tampa Bay for one season in 1978, then reunite with Coryell in San Diego as the as the

Chargers' offensive coordinator. As the behind-the-scenes architect of a powerful San Diego offense that would capture two AFC titles, Gibbs had the resumé, but not the name. That would change.

One of Gibbs's first tasks was to make a trip to Lawrence, Kansas. That's where John Riggins was, and Gibbs wanted him in the Redskins backfield as part of his offense.

Gibbs met Riggins at his home for breakfast and found the big running back wearing hunting clothes and drinking a beer. Gibbs made his pitch without Riggins saying much of anything. Finally, Gibbs said, Riggins told him, "I'll tell you what. If you get me back, I'll make you famous." They would both help each other reach new heights, as it turned out.

Riggins said he wanted to come back, but nothing had been finalized when Gibbs left Kansas. Soon after, though, Riggins showed up ready for training camp, proclaiming, "I'm broke, I'm bored, and I'm back."

Gibbs went into training camp in Carlisle with a lot of new faces, thanks to the work done by himself, Beathard, and the staff. Even though they were penalized by the lack of draft choices, they managed to make the most of the picks they had

The 1982 Washington Redskins, in Joe Gibbs' second year as head coach, put together an 8-1 record during the strike-shortened season and went on to win Super Bowl XVII, the franchise's first NFL championship since 1942. (Washington Redskins)

and also found diamonds in the rough with free agent signings. Joining the team in the draft were offensive linemen Mark May and Russ Grimm; defensive end Dexter Manley; Darryl Grant, who played guard in college but would be switched by the Redskins to defensive tackle; and tight end Clint Didier.

The Redskins would also deal their second-round draft pick for running back Joe Washington and pick up a free agent lineman from Louisville. The story of Joe Jacoby, and how Charley Casserly found him, is illustrative of the personnel work that built the club into a championship team.

"I had seen him as a junior, and like a lot of other scouts, I rated him as a free agent," Casserly said. "Then I saw him late in his last year against highly rated guys, and he played them pretty good," Casserly said. "These guys were not making plays, not getting to the quarterback, and he was blocking them. He was six-foot-seven, 290 pounds, a big guy who could stand on his feet. I thought, 'This guy must be a lot better than all of us think he is, because he is blocking these guys who are going to be high-rated draft choices.'

"I met with him and told him that he needed to get on the weights and work hard in the off-season and that we were coming back in April to see him," Casserly said. "So Joe Bugel and I go back in April. Jacoby walks in the room, and he completely blocks the light out coming through the door. He had transformed his body. He didn't weigh any more, but he had a massive chest, and he didn't have that when we saw him in the fall. He was a guy we had to take a shot at, a big guy with balance, strength, and was competitive."

It may have been Casserly's most successful gamble. Jacoby would play thirteen seasons as the anchor of Washington's great offensive line, a four-time Pro Bowler who is likely on his way to the Hall of Fame. He almost didn't make it on the opening-day roster. As big as he was, the first time Gibbs saw him, he was sure Jacoby was a defensive lineman. When Gibbs learned that Jacoby was an offensive lineman, Gibbs had his doubts that Jacoby could play. Those doubts were soon erased.

The team appeared to be playing well. In the preseason they went 3–1, losing to New England in their final exhibition game 19–10. Gibbs would get an early baptism into the Redskins-Cowboys rivalry, because Washington would open with Dallas at RFK.

With more than 55,000 on hand for the debut of the new-look Redskins on this hot Sunday afternoon, both teams had yet to score after the first quarter. In the second quarter, Danny White connected on a thirty-three-yard scoring pass to Billy Jo Dupree to take a 7–0 lead, and Washington bounced back to tie the game on a fifteen-yard touchdown pass from Joe Theismann to Joe Washington.

The Cowboys would go ahead 14–7 in the second quarter when White hit Drew Pearson from forty-two yards out, and they took that score into the locker room at halftime. During Gibbs's career, he would be recognized for his ability to make adjustments against teams during halftime and turn games around. But the only adjustment in this game was the Cowboys' shutting down the Redskins, holding them to just one Mark Moseley field goal while adding three Rafael Septien field goals to hand Washington a 26–10 opening-game defeat.

Riggins showed a lot of rust in his return, rushing for just twenty-five yards on eight carries, and the team managed a total of just forty-four yards rushing.

Next week the New York Giants came to town, and it seemed as if Washington would be on the way to its first win when, in a scoreless game in the third quarter, Theismann threw a touchdown pass to Ricky Thompson, and Washington took a 7–0 lead. Again, though, Gibbs would taste defeat, this time 17–7. With two straight home losses, Redskins fans were beginning to grumble, still

Joe Gibbs was a highly regarded offensive assistant coach when general manager Bobby Beathard recommended him to Redskins owner Jack Kent Cooke to become the team's head coach in 1981. But he was an unknown commodity to Washington fans, who were nervous after seeing their team get off to an 0-5 start under Gibbs that year. Gibbs proved to be a winning choice, however, bringing three Super Bowl titles to the franchise. (Scott Cunningham)

wondering who Joe Gibbs really was and why the Redskins had hired him.

The losing continued next week in St. Louis. Even though the Washington offense managed 521 yards to only 315 yards for the Cardinals, and although Theismann had an outstanding day, completing twenty-five of thirty-seven passes for 388 yards, the Redskins wound up losing 40–30. Back home, speculation was rampant about how much longer Gibbs would last.

It didn't look good the following week, because the Redskins were going to face the Eagles, the defending NFC champions, in Philadelphia. But the Redskins played the Eagles tough, trailing by just one point 14–13 with about ten minutes to play. What happened then was nightmarish for Gibbs. Philadelphia would score twenty-two points in those last ten minutes to bash Washington 36–13. Now Gibbs was wondering how much longer he would last.

The Redskins returned home the following week to meet the San Francisco 49ers, and the bad times continued. At one point, Washington trailed San Francisco 30–3. Things got so bad that Gibbs benched Theismann in favor of rookie quarterback Tom Flick. It seemed as if the Redskins, who had turned into one of the top organizations in the league under Vince Lombardi and George Allen, were a franchise in trouble. They were coming off a 6–10 record the previous year, had fired one of the franchise's favorite sons, Jack Pardee, and had replaced him with a man unknown to Redskins fans who had gotten off to a horrendous 0–5 start. The calls for a change were heard from every-

Gibbs' first task as Redskins coach was to visit running back John Riggins at his Kansas home to persuade him to return to the team. Riggins had sat out the 1980 season in a contract dispute. The new coach was successful, and the maverick running back would enjoy his best years under Gibbs. (Scott Cunningham)

Joe Jacoby was an unheralded offensive lineman from Louisville when he was discovered on a scouting trip by Charley Casserly in 1980. Casserly signed Jacoby as a free agent, and he, along with Mark May, Jeff Bostic, and Russ Grimm made up the core group called "Hogs" by line coach Joe Bugel. (Scott Cunningham)

where, except from where it counted—the office of Jack Kent Cooke at Redskins Park.

Gibbs feared that that final call for change might have come when Cooke called the coach. But, Gibbs said, Cooke never wavered in his support. "Mr. Cooke was at his best when things were at their worst," Gibbs said. "Every time I thought he was going to fire me, he would find a way to talk to me and pick me up. He would say, 'We're going through a tough time right now, but we're going to pull out of it. We know that what we believe in here is going to eventually win out.'"

Another meeting that took place that week after the Philadelphia loss was key for Gibbs and

the Redskins. Theismann, upset about being benched during the game, met with Gibbs to make his case for another shot.

Neither Gibbs nor Theismann would have to go through another week like that. The following game, in Chicago, they would get their win, 24–7, over the Bears. And the key may have been the improvement of Riggins, recovering from his year off, as he gained 126 yards.

The Redskins would lose again the following game, 13–10 to the Miami Dolphins, but then would go on a streak that would vindicate Cooke, Beathard, Gibbs, and the entire team, winning four straight, including an exciting 30–27 overtime victory over the Giants, the team who had beaten Washington earlier that year.

With the Giants leading 27–24 and just forty-five seconds left in the game, New York, kicking off after adding a field goal by Joe Danelo, surprised everyone with a squib kick, and Darryl Grant picked up the ball and chugged twenty yards to the Washington forty-six-yard line. Theismann quickly moved the ball up the field, with the key play coming on a ten-yard run by the quarterback, and with about five seconds left, the ball was on the Giants' thirty-two-yard line. Mark Moseley, who would deliver so many last-second wins for Gibbs, came on to kick the tying field goal.

New York got possession of the ball first in overtime, but the Redskins defense would stop them, forcing a punt from the Giants' twenty-six. Mike Nelms returned the kick to the New York forty-seven-yard line, then a twelve-yard dash by Joe Washington put the ball on the Giants' thirty-five. After the Redskins moved the ball down to the thirty-two, Moseley finished the job, kicking the winning field goal for the 30–27 win.

"Moseley was the best clutch kicker I've ever seen in the business," Charley Casserly said. "He kicked more with his back to the wall to win or tie games than anyone I've ever seen, with any team, period."

Washington would lose the next two, 24–10 to the Cowboys in Dallas and 21–14 to the Bills in Buffalo.

But the kinks were working their way out of this Gibbs team, and the way Washington ended— with three straight wins, 15–13 over Philadelphia, 38–14 over the Colts, and 30–7 over Los Angeles in

Joe Theismann blossomed into a championship quarterback under the offensive-minded Gibbs. In 1983, Theismann threw for 3,714 yard and 29 touchdowns, receiving a quarterback rating of 97.0, which is the third highest in Redskins history. He threw 160 career touchdown passes, and completed more passes (2,044) than any quarterback in team history, benefiting from the protection of "The Hogs," with tackle Mark May, shown here, doing the blocking. (Scott Cunningham)

The "Hogs" was the tag that offensive line coach Joe Bugel put on his young offensive linemen; center Jeff Bostic (*opposite left*) was one of the charter members. Fans went hog wild over them. (Scott Cunningham)

The Hogs

Washington Redskins offensive line coach Joe Bugel had a bunch of young offensive linemen at his disposal back in 1982—Mark May and Russ Grimm were drafted in 1981, Joe Jacoby signed as a free agent, and Jeff Bostic was signed as a free agent in 1980. Mixed in with veteran George Starke, this would be the first unit to be known as "The Hogs," the name for Washington's offensive line that would come to be more recognizable than perhaps any other part of this team.

How did they get the name?

"Joe Bugel was looking at Russ Grimm's body one day during training camp in Carlisle, then he called us all hogs," Bostic said. "He said, 'Hey, you bunch of hogs, let's go,' calling us over to what he called his bullpen, which was the most remote place on the practice field at Carlisle. That's where we worked.

"It kind of started out as a joke," Bostic said. "On his own, Bugel had T-shirts made, with this nasty-looking hog in between goalposts, with Redskins colors. He passed them out in a meeting at training camp, and it gave us a sense of identity. We had no idea what it would turn into."

The Hogs became one of the biggest promotions the franchise had ever seen, and they continued for a number of years, although there was some changeover. Jim Lachey, Mark Schlereth, Ed Simmons, Raleigh McKenzie, and others would join the Hogs along the way, and John Riggins, though a fullback, was truly a Hog in heart and soul and was considered part of the group. "He would sit in the meetings with us and watch our films," Bostic said. "He wanted to see where the blocking schemes were coming from and where he needed to be. And John liked hanging out with us."

The Redskins possessed many powerful offensive weapons; one of the best was running back Joe Washington, who rushed for 916 yards, averaging 4.4 yards a carry, in Gibbs' first season. Two years later he averaged 5.3 yards every time he ran the ball in the 1983 NFC title season. In four years with the Redskins, Washington rushed for 2,070 yards, capturing the hearts of Redskin fans with his scintillating play. (Scott Cunningham)

the season finale—had shown Redskins fans enough to give them hope for the following year. And the 8–8 record prevented Gibbs from having a losing season in his first year, a small psychological victory.

However, looking back on that year and the 0–5 start, Gibbs might not have traded the experience for anything else. He believes it had something to do with putting the franchise on the road to victory that it often traveled during his tenure as coach.

"That 0–5 start was the worst period I ever experienced in my career, occupationally," Gibbs said. "But in life many times, when you go through those times, thinking that this is the worst thing that ever happened to me, I found out later in life that lots of times, if you go through them the right way, they wind up being a blessing down the road and something you wouldn't trade.

"That's really what that time was," Gibbs said. "Looking back on it, I think it motivated my team. I know it caused me to make some changes I should have made. It gave me a chance to analyze the people around me. And it gave me a chance to see what our owner was like under severe difficulties. I learned all of those things in that 0–5 start.

"Then, when we turned it around, it's almost like from that point on, it helped motivate us for years," Gibbs said. "None of us wanted to go back to that."

Joe Washington brought some excitement to the Redskins with his reckless abandon and 916 yards rushing. Riggins finished up strong with 714 yards after his slow start. Theismann's finishing numbers were erratic but impressive. He completed 293 of 496 passes for 3,568 yards and nineteen touchdowns, but also with twenty interceptions.

Although the strong ending promised hope for 1982, those hopes were disappearing during the preseason. Washington lost its first exhibition game 24–7 to Miami and finished with a 28–21 loss to Cincinnati for an 0–4 preseason record. Memories of the 0–5 start from the previous year were in everyone's mind.

But one of the most important games in the history of the franchise would send the Redskins on the way to a championship year. At the time, no one knew how important it would be. But it sticks in the minds of the men who would help lead this franchise.

"That was one of the most exciting games I've ever seen," Charley Casserly said.

The Eagles, NFC champions two years before, were still a powerful team, with offensive stars like quarterback Ron Jaworski, running back Wilbert Montgomery, and receiver Harold Carmichael. They would be a good test, particularly on the road at Veterans Stadium before 68,000 Eagles fans.

Philadelphia had those fans roaring when

Jaworski moved the team down the field, and Montgomery took it over from the four-yard line in the first quarter for a 7–0 lead. The Eagles made it 10–0 shortly after on a field goal by Tony Franklin.

These were Washington players, though, who had discovered something about themselves the year before, and they were not a team to quit. On a second-quarter possession, several runs by Riggins moved the ball to midfield, and then Theismann connected with Art Monk on a forty-three-yard pass. Two plays later Theismann and Monk hooked up again for a five-yard scoring pass, and the point after by Moseley put Washington on the board 10–7.

The Redskins defense would hold the Eagles, and Philadelphia had to punt with less than two minutes remaining in the half. Washington started a drive from the Eagles' forty-six-yard line with a nineteen-yard pass to Don Warren, a ten-yard run by Clarence Harmon, and an unsportsmanlike penalty call, and, with less than a minute left, the Redskins had the ball on the Philadelphia eight-yard line. Theismann found Charlie Brown in the end zone to take a 14–10 lead.

But with about thirty-five seconds remaining, Jaworski managed to move his team to within field goal range, and Franklin connected on a forty-four-yard field goal to make it a 14–13 game at halftime.

The Eagles would score first in the third quarter on a two-yard run by Montgomery to go ahead of Washington 20–14. And Jaworski seemed to be able to pass at will, finding Montgomery on the Eagles' next possession for a forty-two-yard scoring pass. Now Philadelphia led 27–14 going into the fourth quarter.

But the Redskins played like a team determined not to open the 1982 season like they had the year before. Theismann tossed a deep pass to Charlie Brown for a seventy-eight-yard touchdown, and now Philadelphia led by just six points, 27–21.

The Redskins defense stopped the Eagles on their next possession, as Dave Butz and Tony McGee sacked Jaworski on a third-down play, forcing Philadelphia to punt. Mike Nelms returned the kick twenty-eight yards to the Eagles' forty-eight-yard line. Theismann hit passes to Warren and

Mark Moseley may have simply been the best clutch placekicker in the history of the NFL. "He was the best clutch kicker I've ever seen in the business," Charley Casserly said. "He kicked more with his back to the wall to win or tie games than anyone I've ever seen, with any team, period." Moseley was the league MVP in the 1982 championship season. (Scott Cunningham)

Wilbur Jackson to get down to the Philadelphia ten-yard line, and Riggins took the ball over two plays later. The extra point put Washington ahead 28–27. They added three more after stopping the Eagles again, and Moseley connected on another field goal for a 31–27 margin.

But Philadelphia managed to take back the lead with about a minute left after Jaworski completed several passes and a pass interference penalty put the Eagles on the thirty-eight yard line. Several plays later, down near the end zone, Jaworski found Carmichael for a touchdown and a 34–31 victory in sight.

In a day for the ages, running back John Riggins bows to acknowledge the standing ovation of the fans at RFK Stadium after rushing for 185 yards in a 21-7 playoff win over the Minnesota Vikings on Jan. 15, 1983. "It seemed like the appropriate thing to do," Riggins said. (NFL Properties)

The Redskins took the ball on their thirty-seven-yard line, and, with less than a minute remaining, Theismann went to work. After he made several completions, with six seconds left Moseley came in to try to tie the game. He came through with a forty-eight yarder, and when the clock ran out, it was a 34–34 game.

Washington won the coin toss in overtime, and passes from Theismann to Brown and Monk helped put the Redskins at the Philadelphia nine-yard line. Moseley was called upon to seal the win, a 37–34 remarkable victory.

What's remarkable is that going into the season, Moseley was fighting for his life as a Redskin, because the team had drafted kicker Dan Miller from the University of Miami. "We had kept Miller on our roster for that opening game," Casserly said. "He didn't dress, because we made him inac-

tive. But we made the decision to keep Miller because we didn't know how Moseley would do." Miller would be released, and Moseley would go on to be the team's Most Valuable Player.

"I felt that game was one of the key turning points in all of our games we ever played with the Redskins," Gibbs said. "It was a tremendous victory that got us rolling."

But the rolling didn't last long. The Redskins would go to Tampa Bay and defeat the Bucs 21–13. But in the background of the team's success in the first two weeks was the threat of a players strike. That threat became reality after the Tampa Bay game, and the games stopped, leaving Redskins fans with a team who was undefeated but whom fans had not had a chance to see live, because the first two games of the season had been on the road.

It was a difficult time, particularly for a team

with so many key young players still trying to come together as a unit. But the group of young offensive linemen—now and forever known as the Hogs—were a tight unit that was determined to stay together during the strike.

"The offensive guys, the defensive guys, receivers, and others held their drills," Joe Jacoby said. "But as far as the line, there wasn't much we could have done as far as practicing. We stayed in shape together, had dinners together, played cards together. We were young and just out of college, and to us, it was still a college atmosphere. We kind of bonded together then."

It would be eight weeks until the strike ended and the Redskins took the field again, and to the chagrin of Washington fans, their team would be on the road once more, this time in New York. Moseley delivered two field goals, Riggins rushed for seventy yards, and Theismann completed six-

teen of twenty-four for 185 yards. In all, it was a satisfying win, one that Gibbs was eager to have. "We felt a lot of pressure coming into that game," he said. "We were relieved to win it."

Finally, on November 28, Redskins fans would get a chance to see their undefeated team in action—in the first home game of the season, facing the Eagles again. On a rainy day, Washington slopped out a 13–9 win on two Moseley field goals and a sixty-five-yard touchdown pass from Theismann to Brown. With the Redskins now 4–0, the city was getting turned on by its undefeated team, and Redskins fever raged in the next week when the Cowboys came to town.

The game would turn out to be a setback, though, as Dallas came away with a 24–10 victory. The turning point in the game came when, with a 17–10 lead in the fourth quarter, Danny White faked a punt and ran for a first down. The play

RFK Stadium nearly came off its foundation when the Redskins defeated the Dallas Cowboys 31-17 to capture the 1982 NFC title and go on to Super Bowl XVII. "The stadium felt like it was moving," Charley Casserly said, as the fans rocked to the heroics of players like wide receiver Charlie Brown, getting a ride here following the victory. (NFL Properties)

This is the image forever etched in the minds of Redskins fans from Super Bowl XVII: With Miami up 17-13 in the fourth quarter, John Riggins turns the left corner and shakes off Miami cornerback Don McNeal on his way to a 43-yard touchdown run. Riggins racked up 166 yards rushing and earned Super Bowl MVP honors. (NFL Properties)

kept the ball away from Washington, and along with two Redskins fumbles, led to a Dallas win. Now 4–1, Washington faced another test. How would they recover from this loss? "At that point, we had to prove that we could bounce back from a tough loss," Gibbs said.

As they did much of the season, they rode Moseley's foot as the kicker connected on four field goals for a 12–7 win over the Cardinals in St. Louis. Now, a 5–1 record was worth celebrating, but Gibbs had concerns about the lack of offense, the team scoring a total of just thirty-five points over the past three games. "We're not scoring enough points to win consistently," Gibbs said.

Fortunately, he had Moseley. The kicker had hit on fifteen straight field goals so far in 1982 and

eighteen straight going back to the previous season. By the end of the 1982 season, Moseley would be the difference in six of the eight Washington victories.

The next test would be at home against the Giants, and the Redskins appeared to be failing that test. New York forced five first-half turnovers, including four interceptions of Theismann passes, to take a 14–3 lead. This year, though, the Redskins would win such games, not lose them.

With the snow falling on RFK, Washington bounced back with a twenty-two yard run by Joe Washington, but Moseley would not hit the extra point, as the Redskins came closer, 14–9. But Moseley, of course, would prove to be the difference, nailing two field goals, including the game-winner from forty-two yards out with just four seconds left, for a 15–14 win. Moseley's field goal was his twentieth straight, setting a new NFL record.

Washington's defense, under the guidance of defensive coordinator Richie Petitbon, enabled Moseley to deliver the win, as they sacked Giants quarterback Scott Brunner five times.

The winning would continue with a 27–10 victory over the Saints in New Orleans and a 28–0 shutout of the Cardinals at RFK that clinched home field advantage in the playoff with a 8–1 mark. Moseley would finally miss in that game, ending his record field goal streak at twenty-three. Theismann completed 161 of 252 passes for thirteen season touchdowns, and Riggins would end the regular season with 553 yards rushing. Monk caught thirty-five passes for 447 yards, and Brown brought in thirty-two passes for 690 yards. Joe Gibbs was named NFC Coach of the Year. And the defense, led by tackle Dave Butz, held the opposition to 128 points, the lowest in the league.

All in all, they had a pretty good year, but you couldn't prove that by the Detroit Lions, the Redskins' first opponent in the playoffs. Lions coach Monte Clark declared, "The Redskins are not a great football team. If we were a little healthier, we'd match up well with them."

That remark didn't sit well with the Redskins. "Detroit came in with a 4–5 record, and we're 8–1, and they acted like they were the favorites," Casserly said.

Washington humbled Detroit in that playoff contest 31–7, starting early in the game when cornerback Jeris White cut in front of Billy Sims to intercept a pass from Eric Hipple and take it seventy-seven yards for a touchdown. With Art Monk sidelined with a broken foot and fellow receiver Virgil Seay also hurt, Alvin Garrett got the start, and the "Smurf" responded with six catches for 110 yards and two touchdowns.

Riggins also carried the ball twenty-five times for 119 yards. It was the beginning of four of the biggest games a running back would have in championship play, and it started when, during practice before the Detroit game, Riggins told Gibbs he wanted the ball more. Riggins, who had been sitting out the last two games, told Gibbs, "I'm really getting down the road. I don't have many of these

left. I've been out for two weeks, and I'm ready. Give me the ball."

Also, toward the end of the Detroit game, the chant that would become the rallying cry for an entire region started: "We want Dallas. We want Dallas."

Bur first, the Redskins would have to deal with Minnesota. But as Washington took the opening drive and methodically moved the ball down the field, ending with a short pass from Theismann to Don Warren, taking a 7–0 lead, Redskins fans couldn't resist taking up the call again. "We want Dallas. We want Dallas," they chanted in the first quarter of the Vikings game.

Riggins would give them Dallas. he ran through the Minnesota defense for 185 yards on thirty-seven carries, more than double the Vikings total of seventy-nine. And he put the icing on the cake in one of the most memorable moments in Redskins playoff history. With the game well in hand 21–7 and time running out, Riggins was taken out of the game by Gibbs to give the fans a chance to acknowledge the fullback's outstanding game.

With more than 54,000 fans standing and roaring their approval of his performance, Riggins stopped on the field, and took bows. The crowd was now in a frenzy. "It seemed like the appropriate thing to do," Riggins said after the game.

Now the fans would get what they wanted. The Dallas Cowboys would be coming to RFK on January 22 for the NFC title game.

The city was turned upside-down by the prospect of facing the Cowboys. People hung signs from office windows, held downtown rallies, and were caught up in the hysteria of Redskins fever. "As you would drive to Redskins Park, the buildings on the way were covered with signs for the Redskins," Casserly said. "It was like a high school pep rally. I got goosebumps driving to work."

Some of the Redskins got into the pregame hype, such as defensive end Dexter Manley, who was never at a loss for words. "I hope they run at me every play," Manley said. "We have the best record in football, and all I hear is 'Dallas.'"

The Cowboys shot back with rhetoric of their own. "Washington wants us, they got us," wide receiver Tony Hill said.

Finally, the day of the game came, and Manley put it into perspective. "This is our Super

Bowl," he said. "It's the game we've all waited a long time to play. How can it get any bigger than this?"

The fans knew that and were already chanting at a deafening level, "We want Dallas. We want Dallas," an hour before the game started as the Cowboys worked out on the field at RFK.

The Cowboys opened up the scoring with a field goal by Rafael Septien, taking a 3–0 lead. But when Washington got the ball back, the offense, led by the Hogs and Riggins, picked up where they had left off against Minnesota.

"Our first play was a straight handoff up the middle," tackle Joe Jacoby said. "It looked like a nothing play, maybe a yard or two. The next thing you know the whole pile is moving. That's how pumped up we were. We all got up, and it was second and one. It was like a scrum in a rugby game. They couldn't get John down, and we all kept moving. It was that kind of game, with plays like that."

Theismann would connect with Brown for the first touchdown for a 7–3 lead. Washington took a 14–3 lead in the second quarter when Dallas's Rod Hill fumbled a punt and Monte Coleman recovered on the Cowboys' eleven-yard line. Riggins would take the ball in four plays later.

One of the biggest plays in the game came toward the end of the first half, when, with twenty-two seconds left on the clock, Manley backed up his tough talk by sacking Dallas quarterback Danny White, knocking him out of the game. Manley would play yet another key role later in the game.

Dallas would come back to within 14–10 in the third quarter when they got good field position after Mike Nelms muffed a punt, putting them deep in their own territory. When Dallas got the ball, Gary Hogeboom, White's replacement, moved them into position for a six-yard scoring pass to Drew Pearson.

Nelms would atone for his mistake, though, when he returned the Cowboys' kickoff seventy-six yards. Five plays later, Riggins scored, and Washington now had a 21–10 lead.

The crowd continued its roaring cheers, but Dallas did not prove to be intimidated. They cut the Redskins lead to 21–17 on a twenty-three-yard touchdown pass from Hogeboom to Butch Johnson. Dallas was on its way to another score

when linebacker Rich Milot intercepted a Hogeboom pass, and about halfway through the fourth quarter, Moseley extended Washington's lead to 24–17 with a twenty-nine-yard field goal.

Dallas took over again on its own twenty-yard line. Hogeboom went back to pass, but Manley came in again, this time tipping a pass into the air. Fellow defensive lineman Darryl Grant intercepted it at the ten and rushed in for the touchdown and a 31–17 Redskins lead.

RFK nearly either fell down or rose off the ground after that. No one could speak above the mocking chants of "We want Dallas," and the stands visibly shook up and down, a scene forever etched in the memories of everyone who was at RFK that day.

"The stadium felt like it was moving," Casserly said. "Those stands really rocked. The crowd that day, there's never been another one like it."

When Washington got the ball back with less than five minutes remaining, the plan was to simply hand off to Riggins and let the Hogs pave the way. Dallas would not get the ball back until a bizarre ending gave them one second of possession.

"We're killing them on that last drive," Jacoby said. "We're running to Russ's and my side, against Randy White and Harvey Martin. Ernie Stautner, the Dallas defensive line coach, was yelling at them, 'Dig in, dig in.' They couldn't stop us, even when we were telling them where the play was coming. That line just came together during that playoff run."

Center Jeff Bostic also marks that Dallas game as the day the Washington squad truly emerged as a force in the league. "That game was really a turning point in Redskins football," Bostic said. "It showed that we belonged in the upper tier of football teams. Dallas had been a dynasty for a long time, and we handled them pretty well that day."

With just a few seconds left, Washington lost possession of the ball on downs, and the clock had stopped. But Redskins fans swarmed the field, thinking the game was over, and the Cowboys went to the locker room defeated. However, the referees declared there was still time on the clock, cleared the field, and forced Dallas to suffer the

The Redskins "Fun Bunch," the team's receiving corps, celebrates a score in Washington's 27-17 win over the Miami Dolphins in Super Bowl XVII. The fans adore their Redskins, but this team stirred them more than usual. (NFL Properties)

humiliation of having to come back on to the field for one more play. It was hard to find eleven Cowboys willing to go back out, but Drew Pearson was willing to take the snap from center, and when he did, the Redskins were officially NFC champions and going to the Super Bowl for the first time since 1973. On January 30, 1983, in Pasadena, they would be facing the same opponent from ten years before, the Miami Dolphins.

Washington went into Super Bowl XVII with a record of 11–1. Miami finished as AFC champions with a 10–2 mark, led by their young quarterback David Woodley and a tough defense called the "Killer Bees."

"Hogs versus Killer Bees," Joe Jacoby said. "It sounds more like a movie than a football game."

Add to that the "Fun Bunch"—the name picked up by the Redskins receivers—and the Smurfs, and it did sound like a Hollywood production.

It was a stage, though, for John Riggins. He had basked in the limelight of leading the Redskins during their playoff run. He had rushed for 464 yards over those three games and charmed the national media with his sense of humor and style. At a news conference during Super Bowl week in Pasadena, Riggins was asked, "To what do you attribute your longevity?" Riggins replied, "Formaldehyde." And then he showed up for a party by Jack Kent Cooke wearing top hat and tails.

With just one week in between the title games and the Super Bowl, though, there wasn't as

Defensive lineman Dave Butz clutches the Vince Lombardi trophy while Redskins owner Jack Kent Cooke celebrates his team's Super Bowl win, the first NFL championship for the franchise since 1942 and the start of a run of excellence for the organization. (Washington Redskins)

much time for hype. More than 103,000 fans filled up the Rose Bowl on January 30 for the big game.

Miami scored first on their second possession when Woodley connected with Jimmy Cefalo for a seventy-six-yard touchdown—the second-longest in the history of the Super Bowl—for a 7–0 lead with about seven minutes left in the first quarter.

Manley would come through with the big Washington defensive play later in the quarter when he sacked Woodley, who fumbled the ball. It was recovered by Dave Butz, and Moseley would later connect on a twenty-one-yard field goal to get Washington on the board 7–3. Miami moved back to a seven-point lead with a field goal by Uwe von Schamann, making it a 10–3 game.

Washington would tie the game 10–10 on an eighty-yard drive engineered by Theismann. He hit

Rick Walker for a twenty-seven yarder, then threw a screen pass to Riggins for a fifteen-yard gain. Theismann then ran the ball for twelve yards and hit Alvin Garrett for a four-yard touchdown pass.

The vaunted Washington special teams broke down on the kickoff, as Fulton Walker took the ball on his own two-yard line and broke outside and ran untouched up the left sideline to put Miami on top 17–10 with 1:51 left in the half. The ninety-eight-yard return was the longest in NFL postseason history.

Washington had a chance to score again in the brief time left when a pass interference call on Miami's Lyle Blackwood gave the Redskins the ball on the Dolphins forty-two with forty-eight seconds left. They moved the ball to the sixteen, and Theismann hit Alvin Garrett on the eight-yard line. But Blackwood stopped Garrett from getting out of bounds. Because Washington had already used their three time-outs on the drive, time ran out in the first half and Washington had nothing to show for the opportunity, as Miami still led 17–10.

In the third quarter, Washington cut the Miami lead to 17–13. Then, with time running out in the third quarter, Theismann made the play of the game. Right defensive end Kim Bokamper deflected a pass by Theismann. It looked as if Bokamper was going to come down with the ball, but Theismann make a remarkable play by knocking it away at the last second, and the ball fell to the ground.

"If he [Theismann] hadn't done that, it could have been an interception, and he could have run it in for a touchdown," Casserly said. "It was an instinctive, athletic play that not a lot of guys could have made."

Later, with the score remaining 17–3, Washington made its memorable move to take the game. On fourth and one from the Miami forty-three, Gibbs called Riggins's number. The big fullback turned the left corner, and the only man between him and a touchdown was Miami cornerback Don McNeal. Riggins would shake him off and race down the field for the go-ahead touchdown, 21–17, with about ten minutes remaining. "He was like a train," McNeal said.

Riggins would help finish off the Dolphins by being the horse on a ball-control drive that ended with a six-yard scoring pass to Brown to make the final score 27–17. Riggins ended the game with 166 yards on thirty-eight carries and was named the game's Most Valuable Player.

"We were able to wear them down physically in the second half," Jeff Bostic said. "It was football that Lombardi would have been proud of."

In the locker room, as Jack Kent Cooke received the Vince Lombardi Trophy from Commissioner Pete Rozelle and got a congratulatory call from President Reagan, Riggins declared,

"Ron may be the president, but for tonight I'm the king."

The city of Washington gave its Super Bowl champions a reception never seen before in the city. More than 500,000 people showed up on a rainy day to scream, shout, and show their support for their conquering heroes.

The Washington Redskins were world champions for the first time since 1942. Hail to the Redskins.

Nine

The Battle for Excellence

How do you follow up a season with just one loss, culminating in a Super Bowl win and a world championship? By going back for more.

That was the goal of the 1983 Redskins squad. Many believed that the team was just beginning to show how good it could be during that string of playoff wins in 1982 and that it had come together as a unit then. After a 3–2 preseason, the best, they believed, was yet to come.

And the summer had brought some noteworthy events to further give the franchise a good feeling. On July 30, both Sonny Jurgensen and Bobby Mitchell were inducted into the Pro Football Hall of Fame.

So there were high hopes when the season opened, and, as if the opener needed the added importance, it was at home against Dallas, in front of a national audience on "Monday Night Football."

The crowd of more than fifty-five thousand at RFK was swept up in the euphoria early as Washington opened up a 10–0 lead with a Moseley field goal and a scoring run by John Riggins in the first quarter. The Cowboys nailed a field goal to make it a 10–3 game, but two more Moseley field

goals and a forty-one-yard scoring pass from Joe Theismann to Charlie Brown gave Washington a convincing 23–3 lead at halftime. The Redskins looked every bit like the defending Super Bowl champions on a mission to repeat. After all, when was the last time anyone had scored twenty-one points in two quarters against the Washington Redskins?

So although it was hard for Redskins fans to watch their team blow a twenty-point lead and lose 31–30 on national television, it was brutal for it to happen at the hands of the Cowboys.

Danny White connected on two touchdown passes to Tony Hill, seventy-five and fifty-one yards, in the third quarter to cut the Washington lead to 23–17. In the fourth quarter, Dallas went ahead 24–23 when White took it over himself and added another one that would prove to be important, opening up a 31–23 Cowboys lead. Washington would add a late touchdown but come up one point short. Dallas got its revenge, and, as it turned out, Washington got most of the losing out of its system. In fact, Redskins fans would not see their team lose at home again the rest of the year.

The Redskins came back with a 23–13 win over the Eagles in Philadelphia and, before another

The Washington Redskins picked up right where they left off after Super Bowl XVII, putting together a 14-2 record, another NFC title, and a return trip to the Super Bowl for Joe Gibbs and linebacker Monte Coleman, here celebrating a Redskins win. (Scott Cunningham)

packed house at RFK, got their first home win the following week with a 27–12 victory over Kansas City. After going to Seattle to defeat the Seahawks 27–17, the Redskins would have to fly back home for what turned out to be one of the most exciting games of the year—against the Los Angeles Raiders. Little did anyone know that this would be a preview of the matchup for Super Bowl XVIII. And if they did know, no one would have bet that the two games would be so different.

Washington would be the first to score when safety Curtis Jordan intercepted a Jim Plunkett pass and returned it to the Raiders eleven-yard line. Three runs later, Riggins was in the end zone, and Moseley's point after gave the Redskins a 7–0 lead.

Plunkett threw two more interceptions in the first quarter, but Washington managed to get just three points out of those turnovers, with Moseley missing one field goal and hitting the other for a 10–0 lead in the second quarter.

It seemed as if Washington was about to put Los Angeles away when a punt put the Raiders down on their own one-yard line. But Plunkett wasn't put off by his mistakes, and he connected with Cliff Branch for a ninety-nine-yard touchdown, drawing the Raiders to within three, 10–7.

Washington came back with a drive that ended on a six-yard scoring pass from Theismann to Joe Washington for a 17–7 lead, and that's where it stayed when the half ended.

Washington opened the margin to 20–7 in the third quarter on a Moseley field goal, but Plunkett and the Raiders went on a tear, hooking up with Calvin Muhammad on two touchdowns, a twenty-five-yarder and a twenty-two-yard pass, to take a 21–20 lead, and then made it 28–20 on a short scoring pass to Todd Christensen. Shortly after stopping the Redskins offense, Los Angeles would stun the RFK crowd with a ninety-seven-yard punt returned by Greg Pruitt and a 35–20 lead with about seven minutes left in the game.

John Riggins' status as team leader was never more evident than when he coaxed his teammates into wearing Army fatigues on the trip to Dallas for a key game against the Cowboys in December 1983. The Redskins defeated Dallas 31-10 on their way to another NFC crown. (Washington Redskins)

Defense was just a memory now. Theismann brought his team back with a sixty-seven-yard pass to Joe Washington, putting the ball on the Raiders' twenty. Then, two plays later, Theismann completed a ten-yard pass to Charlie Brown for a touchdown, bringing Washington back to a 35–27 score.

Washington recovered an onside kick to get the ball back, and Moseley would kick a thirty-four-yard field goal to bring the Redskins closer, 35–30. The Washington defense came alive and held the Raiders, and Theismann and company got the ball back with two minutes left and the ball on their own thirty-one-yard line. Two straight passes to Brown put the ball on the Los Angeles six-yard line as fifty-four thousand people at RFK were on their feet stamping and screaming. On a first and goal with about thirty seconds left, Theismann hit Joe Washington in the end zone for the winning touchdown in a 37–35 exhausting victory as the Redskins scored a comeback for the books, putting up seventeen points in the last eight minutes.

The difference was Theismann's accuracy. He threw for 417 yards, whereas Plunkett passed for only 372. Plunkett threw four interceptions, whereas Theismann never gave the ball away. "That's an exciting way to win a game, but you don't want to do that every week," Gibbs said.

After a 38–14 win over the Cardinals in St. Louis, though, Gibbs would go through another offensive war, this time coming out on the losing end, again on a Monday night in a 48–47 loss to the Packers in Green Bay.

It was 10–10 after the first quarter, and the Packers led 24–20 at the half. They extended that lead to 31–20 when Gerry Ellis ran for a twenty-four-yard score in the third quarter. But two field goals and a Theismann pass to Joe Washington would put Washington on top for the first time in the game, 33–31.

In the fourth quarter, Green Bay went ahead 38–33 on a run by Gary Lewis. Washington came back with a Riggins blast to go on top 40–38. Lynn Dickey connected with Mike Meade on a thirty-one-yard touchdown pass, and the Packers now led 45–40. With two minutes left to play, Theismann hit Joe Washington with a three-yard scoring pass, and now it appeared to be a 47–45 Washington victory. Except that the Redskins defense couldn't stop Green Bay, and Jan Stenerud delivered a 48–47 win for the Packers with a twenty-yard field goal. The vital stats read like this: 138 combined offensive plays, fifty-six combined first downs, and 820 combined yards passing. It was hardly a Lombardi-like game for the two teams whom the legendary coach once led.

Coming back home, the Redskins showed no ill effects from the loss, beating Detroit 38–17 and winning their next six games before they would get a chance to avenge one of their two losses. The Redskins, with a record of 12–2, were heading to Dallas to face the Cowboys.

Going into Dallas, John Riggins and company did something that would have made George Allen proud. As the team left Redskins Park to travel to Dallas, they were dressed in Army fatigues, ready for combat.

"It was great," Jeff Bostic said. "Joe Gibbs was a straight-laced guy, and when he saw [special teams coach] Wayne Sevier, Joe said, 'Wayne, they've got Army fatigues on.' Wayne answered, 'I guess they're pretty serious about winning this game.'"

In front of more than sixty-five thousand Dallas fans in Texas Stadium, the Redskins were ready to do battle. After a Washington drive,

Early in Super Bowl XVIII, Joe Theismann and the Redskins had every reason to believe they would come away with another championship. After all, they had already beaten their opponent, the Los Angeles Raiders, during the regular season. But that would not be the case in their second meeting, a Raiders 38-9 championship victory. (Scott Cunningham)

The Washington defense could not stop the Raiders and Jim Plunkett after a devastating interception by linebacker Jack Squirek at the end of the first half. The Redskins never did get on track and went on to suffer their worst defeat of the season. What stung most, however, was that many Redskins believed they were the superior team. "That was probably the best team we ever had," Joe Gibbs said. (Scott Cunningham)

Riggins would bring the ball over from the three-yard line, and the point after put the Redskins on top 7–0 in the first quarter. They made it 14–0 on a pass from Theismann to Clint Didier. Danny White brought his team back with a nineteen-yard scoring pass to Doug Cosbie to cut the Redskins' lead to 14–7 at the end of the first quarter, and the Cowboys would make it a 14–10 game going into halftime after a field goal by Rafael Septien.

In the third quarter, Dallas got the ball and moved it to midfield. On a key fourth-and-one play, the Cowboys seemed to be trying to get the Redskins to jump offsides. At least that's what coach Tom Landry thought. His quarterback had other ideas.

White called an audible play instead, and after Ron Springs took the handoff he was tackled for a two-yard loss. "Tom Landry was on the sideline screaming, 'No, Danny, no,'" Jeff Bostic said.

Washington would add to their lead later in the third quarter when Theismann hooked up with Art Monk for a forty-three-yard touchdown pass, making it a 21–10 game. In the fourth quarter, Greg Williams intercepted a White pass, and after the Redskins got the ball on the Dallas thirty-eight, a pass interference call on cornerback Rod Hill put the ball on the Cowboys' four-yard line. Riggins would score, and Washington now had Dallas defeated and demoralized 28–10. They added a final field goal with about two minutes left for a 31–10 victory.

Washington would beat the New York Giants 31–22 at RFK in the final week of the season, finishing with a record of 14–2 and home field advantage throughout the playoffs.

Their playoff run began with a devastating 51–7 win over the Los Angeles Rams, the largest margin of victory in an NFL playoff game in twenty-six years, as the Redskins either set or tied thirteen playoff records. The Washington defense stopped Eric Dickerson, who had led the league with 1,808 yards rushing. Against the Redskins on this New Year's Day in 1984, Dickerson would run for just sixteen yards. The NFC title game the following week would pit the two offensive coaching geniuses of the 1980s—Gibbs versus Bill Walsh and his San Francisco 49ers and Joe Montana.

These two offensive juggernauts didn't even score in the first quarter, but Washington would be the first in the end zone when, in the second quarter, Riggins scored to put the Redskins on top 7–0, a lead they would take into the locker room at halftime.

Shortly after the start of the second half, rookie Darrell Green knocked the ball loose from wide-receiver Freddy Solomon and recovered the ball himself, which eventually led to another Riggins score and a 14–0 lead. Theismann made it 21–0 with a seventy-yard bomb to Charlie Brown. But they were playing against Joe Montana, the architect of the comeback drive. In the fourth quarter, Montana connected on two touchdown passes to Mike Wilson and one to Solomon, and suddenly it was a 21–21 game about halfway through the fourth quarter.

Redskins fans implored their team to hang tough, yelling, "Defense, defense," and Washington managed to stop the 49ers on their next posses-

The score board congratulates Washington wide receiver Art Monk for pass reception number 106, which set an NFL record for receptions in a season. Monk gained 1,372 yards during that 1984 season, which cemented his reputation as one of the steadiest receivers ever. He also excelled at running with the ball once he caught it. (*right:* Nate Fine; *above:* Scott Cunningham)

ART MONK HAS JUST
SET A NEW REDSKIN
CLUB RECORD FOR
MOST PASSES CAUGHT
IN ONE SEASON

Under general manager Bobby Beathard and assistant GM Charley Casserly, the Redskins were aggressive in finding talent, and they made the most of the demise of the United States Football League, picking up keepers such as wide receiver Gary Clark, who would pull in 549 passes over eight seasons in Washington. (Washington Redskins)

sion, and, with less than a minute remaining, Moseley got into position for a twenty-five-yard field goal, and sighs of relief combined with shouts of joy as he made it to give the Redskins a 24–21 win and a return trip to the Super Bowl. John Riggins had run for 123 yards, marking his sixth straight playoff game in which he gained more than one hundred yards.

This time the big game would be in Florida, in Tampa, and without the strike, there were two weeks, not one, for the hype buildup. Everyone expected a wild and exciting contest, based on the last time the Redskins and the AFC champions, the Los Angeles Raiders, had met during the season in that 37–35 Washington victory.

The Raiders quarterback, Jim Plunkett, had a

shaky game that day but went on to have a remarkable season when most observers believed he was finished. He completed 230 of 379 passes for more than 2000 yards and was complemented by running back Marcus Allen, who gained 1,014 yards rushing. And they had a Raiders-type outlaw defense, led by Lyle Alzado and Howie Long.

This wouldn't be a repeat of the Redskins' previous trip to the big game. Washington knew that early when a punt by Jeff Hayes was blocked and recovered by Derrick Jensen in the end zone for a 7–0 Raiders lead with about ten minutes remaining in the first quarter.

In the second quarter, Plunkett hit Cliff Branch with a twelve-yard touchdown pass to extend the Raiders' lead to 14–0. Washington

November 18, 1985, is a day that will live in infamy for Redskins fans. In front of millions on Monday night, Joe Theismann, sacked by Giants great Lawrence Taylor, suffered an injury so violent in its effect, so ghoulish in its appearance that it ended his career and remains fixed in the memories of all those who saw it. (*Below*): A somber Theismann meets with reporters afterward. Untested backup Jay Schroeder (*left*) took over and led the Redskins to a 23-21 win over New York. Schroeder would go on to quarterback Washington in 1986. (Washington Redskins)

The 1985 season was the swan song for the incomparable, iconoclastic John Riggins. Here he is introduced before his last home game with the Redskins, on Dec. 15, 1985. Riggins set a number of team records during his nine seasons with Washington, including most yards gained in a career (7,472) and most in a season (1,347). He was inducted into the Pro Football Hall of Fame in 1992. (Washington Redskins)

would come back with a field goal to get on the board, 14–3, with about four minutes left in the half.

The Redskins got the ball back late in the half, with about twelve seconds left to play, on their own five-yard line. Then came the one play that Redskins fans would always remember but wish to forget.

Joe Gibbs hoped that his team could break out with a screen pass and then perhaps a long throw by Theismann. He wanted to take a chance and avoid going into the locker room eleven points down with no momentum. So he called a screen pass to Joe Washington, and that gave little-known Raiders linebacker Jack Squirek his place in history.

Squirek stayed with Washington and cut in front of him to intercept the pass and take it five yards into the end zone for a touchdown. The Redskins were stunned, and the Raiders were leading 21–3 at halftime.

Washington would score again in the third quarter on a Riggins run, but they got another sign that it wasn't their day when Moseley's extra point was blocked. The Raiders added two more touchdowns by Marcus Allen, including a seventy-four-yard run at the end of the third quarter, to open up a 35–9 Los Angeles lead. They would add a field goal as the final insult in a 38–9 Super Bowl win.

What made the defeat so difficult for the Redskins is that many believed they were a far superior team than the one who won the champi-

The Redskins, with Jay Schroeder and Doug Williams splitting time at quarterback, battled their way to another NFC title in 1987. Williams, shown here talking strategy with Joe Gibbs in the NFC Title game against Minnesota, led Washington to a 17-10 win over the Vikings with passes such as this scoring toss to Gary Clark. (*above:* Washington Redskins; *left:* Scott Cunningham)

Filling In

The 1987 season, leading up to the victory in Super Bowl XXII on January 31, 1988, was perhaps the most unusual in football history. After the first two games of the year, the players went on strike, and, after one week with no games, replacement teams were fielded.

And as uncomfortable as that may have been, the fact that the Redskins perhaps did it better than anyone else may have helped them reach the Super Bowl that season.

Charley Casserly helped assemble that replacement team. "It was not a pleasant thing," he said. "I don't think anyone wanted to be involved with bringing a replacement team in. But you had a job to do. We had to go play St. Louis, New York, and Dallas, and it was going to make or break our season.

"We went to work day and night, trying to find players, getting people in there," Casserly said. "We were fortunate to have such a great coaching staff."

About ten regulars remained on the Cardinals team in their first game before a crowd of about twenty-eight thousand at RFK against the replacement Redskins, because the players were divided among themselves during the strike. But, with Washington quarterback Ed Rubbert, receiver Anthony Allen, and running back Lionel Vital leading the way, the Redskins won 28–21. Vital caught seven passes for 255 yards. Washington would play the Giants at the Meadowlands the following week and again come out on top, this time 38–12, with Vital rushing for 128 yards.

The strike was about to end during the following week, with players on many teams deciding to return to play. The Cowboys were back and ready to play in time. The Redskins, sticking together as a unit, did not break the picket line until the players decided to return *en masse*, but by then it was too late. It was past the deadline set by the league to return for the October 19 game, so they couldn't suit up.

Bobby Beathard and Charley Casserly watch over the replacement Redskins team's remarkable 13-7 win over the Dallas Cowboys during the 1987 players strike. The Redskins replacement team went 3-0, putting them in a position to win the conference title when the strike ended. (Scott Cunningham)

That meant that the Redskins replacements would be going against Danny White and company—the real Cowboys. It was David against Goliath before a Texas Stadium crowd of more than sixty thousand, and David won, beating the Cowboys in Texas 13–7. Quarterback Tony Robinson completed eleven of eighteen for 152 yards, Vital ran for 136 yards, and the defense forced two Dallas fumbles.

"To beat them down there, in a game nobody thought we had a chance to win, was remarkable," Casserly said. "We didn't think we had much of a chance, but Joe [Gibbs] got those kids believing in themselves.

"We had mixed emotions that night, but we came out with three straight wins from those teams to give us a record of 4–1," Casserly said. "The Giants are 0–3 in those games, and they had lost their first two. They are the defending Super Bowl champions, and they are 0–5."

onship the year before. They had put up 541 points during the season, averaging nearly thirty-four points a game. Moseley led the league and set an NFL record with 166 points, and Riggins was right behind him with 144 points. Riggins also rushed for 1,347 yards. Theismann completed 276 of 459 passes for 3,714 yards and twenty-nine touchdowns. Charlie Brown caught seventy-eight passes for 1,225 yards.

"That was probably the best team we ever had," Gibbs said. "That team was probably the most efficient and strongest we had, if I ever had to pick one. Yet we went and played that game in Florida and got beat by the Raiders. It was one of those things. We had a game on a particular day, and we didn't play real well. But if you look at the stats of that team, it was awesome."

The following year Redskins fans, players, and others believed that the team would return for a third straight trip. Why not? It was the same,

With the NFC championship win over the Vikings, the Redskins faced the Denver Broncos in Super Bowl XXII in San Diego. Here the team is introduced before the game. (Scott Cunningham)

Super Bowl XXII started ominously for the Redskins, especially when Doug Williams left the game with a knee injury. Down 10-0 in the first quarter Williams returned and hit Ricky Sanders for an 80-yard scoring pass. Williams celebrates the touchdown here with guard R.C. Thielemann. (Scott Cunningham)

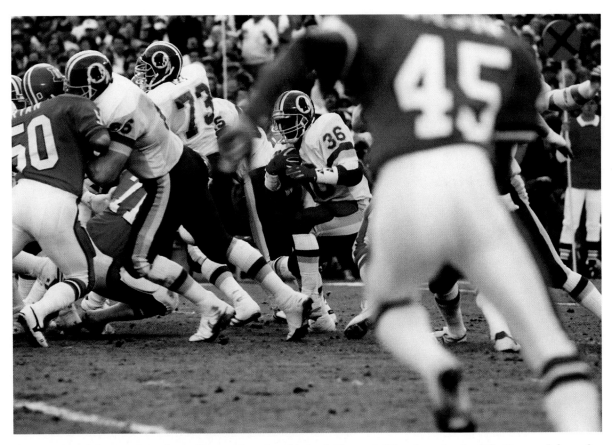

The surprise of the Super Bowl was the running of rookie back Timmy Smith, who pulverized the Denver defense for a record 204 yards. (Washington Redskins)

powerful team. But those expectations disappeared in the first two games of the season—both losses, the first 35–17 to the Miami Dolphins at RFK and the second 37–31 to the 49ers in San Francisco.

Washington recovered to win the next five, including a 34–14 beating of the Cowboys, but lost the next two games on the road, 26–24 to St. Louis and 37–13 to the New York Giants. It turned out that this would be a season when the Redskins clearly enjoyed a home field advantage. Washington won its next two games, both at home, 27–14 over Atlanta and 28–14 over Detroit, for a record of 7–4 before they would take to the road again, and lose again, 16–14 to the Philadelphia Eagles, to fall to a record of 7–5. But a strong finish with four wins (over Buffalo, Minnesota, Dallas again, and St. Louis) gave the Redskins an 11–5 record and a return to the playoffs. It was a short run this time, because the Chicago Bears, with a defense that would emerge as one of the best of all

time, led the Bears to a 23–19 win over Washington at RFK. They sacked Theismann seven times and held the Redskins running game to under one-hundred yards.

Individually, it had been a rewarding year. Art Monk set an NFL record with 106 receptions for 1,372 yards. Riggins had another 1,000-yard season, gaining 1,239 yards rushing. And Theismann completed 283 of 477 passes for 3,391 yards and twenty-four touchdowns.

The 1985 season brought changes from the beginning. With Riggins on his last legs, they traded a first-round draft choice to New Orleans for running back George Rogers. And they added United States Football League players like Gary Clark.

But the season opened with a disappointing 44–14 loss to the Cowboys in Dallas. Then, after a home-opening 16–13 victory over Houston, Washington would lose two straight, 19–6 to the

The Quarter of a Lifetime

It may have been the most perfect 5:47 of offensive football ever played.

Down 10–0 to the Denver Broncos in Super Bowl XXII, the Redskins took the ball in the second quarter. With Doug Williams at the helm, the Redskins offense ran eighteen plays for 356 yards and scored thirty-five points over that span in the quarter. With the score 35–10, the game was over before the half.

"In playing football for twenty years in high school, college, and the professional ranks, I've never been involved in anything like that," tackle Joe Jacoby said. "Everything just worked."

An eighty-yard touchdown pass from Williams to Ricky Sanders. A twenty-seven-yard scoring toss from Williams to Gary Clark. A fifty-eight-yard run by rookie running back Timmy Smith. A fifty-yard touchdown pass to Sanders. An eight-yarder in the end zone to Clint Didier. 35–10. The game would end with a 42–10 Washington victory.

"You have this maybe once in your lifetime," Charley Casserly said. "Everything we worked was perfect. Every execution was perfect. Every time we turned around we hit a home run. In the second half, we could have scored more, but Joe [Gibbs] wasn't going to do that. We just ran the ball."

There's no telling what might have happened if they had kept the pressure on. By the end of the game, the Redskins had broken nineteen Super Bowl records and tied ten others. Some of those records: most yards gained in one quarter (356), most points scored in one quarter (35), most yards passing in one quarter (Doug Wiliams, 228), most yards receiving in one quarter (Ricky Sanders, 193).

They tied several other, including: longest pass completion and reception in a game (eighty yards from Williams to Sanders), most touchdowns passing in a quarter (four), most touchdowns receiving over that period (Sanders, two), and most rushing touchdowns in a quarter (Smith, two).

"We couldn't stop them," Denver coach Dan Reeves said after the game. "It would have been difficult for anyone to beat the Redskins. They're definitely the world champions."

Art Monk and Ricky Sanders celebrate another scoring pass, this one a 27-yarder to fellow receiver Gary Clark, in what was probably the greatest offensive quarter in championship football history. Over a span of 5:47 in the second quarter of Super Bowl XXII, Washington ran 18 plays for 356 yards and scored 35 points. (*Opposite, above:* Washington Redskins; *right:* Scott Cunningham)

Philadelphia Eagles and a 45–10 drubbing to the Chicago Bears. With a record of 1–3, Washington would go 4–2 over its next six games and—coming off another loss to the Cowboys, this time 13–7 at RFK—with a record of 5–5, had a huge contest ahead of them in the New York Giants.

It was a nationally televised Monday night game at RFK. Washington opened the scoring with a ten-yard scoring pass to Don Warren. The Giants tied the game 7–7 when Joe Morris scored on a fifty-six-yard run.

Washington had the ball at the start of the second quarter with the score still tied. They had first down on their own forty-six-yard line when Gibbs sent in the play—fifty gut throwback, which meant that Riggins would take the handoff from Theismann, then turn and pitch the ball back to the quarterback for a long pass.

It worked until Harry Carson broke in and forced Theismann to scramble. Then Lawrence Taylor came down on Theismann for the tackle, resulting in the break that seemed to be heard around the world.

As Theismann went down, his lower leg was bent inward at a horrifying angle, and the sound could be heard all over the field. "It was a sound I will never forget," said guard Ken Huff.

Taylor panicked when he saw what happened to Theismann and quickly motioned for the Redskins trainers to get out onto the field as quickly as possible. "I heard something go snap, and I thought two helmets had hit each other," Taylor said. "It was an ugly sight."

Theismann had started in 71 consecutive

Joe Gibbs and general manager Bobby Beathard celebrate the 42-10 Super Bowl win over Denver—their second NFL championship. Washington set 19 Super Bowl records and tied 10 others. (Washington Redskins)

Doug Williams had the game of his life against Denver, completing 18 of 29 passes for 340 yards and four touchdowns on his way to being named the Most Valuable Player of Super Bowl XXII. (Washington Redskins)

games and was Gibbs's general on the field. "To see him on the ground like that was hard," Gibbs said. "He has meant so much to this town."

Everyone knew how serious the injury was, but no one thought it was the end of an era. It was. Theismann would have a slow recovery, but he vowed to come back. However, he never threw another pass in the NFL.

The team would be handed over to Jay Schroeder, a former major league baseball prospect in his second pro season. The strong-armed Schroeder did not wilt under pressure, leading the Redskins to a 23–21 win over the Giants, connecting thirteen of twenty passes for 221 yards, no interceptions, and one touchdown.

Schroeder would step in and do well the rest of the season, as the Redskins would win four of their last five games for a 10–6 record. But it wasn't enough to make the playoffs, and for the first time

since 1981, Gibbs and company would stay home.

The season would also prove to be the last one for a fan favorite, John Riggins. Rogers got more opportunities to run the ball and finished with 1,093 yards rushing and a 4.7-yard average. Riggins finished with 677 yards rushing and a 3.8-yard average. He would not return but would be recognized for his outstanding career when he was inducted into the Pro Football Hall of Fame in 1992.

It was Schroeder's team in 1986, and the young quarterback started impressively, leading the team to a 5–0 record in their first five games, opening with a 41–14 win at RFK over the Philadelphia Eagles. They would lose, though, 30–6 to the Cowboys in Dallas, and that game marked the end of the career of another great Redskin. Mark Moseley had been missing, including a short field goal and an extra point in the Dallas game, and he was released after the loss.

Washington bounced back with a 28–21 victory over the St. Louis Cardinals, but, in another Monday night meeting with the Giants, Schroeder was not able to work his magic again, and the Redskins lost 27–20. But five more consecutive wins gave Washington an 11–2 record coming into another Giants game, this one at RFK. But New York prevailed 24–14, and Washington would lose again the next week, 31–30 at Denver, before winning the season finale at Philadelphia 21–14, winding up with a 12–4 mark.

It seemed as if Washington might make it back to the Super Bowl. In the wild card game on December 28 at RFK, they played Redskins football against the Los Angeles Rams as they forced six Ram turnovers, and George Rogers carried the ball twenty-nine times for 115 yards in a 19–7 win. "This was the solid game we were waiting for," Gibbs said.

They would have to travel to Chicago next to face the defending Super Bowl champion Bears, the team who had knocked the Redskins out of the playoffs two years before. Chicago led 13–7 at the half, but Schroeder hit Art Monk on a twenty-three-yard touchdown pass to go ahead 14–13, and George Rogers would later cap off an eleven-play, eighty-three-yard march with a one-yard plunge to give Washington a 21–13 lead. Two Jess Atkinson field goals would make the final score 27–13. Waiting ahead in the NFC title game? The Giants, the team who had beaten the Redskins twice already during the season.

This was the Giants team who was on a roll to the Super Bowl, though, and the defense, led by Lawrence Taylor and Harry Carson, shut out Washington in a 17–0 win. The Redskins failed to convert on fourteen third-down situations, and the Giants' running game controlled the ball.

Overall, though, it was a successful season, one game away from the Super Bowl. The Redskins were close enough to believe that they would soon return there.

Changes would come for the 1987 season, most notably the addition of Doug Williams, who was back in the NFL after his stay in the upstart USFL. Williams started out as a backup to Jay Schroeder, but he was more like a relief pitcher, getting his first action early. Schroeder hurt his

shoulder in the opener at RFK against the Philadelphia Eagles, and Williams came in, completing seventeen of twenty-seven passes for 272 yards and two touchdowns. Jess Atkinson, Russ Grimm, and George Rogers were also hurt, but the Redskins would come out on top 34-24.

With Schroeder hurt, Williams got the start in Atlanta against the Falcons but came up short 21–20. It turns out that the difference between losing and getting at least a tie was a missed extra point by Ali Haji Sheikh, signed to replace the injured Atkinson.

All those injured players, though, were about to get a rest they would just as soon have done without. The NFL was about to go through its second players strike in six seasons. And this one would be very different. This time, the NFL would use replacement players.

General manager Bobby Beathard called on Charley Casserly to put together a replacement team. This was a difficult time for many teams, and some clubs fell behind in that effort. The Redskins were not one of them, and their effort paid off. Washington had a 1–1 record when the replacement games began and a 4–1 record when the strike ended and the regular players returned. The replacements beat the St. Louis Cardinals 28–21 before a crowd of nearly twenty-eight thousand at RFK, then followed that with a 38–12 win over the New York Giants at the Meadowlands. The strike ended at the last minute before the third game. Many players began to return to teams, but the Redskins veterans, who stuck together as a unit, did not come back by the league deadline to make them eligible for another Monday night nationally televised game in Dallas against the Cowboys.

The Dallas veterans were there, though. But still the Redskins replacements played an inspired game and shocked the Cowboys with a 13–7 win. Quarterback Tony Robinson completed eleven of eighteen passes for 152 yards, and running back Lionel Vital rushed for 136 yards.

With the regulars back, Washington won its next two games, 17–16 over the New York Jets at RFK and 27–7 in Buffalo over the Bills. In the Bills game, George Rogers rushed for 125 yards, and the defense intercepted Jim Kelly three times and held the Bills to twenty-one yards rushing. "Today we played the best we can play," Gibbs said, but, as everyone found out in San Diego in January, that wasn't the case.

Washington would lose to Philadelphia 31–27, then come back with a 20–13 victory over Detroit, a win for the defense, who had four interceptions, including three by Darrell Green.

They would follow another loss, this one 30–26 to the Los Angeles Rams at home, with three straight victories, including perhaps the turning point for the rest of the season in a 23–19 win over the defending Super Bowl champion New York Giants at RFK. The Giants led 16–0 at halftime, but Schroeder, who had gotten the start when Doug Williams strained his back and had struggled in the first half, had a remarkable second half, completing seventeen of twenty-five passes for 217 yards and three touchdowns. "This was a tribute to the players, hanging in there like they did," Gibbs said. "It showed great courage."

Washington would come out on top in three of their next four games, finishing with another inspirational come-from-behind win, this one in overtime against the Vikings from Minnesota. With the score tied 7–7 midway through the third quarter, Gibbs replaced Schroeder, who started the game, with Williams, healing from his sore back. Williams would hit Ricky Sanders with a forty-six-yard scoring pass to go on top 14–7, but the Vikings scored two touchdowns and a field goal to take a commanding 24–14 lead. But Williams helped Washington put ten points on the board at the end of the third quarter with a thirty-seven-yard field goal by Ali Haji Sheikh and a fifty-one-yard touchdown pass to Sanders to tie the game 24–24 going into the fourth quarter. The defense shut out Minnesota in that final quarter and Ali Haji Sheikh connected on another field goal from the nine-yard line for the 27–24 win.

Washington ended the year with an 11–4 record and a playoff spot with the Chicago Bears in front of them as their first adversary, at Soldier Field. The players were pumped up for the game, particularly because the day before Minnesota had upset the San Francisco 49ers, which meant that if the Redskins won, they would have the home field for the NFC title game. "The players were sky high, because they knew that if we beat Chicago, we're home, and if we're home, we're going to win at

RFK," Charley Casserly said. "That's the attitude."

After Washington fell behind 14–0, Williams engineered a sixty-nine-yard drive that ended with a George Rogers touchdown and a seventy-two-yard march that culminated in an eighteen-yard scoring pass to Clint Didier, tying the game at 14–14.

That set the stage for cornerback Darrell Green to make one of the most important special teams plays in the history of the club, running back a punt fifty-two yards for a touchdown, hurdling one defender before reaching the end zone, tearing a cartilage in his rib in the process.

"It was just instinctive," Green said. "That's all that I could do."

That would seal a 21–17 Redskins victory and a trip to the NFC championship game against Minnesota. Before the game, Gibbs would ask his players to dedicate the game to long time team photographer Nate Fine, who had died after being with the Redskins for fifty-one years. "Joe gives them a speech about winning one for Nate, and there was a feeling that no one could stop us the next day," Casserly said.

Washington controlled the game, to the delight of more than fifty-five thousand fans at RFK, opening the scoring with a forty-three-yard touchdown pass from Williams to Kelvin Bryant in the first quarter. After Minnesota tied the game 7–7 in the second quarter, the Redskins went ahead again in the third quarter on a twenty-eight-yard field goal by Ali Haji Sheikh. Minnesota tied the game again in the fourth quarter, but with the score 10–10 Williams connected with Gary Clark for a seven-yard scoring pass, putting the Redskins on top to stay 17–10. The Vikings were knocking on the door to tie it again, on the Redskins' six with fifty-six seconds left. But on fourth down, Darrin Nelson bobbled a pass in the end zone from Wade Wilson, with Darrell Green putting the hit on him, and the Redskins would return to the biggest game in football again, this time in San Diego to face the AFC champion Denver Broncos.

With more than seventy-three thousand fans on hand, it would turn out to be an unforgettable game, but it didn't start out that way. Washington was down 10–0 in the first quarter. John Elway hit Ricky Nattiel with a fifty-six-yard touchdown pass, and a field goal put the Redskins further in the hole. They could have been buried there. "The pace of a Super Bowl game is ten times faster than a regular-season game," Casserly said. "It's hard to describe how fast that game goes. The intensity is so much higher that teams can get blown out quickly."

But Washington didn't panic, even when they fumbled the kickoff from Denver. Terry Orr managed to come up with the ball from a pile of players to save the day. Finally the offense did something—a fifteen-yard completion from Williams to Art Monk. "It didn't lead to any points, but it gave the team a lift, because it was our first real successful play," Casserly said.

Compared to what came next, it was a blip on a radar screen. The second quarter was one that Redskins fans won't forget.

Doug Williams got the hottest hand in football history—an eighty-yard scoring pass to Ricky Sanders, a twenty-seven-yarder to Gary Clark, a fifty-yard touchdown pass to Sanders, and an eight-yarder to Clint Didier. Add all that to a fifty-eight-yard run by rookie Timmy Smith, who would gain 204 yards on twenty-three carries.

By the end of the quarter, Washington had put a record thirty-five points on the board and had, for all intents and purposes, won the game. The defense would shut out the Broncos for the rest of the game, and Washington would add one more score in the fourth quarter on a four-yard run by Smith for a final score of 42–10.

When the game was over, Williams had completed eighteen of twenty-nine passes for 340 yards and four touchdowns, and the Redskins had broken nineteen Super Bowl records and tied ten others.

"That's the best I've ever seen a team play," Charles Mann said.

"It was like a dream land," guard R.C. Theilemann said. "Everything that Doug threw and everything that we blocked went for big yardage."

"Our whole side of the field had an energy that was difficult to describe," Gary Clark said. "It was like we could accomplish anything. It was like we were all Supermen."

But it wasn't a team of Supermen who won Super Bowl XXII. In fact, it was far from the best of the championship Washington squads. The team had been switching between Williams and Schroeder throughout the season. They were forced to rely on a rookie running back in the biggest game of the year. And there were a number of untested players, like Ricky Sanders, thrown into the mix.

"That team made the most out of its ability," Gibbs said. Redskins fans acknowledged that when they lined the streets of Washington again for another tribute to a championship team and the Redskins' continuing tradition of winning.

Ten

The Fall and Rise Again

So far under Joe Gibbs's tenure, the Washington Redskins had never fallen too far from the top—three trips to the Super Bowl over seven seasons, never winning less than ten games in any full season—so there was no reason to believe that the 1988 season would be any different.

Change, as always, would come. Free agent linebacker Wilbur Marshall signed with Washington, and they drafted a kicker, Chip Lohmiller, in the second round. George Rogers was released, as were linebacker Rich Milot, tight end Clint Didier, and defensive back Vernon Dean, among others. And Jay Schroeder, unhappy with playing time, was traded to the Los Angeles Raiders.

But the season would open on a down note with a 27–20 loss to the New York Giants. It would be a preview of missed opportunities for the year. Washington blew a 13–3 lead in the first half with mistakes like a blocked punt and a fumble recovery and twenty-nine-yard return by Jim Burt. Turnovers would continue to plague the Redskins that year as they committed forty-six to finish with the league's worst turnover ratio at minus twenty-four—not a typical Joe Gibbs team.

The Redskins managed to win the next week before the hometown crowd at RFK, a 30–29 victory over the Pittsburgh Steelers. But it was a tough win as the Redskins' running game turned into a big problem. Throughout the season, none of the candidates—Timmy Smith, Kelvin Bryant, and Jamie Morris—would step forward to take the job. Against the Steelers, Williams had to throw fifty-two times for 430 yards. Ricky Sanders caught five passes for 145 yards and one touchdown.

Williams's arm got a rest the next week, with only twenty-three attempts, as the running game showed some signs of life in a 17–10 win over the Philadelphia Eagles. He would get a lot more time to rest very shortly.

During the week, Williams was hospitalized with appendicitis, leaving untested Mark Rypien to take the snaps against the Cardinals, who had moved from St. Louis to Phoenix in the off-season. Rypien performed well, tossing three touchdowns, but there was no running game to turn to as the offense netted just fifty-three yards rushing on nineteen carries, adding up to a 30–21 loss to the Cardinals in Phoenix.

Washington would suffer its second straight loss the following week, a tough 24–23 defeat to the New York Giants, and had a missed field goal

Not content to sit pat, the Redskins in 1988 signed free agent linebacker Wilber Marshall, on the sidelines celebrating a Redskins win with special teams coach Wayne Sevier. Marshall joined Monte Coleman and later Andre Collins and Kurt Gouveia to form a potent linebacking corps. (Scott Cunningham)

and extra point by Lohmiller to look back on in frustration.

To show how down things were in Redskinland, a win the next week over the Cowboys carried little meaning. Rypien had his best game yet, going thirteen for twenty-one and connecting on three touchdowns for a 35–17 win over Dallas. But these were not the mighty Cowboys. Dallas was on its way to its worst season in twenty-five years.

Rypien continued to grow into the job, leading Washington to a 33–17 win over Phoenix, the team they had lost to four weeks earlier, and a 20–17 win over Green Bay. With a record of 5–3, the Redskins considered themselves fortunate. And though Rypien played well—twelve touchdowns and just three interceptions—Williams returned the following week after his recovery. He struggled, though, and the Redskins dropped a 41–17 game to

Houston. They would win just two of their last seven games and finish the season with a mark of 7–9—their first losing record since 1980, before Joe Gibbs was hired. It didn't go down very easy. "This year was no fun," Gibbs said, evaluating the aftermath. "Our owner isn't used to losing, and our fans aren't used to losing. It isn't a feeling we want to get used to around here."

One noteworthy moment: Defensive tackle Dave Butz broke Len Hauss's record for most games played as a Redskin (196), as Butz would retire at the end of the year having played in 203 games for Washington.

If the organization could turn things around in 1989, it would have to be done without one of its architects. General manager Bobby Beathard retired in May 1989 and went into broadcasting, although Beathard, a native Californian, would later accept a job as GM of the San Diego

Under Joe Gibbs, three quarterbacks would lead the Redskins offense to Super Bowls. In 1988 Doug Williams (*left*), sidelined with injuries, turned the ball over to young Mark Rypien (*right*), who would eventually take the Redskins to a championship season in 1991. (Scott Cunningham)

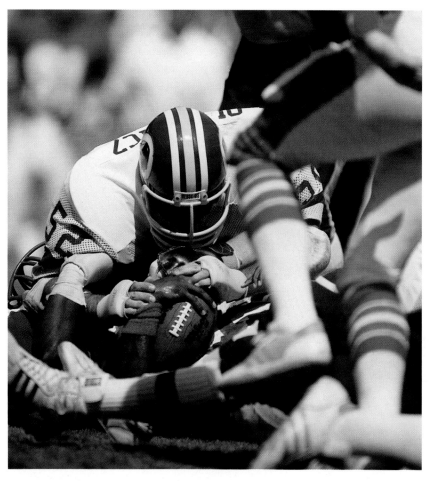

After the 1988 season, Redskins fans said goodbye to the anchor of the Washington defense for 14 seasons when defensive tackle Dave Butz retired. Over that period, Butz appeared in 203 Redskin games. The following year the changing of the guard continued when linebacker Neal Olkewicz (*left*) retired after 11 seasons. (Scott Cunningham)

Chargers. Charley Casserly got his shot now as the Washington GM, having risen from an unpaid intern under George Allen in 1977 to the man in charge of one of pro football's most prestigious franchises.

"I expect Charley will be capable of keeping the Redskins in contention in the National Football League," said Jack Kent Cooke, making the announcement of Casserly's hiring. Cooke would be proved right.

Casserly and Gibbs would make some changes to shore up their running game, trading a first-round draft pick to the Atlanta Falcons for fullback Gerald Riggs and then dealing running back Mike Oliphant to Cleveland in exchange for Earnest Byner, thus acquiring two one-thousand-yard backs. The Redskins went 4–1 in the preseason, and, with Doug Williams suffering from back problems, Mark Rypien got the start in the season opener at home against the New York Giants.

Rypien, a sixth-round draft pick in 1986 from Washington State, continued his impressive play from the previous season, completing twenty-two of thirty-two passes for 349 yards, two touchdowns, and one interception. But it wasn't enough as the defense gave up 159 yards rushing to New York's powerful ground game, and the Giants prevailed 27–24.

After another loss at home, this one 42–37 to the Philadelphia Eagles, Redskins fans were concerned. After all, their team had a four-game losing streak, dating back to last season, and had not won at RFK since November 6, 1988.

The road would offer some relief, though, as Washington won their next two, 30–7 over the Cowboys in Dallas and a hard-fought 16–14 victory over the Saints in New Orleans. It was a tough time for Gibbs, whose father had suffered a massive stroke in California, and after the game the players presented Gibbs with the game ball.

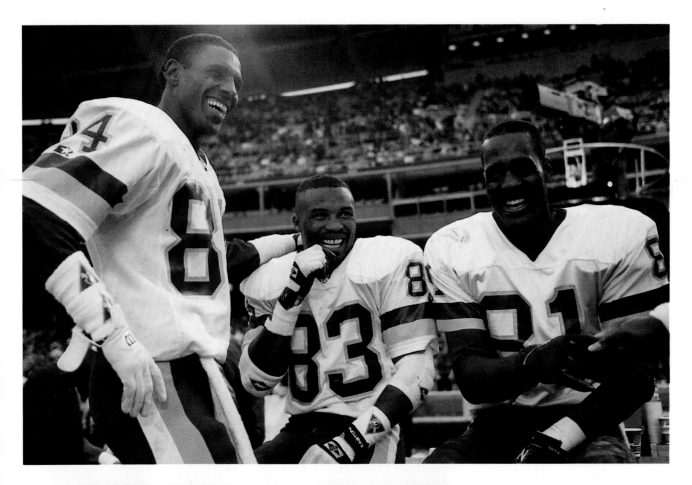

In 1990, the receiving corps of Gary Clark (84), Ricky Sanders (83), and Art Monk (81) enjoyed an epic year, with Clark pulling down 75 passes for 1,112 yards, Monk 68 catches for 770 yards, and Sanders 56 receptions for 727 yards. (Scott Cunningham)

The Greatest Comeback

The Redskins have had many memorable comebacks over their history, but none may have been greater or more dramatic than the one engineered by Jeff Rutledge—a veteran third-string quarterback—in a 41–38 overtime win over the Detroit Lions at the Pontiac Silverdome on November 4, 1990.

The Lions had been demolishing the Redskins, building up a 35–14 lead. Joe Gibbs pulled starter Stan Humphries in the second half for Jeff Rutledge, whose primary purpose at this late date in his career was to serve as the holder for Chip Lohmiller.

Rutledge called on whatever was left in his arm and heart to engineer an improbable comeback. He marched the team down the field, finishing with a three-yard run by Gerald Riggs for the first score, cutting the Detroit lead to 35–21. The Lions added a field goal, but Lohmiller came back with his own three-pointer, and now it was a 38–24 contest. With less than six minutes left, Rutledge connected with Gary Clark for a thirty-four-yard score, and it was now Detroit 38, Washington 31. And Rutledge would top it off with a twelve-yard quarterback draw with eighteen seconds left to tie the game at 38–38 with the clock running out.

After an exchange of punts in overtime, Rutledge directed a seventy-three-yard, twelve-play drive that ended in a Lohmiller field goal from thirty-four yards out for a 41–38 victory.

Having completed thirty of forty-two passes for 363 yards, the thirty-three-year-old Rutledge sealed his place in Redskins history with his performance.

Redskins players always appreciated what Gibbs gave them—the preparation that allowed them to win.

"Joe was an offensive genius," Jeff Bostic said. "I'm convinced that if he had been given two weeks to prepare a game plan for every team, each one would be a masterpiece."

Finally, at home before a crowd of more than fifty-three thousand, the Redskins won, a 30–28 victory over Phoenix. The Cardinals led 21–13 going into the fourth quarter when Rypien brought Washington back, connecting on a twelve-yard touchdown to Art Monk and a twenty-three-yard scoring pass to Gary Clark. And Chip Lohmiller topped it off with a thirty-seven-yard field goal. It was Lohmiller's third field goal of the game, and the defense held off a late Cardinal rally for the win.

The season then took on a roller-coaster pattern—a 20–17 loss to the Giants, a 32–28 win over Tampa Bay, then two straight losses, 37–24 to the Los Angeles Raiders and 13–3 to the Dallas Cowboys. A 10–3 victory over Philadelphia was followed by a 14–10 loss to Denver. But Washington found their mark in the last five games of the season with five straight wins. Rypien established himself as one of the best young throwers in the league, completing 280 passes in 476 attempts for 3,768 yards and twenty-two touchdowns. They set a team record for total yardage (6,253) and were one of only two teams to rank among the league's top ten teams in both offense and defense, the other team being the world champion San Francisco 49ers.

Washington finished with a 10–6 mark—not good enough for a playoff spot but enough to fuel the hopes for better times the next year. And with young players like rookie cornerbacks A.J. Johnson and Martin Mayhew and offensive line newcomers Mark Schlereth and Ed Simmons, Gibbs saw similarities to his first group of players in Washington. "All the young players created an excitement around here," he said. "It reminded me of the first year or two I was here."

The 1989 season also saw the departure of linebacker Neal Olkewicz, retiring after eleven seasons with Washington; the elevation of Art Monk into third place in NFL history in pass receptions, ahead of former Redskins great and then-receiver coach Charley Taylor (649 receptions); and the one hundredth career win for Gibbs, a 26–21 victory over San Diego.

The offense that finished the 1989 season was tuned and ready for the 1990 season opener, as was the defense, in an outstanding 31–0 win over the Phoenix Cardinals at RFK. Mark Rypien threw three touchdown passes—a thirty-seven-yarder to Ricky Sanders, a four-yard toss to Earnest Byner, and a forty-three-yard shot to Gary Clark. Alvin Walton put the defense's stamp on the game with a fifty-seven-yard pass interception, and Chip Lohmiller's twenty-nine-yard field goal extended his consecutive-game field goal streak to twenty-one.

The new-look Redskins got a lesson in championship play the next week, though, as they were defeated 26–13 by the world champion 49ers in San Francisco as Joe Montana picked them apart for 390 yards.

Back home the next week, the Redskins' best-laid plans seemed to fall apart against the Dallas Cowboys at RFK when Rypien went down with a knee injury in the second quarter. But backup Stan Humphries gave them enough to pull out a 19–15 win. With Rypien out, Humphries started the next five games, and the team went 3–2 over that period for a season mark of 5–4. When Rypien returned, he picked apart the New Orleans Saints defense for 311 yards in a 31–17 win before a pumped-up RFK

Before the start of the 1991 season, the core group of the Hogs—Russ Grimm, Joe Jacoby, and Jeff Bostic—sensed that this might be their last shot at a championship. Thus, the entire team met voluntarily every Saturday night during the season to focus on their mission. (Scott Cunningham)

crowd of more than fifty-two thousand fans.

The Redskins would go on to win four of their final six games, repeating their mark of 10–6 in the previous year. This time, though, it was good enough to earn them a wild card playoff spot. Gibbs would be squaring off against Buddy Ryan on Philadelphia's home field, and it proved to be no contest. The Eagles got on board first with a Roger Ruzak field goal to take a 3–0 lead in the first quarter.

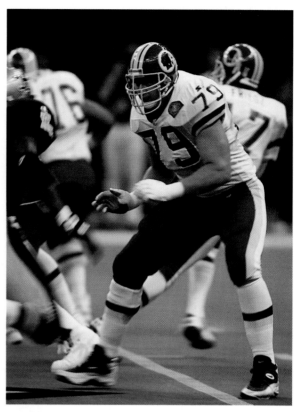

The Hogs changed faces a number of times over their run, and the new faces, such as Mark Schlereth (*left*) and Jim Lachey (*right*), carried on the tradition well. (Scott Cunningham)

Washington opened up a 10–6 lead in the second quarter on a sixteen-yard scoring pass from Mark Rypien to Art Monk and a twenty-yard field goal by Chip Lohmiller. But it nearly turned out to be an Eagle win, when, in the second quarter, Philadelphia's Ben Smith picked up what appeared to be a fumble by Earnest Byner and ran ninety-four yards for an apparent touchdown. But instant replay determined that there was no fumble, and the play was called back. The final score would be 20–6, and it was particularly satisfying after the Eagles had beaten Washington in Philadelphia nearly two months before. "We all wanted the game badly after the way we were beaten earlier," Gibbs said.

But the road to the Super Bowl would have to go through San Francisco, and it would stop there for the Redskins. In the first quarter it seemed as if Washington was primed to upset the defending champions as they marched down the field seventy-four yards in eight plays on their first

possession, finishing with a thirty-one-yard touchdown pass from Rypien to Art Monk. The 49ers came back with their own drive to tie the score at 7–7, but Rypien moved his team into position for another score, this time a forty-four-yard Chip Lohmiller field goal to take a 10–7 lead at the end of the first quarter.

This was Joe Montana and the 49ers, though, and they methodically picked apart Washington's defense as Montana hit Jerry Rice with a ten-yard touchdown pass and Mike Sherrard with an eight-yard scoring toss for a 21–10 lead. In the fourth quarter, nose tackle Michael Carter intercepted a Rypien pass and rumbled sixty-one yards for the final touchdown and a 28–10 victory.

Still, it was a season of renewed rewards for the Redskins, getting back to the playoffs and coming within one game of the Super Bowl. Though Rypien missed five games, he completed 16 of 304 passes for 2,070 yards and sixteen touchdowns. Earnest Byner broke through as the primary force in the Washington running game, gaining 1,219 yards, averaging 4.1 yards per carry. And the receiving corps had an outstanding season—Gary Clark pulled down seventy-five passes for 1,112 yards, Art Monk caught sixty-eight passes for 770 yards, and Ricky Sanders had 56 receptions for 727 yards.

In 1991 an interesting momentum was taking place during training camp. In the past ten years of Redskins success, some players were constant throughout the run—basically, the Hogs, men like Jeff Bostic, Joe Jacoby, Russ Grimm, and Don Warren.

But time was running out for these men. They were all close to the end of their careers.

They sensed that this year, with the high-powered offense at their disposal, would most likely be their last chance at another championship.

"The older guys, we had our own meetings every Saturday during the season, from the first game, after the team would meet, and we talked about things, how important this is and all that," Jacoby said. "We kept going week after week. We were on a mission."

They made that clear in the first game before their hometown fans at RFK by blowing the Detroit Lions out of the water 45–0. Rypien started as soon as they got the ball with a twelve-play, sixty-two-yard drive, topped off by a one-

The Best Man

The Redskins have had some great coaches over their rich history, from Ray Flaherty to Vince Lombardi to George Allen. But none put together a greater record of excellence than Joe Gibbs.

When Gibbs, fifty-two, stepped down on March 5, 1993, he finished with a career coaching record of 140–65, four NFC titles, and three Super Bowl championships.

He was considered among the best there ever was at his job, as witnessed by his induction in 1996 to the Hall of Fame. Yet he decided to leave, surprising the sports world and the Washington community.

Why? "The biggest reason was my family," Gibbs said. "My kids used to come to camp with me, but they didn't now. They were away at college. J.D. was just graduating from college and starting a business, and if I was going to see Coy play—I missed seeing J.D. play—then I needed to get out then, because he only had two years left in college. It was mostly for family reasons.

"When I coached when I was younger, my kids went with me to camp. It was something we all did together. If I was going to continue coaching, it would have been pretty much by myself, and I wasn't ready to do that.

"I have a lot of memories," Gibbs said. "People will ask, 'Who are the players you remember the most, the one or two players?' I can't do that because when people ask me who were the great players, I start off with Otis Wonsley, Greg Williams, and Pete Cronin, and they'll go, 'Who?' Those are the special teams guys I remember, probably more than the starters. You can't separate all the memories.

"When you talk about special moments, I grabbed my kids after two of those Super Bowls, and I've got pictures of that, one with J.D. and one with Coy," Gibbs said. "Then for the third one we were all together on the sidelines. I remember those moments the most."

Chip Lohmiller was a key part of the Redskins success in their march to the Super Bowl in 1991, scoring 149 points, including four field goals in a 33-31 win over Dallas in the second game of the season.
(Scott Cunningham)

yard plunge by Gerald Riggs. Soon after, tight end Jimmy Johnson caught a four-yard touchdown pass, and in the final minute of the first quarter Brian Mitchell took a Detroit punt sixty-nine yards down the right sideline for a 21–0 lead, and the Redskins were on their way to an impressive victory.

"We played about as well as we're ever going to play," Gibbs said.

He would have to say that quite a few times this season, but first there would be Dallas in Texas in a Monday night game.

The Cowboys weren't impressed. They jumped out to a 21–10 lead in the second quarter, but the Redskins had supreme confidence in their offense. Before the day was out, Chip Lohmiller would kick four field goals, including a fifty-three- and a fifty-two-yarder. And Washington took the lead for good in the fourth quarter when Mitchell ran for a first down on a fake punt, and, several plays later, Riggs took the ball over from the one-yard line. The Redskins would prevail 33–31.

"This has to be one of the best days of my life

in football," Lohmiller said after the game.

The juggernaut picked up where it left off with a 34–0 bashing of Phoenix, now coached by former Hog head Joe Bugel. The offensive line coach had taken the head coaching job with the Cardinals, who came to RFK with 2–0 record.

The Redskins were not kind to their old friend. The first time they had the ball, they ended their possession with a two-yard touchdown run by Earnest Byner for a 7–0 lead. They made it 14–0 on a ten-yard reverse by Ricky Sanders and added two more touchdowns in the third quarter on a twenty-eight-yard connection from Mark Rypien to Gary Clark and a fifty-four-yard interception return by linebacker Wilbur Marshall. Chip Lohmiller kicked two fourth-quarter field goals to wrap up the scoring.

"We wanted to come out and establish control," Byner said after the game. "Last year we struggled some in these situations, but everyone is really concentrating a lot more this year. We need

Redskins fans at RFK celebrate their team's impressive 41-10 win over the Detroit Lions in the NFC Title game. The Redskins defense was superb, holding the slippery Barry Sanders to just 44 yards rushing.
(Scott Cunningham)

Climbing Up

There are few success stories in sports more impressive than the rise of Redskins general manager Charley Casserly. In 1989, after GM Bobby Beathard resigned, owner Jack Kent Cooke named Casserly to be the team's new general manager.

That's quite an accomplishment for a former Massachusetts high school coach who started for the Redskins as an unpaid "gofer" for George Allen.

"I had written to all twenty-eight teams and got twenty-two responses," Casserly said. "Out of those, I got twenty rejections and two interviews, one with the Patriots and Chuck Fairbanks, and one here with George Allen. I was thrilled at the time to just get answers. I was thrilled to have the autographs of great people like Don Shula, Bart Starr, and Chuck Noll.

"George Allen was my hero, and here I was getting a chance to meet the guy. The first thing he said was write up three ways you can help the Redskins. I'm thinking, 'Wait a minute, coach. You've got this backwards. You're supposed to help me. How am I going to help you? I'm a high school coach from Massachusetts.

"I wrote up my three ways," Casserly said. "We spent quite a bit of time together that day, and at the end he told me he wanted me to go home and rewrite the three ways I could help the Redskins, in more detail, what I haven't done in football, and what I'd like to do, and what changes I would make in the National Football League. These were his standard three questions for everyone he interviewed, but I didn't know that at the time. I went home and wrote it up and mailed it to him. I met with the Patriots next week, and they offered me a position. I talked to the Redskins, and they offered me a position, too. The position was to work for nothing. I worked eight months for nothing until I got a scouting contract.

"In April 1977 I wrote the letter," Casserly said. "In May 1977 I had the interview and came here the end of June 1977. I lived at the YMCA in Alexandria for eight dollars a night until training camp started.

"At training camp I was the 'gofer,' among other things. I answered the phones for George Allen. I was the 'Turk' in training camp. I had to run errands. I had to work in the public relations office because we only had one person in that department. And I worked in scouting. I did preseason scouting. I did film breakdowns. I did a little bit of everything. George left in January 1978, and I was hired in February as a scout."

Casserly would leave his imprint on those championship Redskins teams, scouting such players as Joe Jacoby and Jeff Bostic. He was promoted to assistant GM in 1982 and, after taking over in 1989, was the architect of the 1991 team that went on to win Super Bowl XXVI.

Charley Casserly started out as an unpaid worker for George Allen, doing whatever needed to be done. He worked his way up in the organization and, with his strong skills in player development, was named general manager in 1989. (Scott Cunningham)

After big playoff wins over Atlanta and Detroit, the Redskins were on their way to Super Bowl XXVI in Minneapolis. Some team members took advantage of the outdoor winter activities to stay loose before the big game, such as Art Monk, here getting ready to go ice fishing. (Scott Cunningham)

time lead over the Cincinnati Bengals on a Lohmiller field goal, two one-yard touchdown dives by Gerald Riggs, their goal line specialist, and a sixty-six-yard punt return by Brian Mitchell.

But the Bengals didn't know the game was supposed to be over. They came back with a no-huddle offense and, helped by Redskins penalties, put together drives of ninety-two and ninety yards, both ending in scores. After the teams traded field goals, it was 27–27.

However, with two minutes left, Rypien moved his team fifty-three yards on six running plays, fooling the Cincinnati defense by lining up four wide receivers, but never throwing to them on the drive. Riggs scored the go-ahead touchdown on a seven-yard run.

The next week, one might argue that a pattern was developing—alternating shutouts. Washington won its third shutout of the season, this time a 23–0 win over the Philadelphia Eagles.

There was another pattern—all three shutouts came at RFK, which meant that after five weeks into the season, Redskins fans had yet to see their team scored on live. That may not have been a coincidence.

"I think it was the loudest I've heard it in the nine years I've been here," Charles Mann said of the fanatical crowd basking in the glow of their high-powered team that Monday night.

The defense limited Philadelphia to just four first downs and eighty-nine total yards. Chip Lohmiller's hot foot didn't cool off as he connected on three field goals. Mark Rypien found Art Monk on a nineteen-yard scoring pass, and Earnest Byner scored on a seven-yard run.

At that point, there seemed to be no stopping this Redskins team—20–7 over the Chicago Bears, 42–17 over the Cleveland Browns—but then came the New York Giants, the defending Super Bowl champions, and Washington's undefeated record (7–0) was in jeopardy at the Meadowlands.

The Giants had one of the all-time ball-control offenses, with Rodney Hampton carrying the ball. At the end of the first quarter, New York had gained 125 yards in total offense to one for the Redskins. By the end of the first half, the Giants had 205 yards of offense, Washington had 35. And when both teams went into the locker room at halftime, New York had a 13–0 lead on two field

to maintain our concentration and let other people do the talking."

Concentration didn't seem to be much of a problem, and with a 3–0 mark and 112 points scored in those three games, the Redskins had plenty of fans around to do the talking for them.

It looked as if the Redskins were on their way to another lopsided victory in week four at Riverfront Stadium as they jumped to a 24–10 half-

Washington's Super Bowl XXVI game plan was to apply constant pressure to Buffalo quarterback Jim Kelly. Wilber Marshall and Charles Mann did just that, contributing mightily to the Redskins 37-24 victory. (Scott Cunningham)

goals by Raul Allegre and a one-yard run by Hampton. The way the game had been going, that seemed good enough to win.

But the Redskins gave New York some of their own medicine with a time-consuming (8:55) eighty-four-yard drive in the third quarter that ended with a seven-yard scoring pass from Mark Rypien to Gary Clark, and then they came back with the opposite style of scoring, hitting quickly on a fifty-four-yard pass from Rypien to Clark in the fourth quarter, giving Washington a 14–13 lead. A thirty-five-yard field goal by Chip Lohmiller sealed a 17–13 victory.

Though it was not the blowout they had become accustomed to, some Redskins found this win just as satisfying. "That was a sweet feeling on the sidelines," Jeff Bostic said. "We came up here

and found ways to lose in the past. To come here and spot them thirteen first-half points and come back and win, it's a great feeling."

They may have gotten some satisfaction out of the Giants win, but they were breathing sighs of relief everywhere at RFK the following week when Redskins fans finally saw that their team was mortal when Washington went against the Houston Oilers, themselves an impressive team with a 7–1 record. They were coached by a familiar face—former Redskins player and coach Jack Pardee.

After Chip Lohmiller put Washington in the lead with a twenty-one-yard field goal in the second quarter, the Oilers came back with two field goals of their own by Ian Howfield to take a 6–3 lead into halftime.

The low scoring—a surprise, considering

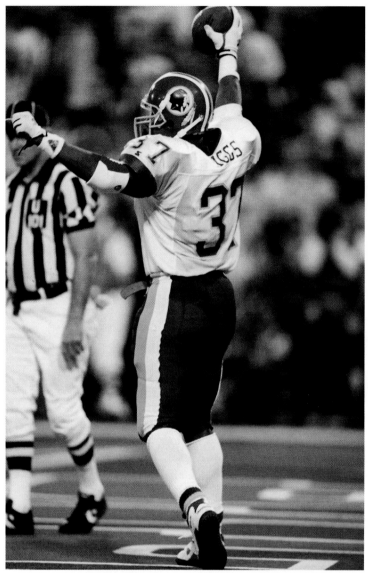

Gerald Riggs was the Redskins' goal line specialist. (Scott Cunningham)

haps the best offense ever to take the field for the Redskins—56–17 over Atlanta and 41–14 over Pittsburgh—the city was consumed by Redskins fever and the team's undefeated record (11–0) and ready to take special pleasure in watching the fall of the next opponent—Dallas.

This was the Cowboys team that was on the verge of making their own championship run, led by Troy Aikman and Emmitt Smith, who ran on the Washington defense for 132 yards. And though Dallas lost Aikman to a knee injury early in the second half with a 14–7 lead, Dallas backup quarterback Steve Beuerlein kept throwing to Michael Irvin and Alvin Harper, hitting on seven of twelve passes for 109 yards and one touchdown.

these two powerful offenses—continued as Lohmiller tied the game in the third quarter. With the score 6–6 going into the final quarter, Washington went ahead on a twenty-three-yard run by earnest Byner. But Houston came back to tie it again in the fourth quarter on a touchdown by Lorenzo White, and, with the score 13–13, the game went into overtime.

In overtime, cornerback Darrell Green intercepted a Warren Moon pass that set up the game-winning field goal, a forty-one-yarder by Lohmiller, for a 16–13 victory and a 9–0 record.

After two more blowouts and displays of per-

Mark Rypien and Earnest Byner celebrate their Super Bowl win with the Vince Lombardi trophy held high. Rypien capped off a remarkable season (28 touchdown passes and 3,564 yards) with an 18 of 33 day for 292 yards and two touchdowns in the Super Bowl, which earned him MVP honors. (Scott Cunningham)

The Cowboys offense just outdid the Redskins this day, with twenty-three first downs to fourteen for Washington, 399 yards to 262, and a 24–21 win. The Redskins made it close when, down 21–7, Rypien moved the team ninety-two yards on thirteen plays, finishing with a one-yard score by Gerald Riggs to cut the Dallas lead to 21–14. But the Cowboys added a field goal, which proved to be the difference. A last-minute twenty-nine-yard touchdown pass from Mark Rypien to Ricky Sanders would end the game and Washington's unbeaten streak. And it was the first time that fans in Washington had seen their team lose at RFK since October 14, 1990.

"You would like to go undefeated, but these things happen," linebacker Matt Millen said. "But our main goal wasn't to go 16–0. It was to make the playoffs, and we've done that. . . . It was good while it lasted, but now it's over."

With that out of the way, Washington got back on track with three straight wins—27–6 over the Los Angeles Rams, 20–14 over the Phoenix Cardinals, and this time a 34–17 victory over the Giants. The Redskins took a 14–1 record into the final game of the season against the Eagles in Philadelphia.

This was a strange finale for Washington. Gibbs did not want to take a chance on risking his

Washington Redskins owner Jack Kent Cooke was the architect of the three Super Bowl wins. (Scott Cunningham)

starters in a meaningless game. On the other hand, he didn't want to go into the playoffs on a losing note. Unfortunately, it didn't work out the way he had hoped. After taking a 16–7 lead, Gibbs sat down starter Mark Rypien and several other starters. The Eagles would come back to score seventeen fourth-

Redskins fans, in typical rabid fashion, honored their Super Bowl champions with a celebration on The Mall in Washington. (Scott Cunningham)

quarter points to defeat Washington 24–22. Washington would have to put the loss behind them and concentrate on the goal at hand. With a 14–2 record and such a dominant team, nothing less than a trip to the Super Bowl would do.

Jerry Glanville and his Atlanta Falcons would be their first opponent at RFK. The Redskins had already disposed of the Falcons earlier in the year by a whopping 56–17 score, but Atlanta went on to win six of their next seven games and believed that the outcome would be different this time. Glanville would say as much, but with the rain falling at RFK, this was Hog weather, and the Redskins would crush the Falcons with a running onslaught—162 yards rushing—combined with a defense that forced four interceptions against Atlanta quarterback Chris Miller. Washington won 24–7 before a raucous crowd of more than fifty-five thousand and two noteworthy and disappoint-ed Falcons fans on the sidelines—heavyweight champion Evander Holyfield and rap artist M.C. Hammer.

"We're basically a running team that can pass," center Jeff Bostic said after the game. "They're a passing team. It was advantage, Redskins."

The following week came the NFC title game against the Detroit Lions at RFK. It would be the last time Redskins fans would be able to see this historic team play in RFK that year, and the team gave their fans a game for the books.

This was the Lions team that Washington had disposed of in the season opener by a 45–0 score, but that was with running back Barry Sanders side-lined. Sanders was ready, but so were the Redskins. They held the running back to just forty-four yards rushing, and linebacker Wilbur Marshall sacked quarterback Eric Kramer three times in a 41–10 championship victory.

And although the score would seem to indi-cate another offensive explosion, the two offenses were actually close in statistics. The Lions had twenty first downs, compared to seventeen for Washington; the Redskins rolled up 345 total yards, just 41 more than the Lions had.

No, this was a defensive win all the way. "Gamewise, it was defense," Gibbs said after the game. "The offense made enough things happen, special teams kept them in check and made some

special plays themselves, but it seems like lately we've just had some great defense, especially at home."

Two weeks later, Gibbs and company would hope that the Metrodome in Minneapolis would feel like home. They were on their way to Super Bowl XXVI. "I never though I would hear myself say this, but I'm looking forward to Minneapolis," Gary Clark said. "I don't care if it snows twelve feet."

The meetings each week during the season had paid off with another trip to the Super Bowl for veterans like Bostic and Jacoby. They would make the most of it.

The Buffalo Bills, losers in the previous Super Bowl by one point to the New York Giants on a missed field goal by Scott Norwood, returned as AFC champions to avenge that loss. They were led by quarterback Jim Kelly and the Most Valuable player in the AFC, running back Thurman Thomas. Buffalo had no lack of motivation to win.

But Jacoby said his team was on a mission from the start of the season, and the only way to finish that mission was a Super Bowl victory.

But before a crowd of more than 63,000, the Redskins looked like a team that would come up short of its goal early in the game. After both teams traded punts, Washington took the ball from their own eleven-yard-line on a mixture of passes by Mark Rypien and runs by Earnest Byner. The big play came on third and fourteen from the Redskins' forty-eight-yard line when Rypien con-nected on a nineteen-yard pass on the right side-line to Art Monk. The pair connected again on a thirty-one yarder to give Washington first and goal from the Buffalo two-yard line. After two attempts by Gerald Riggs to get the ball into the end zone failed, Rypien hit Monk in the back of the end zone for an apparent touchdown. But the play was reversed after a look at the instant replay revealed that Monk was out of the end zone.

It looked as if the Redskins would have to settle for a field goal, but Jeff Rutledge mishandled the snap from center, and they came away with nothing to show for that drive.

But Washington had little time to grouse over that futility, because on Buffalo's first play after taking over on their fourteen-yard line, Kelly's pass was tipped by Darrell Green and intercepted

The 1991 Washington Redskins posted a 14-2 record on their way to a Super Bowl championship season. The offense scored an astounding 485 points that year, while the defense held opponents to just 224 points. (Washington Redskins)

by Brad Edwards on the Bills' twelve-yard line. It seemed as if the Redskins would get their chance again to get on the board.

However, more frustration was ahead. On third and nine from the Buffalo eleven, Mark Rypien's pass was tipped and intercepted. The Bills would take over and punt again, and the score at the end of the first quarter was 0–0. At that point, few people in the Metrodome could have been convinced that sixty-one points would be put on the scoreboard that day.

Early in the second quarter Washington finally had a drive with something to show for it. After Rypien connected with Ricky Sanders on a forty-one-yard pass to the Bills' seventeen, Chip Lohmiller connected on a thirty-four-yard field goal to give the Redskins a 3–0 lead.

Another Buffalo punt after three plays put Washington into good field position on its own forty-nine-yard line. Six plays later, Rypien would find Byner in the end zone for a touchdown and a 10–0 lead, and the Redskins were now on a roll.

They quickly got the ball back when Green intercepted a Kelly pass on the Washington forty-

five yard line, and another drive down the field led to a Redskins touchdown and a 17–0 lead, the margin at the end of the first half.

Buffalo found no solace in their locker room at halftime. When they took the ball first in the third quarter, Kelly's first pass was intercepted by linebacker Kurt Gouveia on the Bills' twenty-five-yard line. Gouveia would return the ball twenty-three yards to the two, and Gerald Riggs took it over to extend Washington's lead to 24–0.

The Bills came back to score twice on their next two possessions—a twenty-one-yard field goal by Norwood and a one-yard plunge by Thomas—to make it a 24–10 game.

But Rypien got the Redskins' scoring machine back on track when they got the ball back, moving seventy-nine yards down the field. The drive was capped off by a thirty-yard scoring pass to Gary Clark, putting Washington on top 31–10.

The defense would force yet another Buffalo mistake as Kelly fumbled, and that would lead to a Lohmiller field goal and a 34–10 lead in the beginning of the fourth quarter. Washington would add

Some of Joe Gibbs' fondest memories as Redskins head coach were those moments on the sidelines with his sons Coy and J.D. after each of the three Super Bowl wins. (Scott Cunningham)

another field goal, and the Bills would put two meaningless touchdowns on the board, but at the end it was Washington 37, Buffalo 24. Gibbs and the Hogs had their third Super Bowl victory in ten years.

"This team had great chemistry, a great feeling for each other," Gibbs said in the postgame celebration. "From day one, no one was fighting for individual goals."

In the wild Redskins locker room, the heart of this great team took a moment to savor their run, sensing that it was at an end. "Jacoby, Grimm, and I sat together and pulled out big cigars and lit them while we were still in our uniforms," Bostic said. "I don't think anybody would admit it, but in the back of everyone's mind, I think the idea was there that this might be the last time we get there."

Grimm would retire after that, coming to Gibbs's staff as an assistant coach the following year. Bostic and Jacoby would follow him into retirement two years later. The Hogs were now part of Redskins legend and lore.

That Super Bowl team, in the mind of Charley Casserly, the architect of the group, was the best in the history of the franchise. "That was the greatest team in the history of the Redskins, in my opinion," Casserly said. "We led the league in scoring [485 points]. We were second in defensive points allowed [224]. We're 14–1 going into the final game of the year. We're ahead of Philadelphia, and Joe pulls Rypien from the game. The Eagles come back and beat us on a field goal. That's how close we were to 15–1."

It was a hard act to follow. The Redskins fell back in 1992 to 9–7 as the offense struggled, putting just three hundred points on the board. But there was a moment of history during the season that Redskins fans will always remember. On October 12, 1992, at RFK in a Monday night game against the Denver Broncos, Art Monk would become the NFL's all-time leading pass receiver with his 820th career reception, a ten-yarder with 3:12 left in the game.

"It was important for me to do it in front of the Washington fans because they've been so supportive over the years."

Gibbs still managed to get his team into the playoffs and, with a 24–7 win over the Minnesota

Vikings in the wild card game, had a shot to get to the NFC title game. But Washington would lose to San Francisco 20–13 to end the season. No one knew what lay ahead.

After the season ended, Gibbs was exhausted. He had a physical exam that showed no problems, but he took some time to step back and look at his future and made an important personal decision that would shock the Washington area: He would retire from coaching to spend more time with his family.

It was front page banner headline news when Gibbs announced on March 5, 1993, that he was leaving his coaching job with the Redskins.

"I think there is a window of opportunity now with my family," Gibbs said at a news conference. "I stopped and backed up and started thinking I've got two boys [Coy and J.D.] that I'd like to spend more time with. The same thing with Pat. There are some things we've put off for a long time."

He retired with a legacy unmatched in Redskins history: a 140–65 career record, 16–5 in the playoffs, four NFC championships, and three Super Bowl victories. Gibbs would continue with his other passion, auto racing, with his two sons as part of a successful racing team. He has also become a successful television football analyst.

Owner Jack Kent Cooke, the man who hired Gibbs, described the importance of the coach as he retired. "He has been a friend, a confidant, an aide of incomparable professional talent and wisdom," Cooke said. "He has simply been the best head coach in the history of the Redskins."

The obvious choice to replace Gibbs was his assistant head coach and the master of the Redskins defense over those successful years, Richie Petitbon. He was a former Redskins player, coming over with George Allen as one of the "Ramskins" from the Los Angeles Rams, and later became Washington's defensive coordinator in 1978.

Petitbon had been a candidate for numerous head coaching jobs, so when Gibbs retired, he was the natural choice to succeed him.

But circumstances did not work in Petitbon's favor. He caught some tough breaks with a team in transition and finished with a 4–12 mark, the club's worst record since 1963. Cooke believed that the franchise was at a pivotal moment and needed new direction on the field. Despite his strong feelings of friendship and loyalty for Petitbon, Cooke made the move he felt had to be made. Petitbon was fired, and Cooke looked to a young man from Dallas, of all places, to coach the Washington Redskins—Cowboys offensive coordinator Norv Turner. The future was about to begin again.

Eleven

A New Era

Washington Redskins fans found out that the 1990s would be a different time in professional football when the next Redskins coach was hired: a Dallas Cowboy, Norv Turner.

Turner had worked as the Cowboys' offensive coordinator under Jimmy Johnson on two Super Bowl teams and was on the top of everyone's list as a head coaching candidate after the 1993 season. But he was a Cowboy, and at one time it might have been unthinkable for Washington fans to welcome such a rival.

But in the new world order of the NFL, with free agency, salary caps, and other issues that never faced teams before, fans were savvy enough to realize that their owner, Jack Kent Cooke, remained committed to bringing them a winner again, and Turner was a strong candidate to do that.

Just to show how different football was in these new times, few people said, "Norv who?" when he was hired, unlike the reaction after Joe Gibbs had been hired after the 1980 season. Few fans knew who the offensive coordinators of teams were in those days, even though Gibbs had a reputation within the game as head coaching material. But in this new information age and with increased

media coverage of all aspects of sports, Turner was well known to football fans as the hottest head coaching candidate around.

There were similarities in the way Gibbs and Turner came up through the ranks, with a mixture of college and pro experience. Turner had been the offensive coordinator under John Robinson at USC and later joined the Los Angeles Rams with Robinson in 1983 as a receivers coach. The Rams had not passed for 3,500 yards in a season since 1950. After Turner arrived as receivers coach, they did it in each of his last three seasons there, finishing third, fourth, and third in the league in 1988, 1989, and 1990. The year before his arrival, the Rams were 27th in the league in passing yards and completed thirty fewer passes than any other NFL club. It was under Turner that Henry Ellard and Flipper Anderson each went over 1,000 yards in 1989 and 1990.

He joined Jimmy Johnson in Dallas in 1991 to become the offensive architect of two Super Bowl champions, and he was credited with the development of Troy Aikman at quarterback. "His biggest strength is that he puts people in a position where they have a chance to be successful," Aikman said.

That's the same sort of praise Dan Fouts had for Gibbs when they were paired together in San

 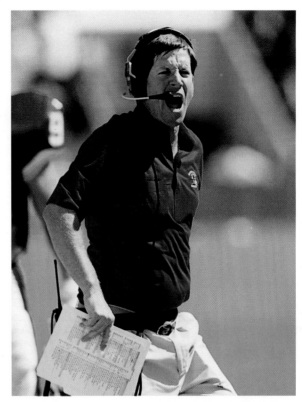

The Redskins underwent massive changes shortly after their Super Bowl win against Buffalo. Joe Gibbs retired, and after a 4-12 record under Richie Petitbon (*left*) in 1993, they decided to change course. That led them to former Dallas offensive coordinator Norv Turner, who in 1994 became their head coach.
(*left:* Scott Cunningham; *right:* Bill Wood)

Diego. There were other similarities between the two coaches. Both learned the passing game from offensive technician Ernie Zampese, who was with Gibbs in San Diego and with Turner in Los Angeles.

But Cooke made a point not of forcing the comparison with Gibbs, but rather of judging Turner as his own man after he was hired. "He is not a replica of Joe Gibbs, but what he is is the most professional, dedicated, intelligent young football brain I have run across," Cooke said. "I have total confidence in Norv Turner."

Turner also has a determination to succeed that motivates most successful coaches. "The number one thing that drives me is the fear of failure, the fear of not finishing what I've started. The fear of not being successful."

That determination is one of the reasons the Redskins are in a revival after several seasons of transition. They were 3–13 under Turner in his first season in 1994 and improved to 6–10 the following year. Along the way, Turner and general manager Charley Casserly have brought in some talented young players like receiver Michael Westbrook and the team's two young throwers, Heath Shuler and Gus Frerotte. And with other player development and moves, the organization is optimistic about the future.

"I have nothing but bright hopes for the future of the Redskins," Cooke said. "The collaboration of two outstanding men, Norv Turner and Charles Casserly, will turn us around. They have shown a rare level of intelligence with regards to what kind of players we're going after."

It's a different challenge to build a winner in the 1990s, but Casserly believes the Redskins are on their way. "I think we have a real good young group of players," Casserly said. "I think we will get better as the years go by. I think we're one of the coming teams in this league. And Norv is an outstanding football coach, a real innovative guy."

Though the league has changed, Turner

Washington found itself with two talented young quarterbacks coming out of the 1994 draft: Gus Frerotte (12), a seventh-round pick out of Tulsa, and Heath Shuler (5), a first-round selection from Tennessee. (Scott Cunningham)

The new-look Redskins have featured a number of young, talented players, such as cornerback Tom Carter, selected in the first round of the 1993 draft out of Notre Dame. (Scott Cunningham)

believes the basics for a winning football team are the same. "You've got to have a solid organization, which we have, that is going to work together. Whether from the financial aspect, administrative, scouting, or coaching, everyone has to be on the same page to have the best chance," Turner said. "And I still think teams are built through the draft and through your pro personnel department, in exhausting all resources to find football players.

"And then I think the key difference is what has happened with free agency," Turner said. "The first two years I was here we were very involved in free agency, using it recently to supplement our young players. Ideally you would like to be in a situation that you're only in the market for one or two free agents.

"Then, when you get to the point of trying to keep players, you have a nice problem, because that means you've had success," Turner said. "It means you're playing with good football players, and

other people are interested. That's a problem we hope to have three or four years down the road. That means you've had success and that we have a lot of good players, and you deal with it then."

Besides the change in coaching, the Redskins franchise underwent another significant change—moving its training camp from Carlisle to Frostburg in western Maryland.

In 1995, the Redskins began training at Frostburg State University, after thirty-two seasons in Carlisle. They were welcomed with open arms, with a parade, and with a community looking forward to embracing its new summer residents.

Longtime Redskins who spent all their summer camps in Carlisle were impressed with the reception they received in Frostburg. "Carlisle was great, but if you want to forget a place, you forget it by coming to a reception like this," said cornerback Darrell Green after a parade welcomed the team to the mountain town of about eight thou-

Jack Kent Cooke

There have been many good days in the history of the Washington Redskins franchise, but perhaps none better than in January 1961, when stockholder Milton King sold some of his shares to someone described as a "Toronto baseball executive" by reporters.

That minor league baseball owner—Jack Kent Cooke—would become a major player not just in professional sports, but also in the world business scene, with financial holdings in newspapers, cable television, real estate, and numerous other endeavors.

But none has been closer to his heart and soul than the Washington Redskins, as the owner has been committed to bringing Redskins fans a winning franchise. He has accomplished that task with tremendous success, with three Super Bowl championships and four NFC titles during his tenure as owner.

In fact, Cooke's influence on the success of the franchise dates back to 1971, when he was the key figure involved in bringing George Allen to Washington.

Jack Kent Cooke has been one of the most successful owners in all of professional sports. Joe Gibbs, Charley Casserly, and others give Cooke the credit for the team's success over the years. (NFL Properties)

"I'm very proud of this team," Cooke said. "I enjoy owning this team, more than anything else I've ever owned."

That says a lot, because Cooke has owned and been involved in some very exciting projects. He owns *Los Angeles Daily News.* And he can walk down the streets of Manhattan, look upward, point to the Chrysler Building, and say, "I own that, too."

Cooke is the proverbial self-made man, a former encyclopedia salesman who used his drive and intelligence to rise to the top of the business world.

He was born on October 25, 1912, in Hamilton, Ontario. Cooke grew up in sports, an avid hockey player who once played in the Ontario Hockey Association and was offered a scholarship to play for the University of Michigan. But the tough economic times of the era meant money was tough to come by, and Cooke instead began working, starting out selling encyclopedias.

That wouldn't last long. He joined Northern Broadcasting and Publishing, Ltd., and before he was twenty-six, he was a one-third partner in Thomson Cooke Newspapers. He later became a half partner with Roy Thomson, operating radio stations and newspapers throughout Canada.

Cooke also kept his interest in sports,

purchasing the Toronto Maple Leafs minor league baseball team in 1951 and later being named Minor League Executive of the Year by *The Sporting News*. He once hired Sparky Anderson as the manager of his minor league club.

He would later move to the United States and become owner of another sports team, also one that he would build into a premier franchise, the Los Angeles Lakers. He brought Wilt Chamberlain to the team and helped oversee the world champion 1971–1972 Lakers squad. Like he is doing in Washington, Cooke also made a bold move by building the first privately funded indoor arena in the United States, the Los Angeles Forum, which remains one of the country's top arenas.

His other sports interests include horse breeding and racing. He purchased the Elmendorf Racing and Breeding Farm, one of the country's top farms, and remains involved in the sport of kings.

One of the keys to his success in such a volatile business as sports is recognizing talent and knowing the role of the talent he hires. "It's foolish to hire top-flight, expert talent and then interfere with them," Cooke said. "This is a business concept that is very sound."

He is deeply involved in the franchise, but, according to some of the "top-flight, expert talent" who have worked for him, his involvement has contributed to the success of the franchise.

Joe Gibbs remembers Cooke's support when, in Gibbs's first five games as the Redskins coach, he was 0–5. "Mr. Cooke was at his best when things were at their worst," Gibbs said. "Many times when I was at my lowest, and I was thinking that he was going to come in and jump on me, that's when he would surprise me. He would come in here and say, 'Look, things are going to be okay. We're going to get through this.'

"That's what happened when we went 0–5," Gibbs said. "Every time I thought he was going to fire me, he would try to find a way to talk to me and pick me up. Many times during my years there, that is what he would do."

It was that sort of dedication and commitment that swayed Norv Turner to take the head coaching job with Washington.

"One of the major factors that I weighed most heavily when I pursued this job and decided it was the one I wanted was the ownership," Turner said. "You look at Mr. Cooke's record and what he has accomplished and the commitment he is willing to make, you want to work for a person like that."

Charley Casserly is an example of the rewards that go to talented people who work for Cooke. He rose through the organization from an unpaid helper for George Allen to a scout to assistant general manager and now is the GM of the organization.

"I'm fortunate enough to be in a strong organization with a great owner," Casserly said. "Owners win football games."

Owners rarely build stadiums anymore, but Cooke is privately financing a new 78,600-seat stadium in Prince Georges County. And he built his team a new headquarters several years ago, Redskins Park, the 161-acre complex that opened in August 1992.

Cooke has a variety of other personal interests. He has a love for literature and is an avid reader, and he collects antiques and wine.

But what he most likes to collect are championships. Says Cooke, "I have nothing but bright hopes for the future of the Redskins."

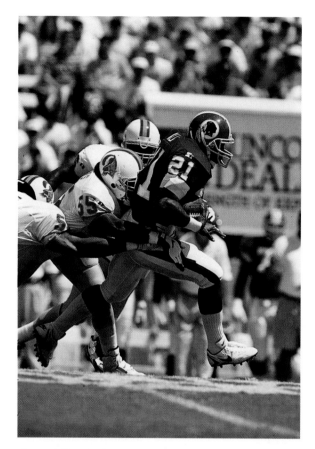

The Redskins had to rely on the free agency market in the changing world of the NFL. They were fortunate to find two solid ones in running back Terry Allen and linebacker Ken Harvey. (Scott Cunningham)

sand people. "This is new excitement, and that excitement can be transferred to the team. That's what football is all about, having high energy."

Frostburg is the Redskins' eighth summer training site since moving to Washington in 1937. During their first season in Washington, the team trained at Fairlawn Playground in Anacostia. In 1938, they moved to a softball field in Ballston, Virginia.

The following year, owner George Preston Marshall began running his team's training camps on the West Coast. In 1939 and 1940, they trained in Spokane, Washington and moved to San Diego from 1941 to 1944. The following year they were forced to stay in Washington, training at Georgetown University because of wartime travel restrictions, but returned to the West Coast in 1946, calling Occidental College in Los Angeles their training home until 1962. The next year, they moved to Carlisle.

Though the move to Frostburg was exciting, it didn't take away from the memories that fans and players have of Carlisle. There was a time when the rookie class of Russ Grimm, Joe Jacoby, and others was so great in numbers and bravado that they gave the veterans—who traditionally harassed the rookies on the last night of camp—more than they bargained for. "We turned the tables on them," Jacoby said.

The fallout from the battle that night: water on the floor of the dorm at Dickinson College was nearly an inch deep. Joe Gibbs learned his lesson from that and would never again tell the team when they would be breaking camp, thus avoiding last-night hijinks.

The Gibbs family also became a target of those hijinks, as the coach would bring his two sons, J.D. and Coy, to training camp. "I remember we taped Coy Gibbs to the training table and put him in a field," Jacoby said.

John Kent Cooke

The success of the Redskins is very much a Cooke family affair, and the Cooke behind the scenes is John Kent Cooke, Sr., executive vice president, and son of owner Jack Kent Cooke.

After Norv Turner joined the Redskins, he said, "I'm amazed at just how much John Kent Cooke does to ensure this organization runs so smoothly."

Added GM Charley Casserly, "Without John's involvement, support, and experience, we would not have achieved what we have over the years."

Professional sports became Cooke's playground as a youth when his father became owner of the minor league baseball team, the Toronto Maple Leafs, and they also provided the backdrop for the beginning of his business education. "I was around ten years of age when Dad got into baseball," Cooke said. "That was my introduction into professional sports: spending my summers at the stadium, being a ballboy, selling hot dogs in the stands, and handing out giveaways at the gate."

Cooke joined his father in Los Angeles as vice president of sales to help establish the NBA Lakers and the NHL Kings in the new L.A. Forum. After working with those sports operations, Cooke operated the family 13,000-acre cattle ranch in California, then moved to Washington in 1978 to work with his father in organizing the family holding company. In 1981, he became the Redskins' executive vice president and has been supervising the daily operation of the club and running the club at the league level ever since.

Like his father, John Kent Cooke, Sr., has a varied background. He attended Waterloo College in Canada, majoring in English and journalism, and would later work in television production and cable television. His work in communications has served the team well, as he has been responsible for negotiating the club's radio and television contracts for the past fifteen years, being the first in the league to televise scrimmages, syndicate preseason games, and develop football specials and community programs locally.

Among the milestones of his tenure as executive vice president, in addition to the record local radio and television contracts, is the construction of Redskins Park, one of the league's top training facilities, and the appointments by the National Football League to the special committee to select the new League Commissioner and to the Management Council Executive Committee, which negotiated the present NFL Labor Agreement—not to mention, of course, the team's eight playoff years and four Super Bowl appearances.

In 1996, Marymount University recognized Cooke's business leadership and involvement in the community by conferring on him an honorary degree of Doctor of Humane Letters.

Cooke hopes that the Redskins future will be as glorious as the past with the third generation of Cookes at the helm. Cooke's son, John, has been director of stadium operations and club promotions since 1990. The success of the Redskins is and will be very much a Cooke family affair.

John Kent Cooke, Sr., has been an integral part of the success of the franchise with his work running the daily operations of the team. He was instrumental in the development of the team's state-of-the-art training complex, the new Redskins Park, which opened in 1992. (Washington Redskins)

Both Norv Turner and Charley Casserly believe that the foundation has been laid for a return to the success the Washington Redskins have enjoyed under owner Jack Kent Cooke. (Scott Cunningham)

Now, Frostburg will create a whole new set of tales and memories for a new generation of players and fans.

And more change is yet to come. The Washington Redskins will have a new place to play in 1997, as owner Jack Kent Cooke's dream of a new stadium will finally come true.

Cooke is financing the construction of a state-of-the-art 78,600-seat stadium on the Wilson farm in Landover, just inside the Capital Beltway, on a site that will be called Raljon, a combination of the names of Cooke's sons, Ralph and John.

Cooke had been trying for many years to build a new stadium, and in a move unheard of these days, has been willing all along to pay for the facility himself. But he ran into hurdles in Virginia, the District, and other Maryland sites before meeting success in Prince Georges County.

RFK has been a good home to the Redskins since it opened in 1961, with many memorable moments. But the owner has always had a vision of a new home for his team, based on Giants Stadium in New Jersey's Meadowlands, but with its own unique features. "We have had twenty years of experience and know-how since that stadium was built to make improvements," Cooke said. "So just imagine how wonderful this stadium will be."

The stadium will accommodate many more fans than RFK, which is limited to fifty-five thousand capacity. And the new facility will have more than three hundred luxury boxes and about fifteen thousand club seats, moving into the modern era of serving both the corporate community and individual ticket holders.

The excitement over the future of this organization is in part based on the success of its past. Today's change becomes tomorrow's tradition, and the Washington Redskins is a franchise rich in tradition. That's one of the factors that brought Norv Turner to Washington.

"I've been fortunate in my career to coach in places like the University of Southern California and with the Cowboys, who have their own tradition, and if you can be involved in an organization like the Washington Redskins, it's great," Turner said. "When you walk into the offices and see pictures of Vince Lombardi and George Allen and Joe Gibbs, and you see pictures of players like Sam Huff and Joe Theismann, it gives you a great feeling and is a great motivator. You see the pictures of the Super Bowl teams, and it's obvious there is a tradition here. We'd like to be a part of it."

The tradition is what former Redskins look back on with pride, because they helped build it. "I was proud of being part of that organization and the teams I was on," Joe Jacoby said.

It's a tradition that the Cooke family is determined to continue. "No one person should take credit for the success of the Washington Redskins in the past fifteen years, or its reputation buildup since 1937 in Washington," said executive vice president John Kent Cooke, Sr. "It's just a whole bunch of people who have done this. As far as the reputation of the team, it's been George Preston Marshall, Edward Bennett Williams, and Jack Kent Cooke, my father. We hope we can continue on as successfully as we have in the past."

From Sammy Baugh to Al DeMao to Dick James to Sonny Jurgensen to John Riggins to Joe Jacoby to Art Monk to Monte Coleman to Darrell Green—the Washington Redskins have an honor roll that fans can point to with pride, and with the hope that more names will be added in the future.

RECORDS AND STATISTICS

HALL OF FAMERS

Since the Hall of Fame opened its doors in Canton, Ohio, on September 7, 1963, 180 NFL players/coaches/administrators have been inducted for enshrinement into the Hall of Fame. The 18 Redskins enshrined in the Hall are the fourth most of any team.

Cliff Battles
Running Back . . . . .1932–37 . . . . .Inducted in 1968
(West Virginia Wesleyan)

Sammy Baugh
Quarterback . . . . .1937–52 . . .Charter Member in 1963
(TCU)

Bill Dudley
Running Back . . . . .1950–51, 53 . . . . . . .Inducted in 1966
(Virginia)

Turk Edwards
Tackle . . . . .1932–40 . . . . .Inducted in 1969
(Washington State)

Ray Flaherty
Coach . . . . .1937–42 . . . . Inducted in 1976
(Gonzaga)

Joe Gibbs
Coach . . . . 1981–92 . . . . Inducted in 1996
(San Diego State)

Otto Graham
Coach . . . . 1966–68 . . . . Inducted in 1965
(Northwestern)

Ken Houston
Safety . . . . .1973–80 . . . . .Inducted in 1986
(Prairie View)

Sam Huff
LB–Coach . . . . .1964–67, 69 . . . . Inducted in 1982
(West Virginia)

David (Deacon) Jones
Defensive End . . . . .1974 . . . . Inducted in 1980
(Mississippi Vocational)

Stan Jones
Defensive Tackle . . . . .1966 . . . . .Inducted in 1991
(Maryland)

Christian (Sonny) Jurgensen
Quarterback . . . . 1964–74 . . . . Inducted in 1983
(Duke)

Earl (Curly) Lambeau
Coach . . . . 1952–53 . . .Charter Member in 1963
(Notre Dame)

Vince Lombardi
Coach . . . . .1969 . . . . .Inducted in 1971
(Fordham)

George Preston Marshall
Founder of Redskins . . . . Charter Member in 1963

Wayne Millner
End . . . . .1936–41, 45 . . . . . . .Inducted in 1968
(Notre Dame)

Bobby Mitchell
Flanker . . . . 1962–68 . . . . Inducted in 1983
(Illinois)

John Riggins
Running Back . . . . 1976–79, 81–85 . . . Inducted in 1992
(Kansas)

Charley Taylor
Wide Receiver . . . . 1964–77 . . . . Inducted in 1984
(Arizona State)

HONOR ROLL

Absher, Dick, LB, Maryland 1967
Adams, John, T, Notre Dame 1945–49
Adams, Willie, LB, N. Mexico State . .1965–66
Adickes, Mark, G, Baylor 1990–1991
Aducci, Nick, B, Nebraska 1954–55
Aguirre, Joe, E, St. Mary's (CA)1941, 1943–45
Akins, Frank, B, Washington State . .1943–46
Alban, Dick, B, Northwestern 1952–55
Aldrich, Ki, C, TCU 1941–43, 1945–46
Alford, Bruce, K, TCU 1967
Allen, Gerry, B, Nebraska–Omaha . .1967–69
Allen, Terry, RB, Clemson 1995
Allen, John, C, Purdue 1955–58
Alston, Mack, TE, Maryland State . .1970–72
Ananis, Vito, B, Boston College 1945
Anderson, Bill, E, Tennessee 1958–63
Anderson, Bob, RB, Colorado 1975
Anderson, Bruce, E, Willamette 1970
Anderson, Erick, LB, Michigan 1994–95
Anderson, Gary, G, Stanford 1980
Anderson, Stuart, LB, Virginia 1982–85
Anderson, Terry, WR,
  Bethune–Cookman 1978
Andrako, Steve, C, Ohio State 1940–41
Apsit, Megs, B, USC 1933
Archer, David, QB, Iowa State 1988
Arenz, Arnie, LB, St. Louis 1934
Ariri, Obed, K, Clemson 1987
Arneson, Jim, G, Arizona 1975
Arnold, Walt, TE, New Mexico 1984
Artman, Corrie, T, Stanford 1932
Asher, Jamie, TE, Louisville 1995
Atkeson, Dale, B, No College 1954–56
Atkins, Pervis, RB, New Mexico State . . .1964
Atkinson, Jess, K, Maryland 1986–87
Audet, Earl, T, USC 1945
Aveni, John, K, Indiana 1961
Avery, Don, T, USC 1946–47
Avery, Jim, E, Northern Illinois 1966

Bacon, Coy, DE, Jackson State 1978–81
Badaczewski, John, G,
  Western Reserve 1949–51
Badanjek, Rick, RB, Maryland 1986
Bagarus, Steve, RB,
  Notre Dame 1945–46, 1948
Bagdon, Ed, G, Michigan State 1952
Bailey, Robert, CB, Miami 1995
Baker, Sam, K, Oregon State . .1953, 1956–59
Baltzell, Vic, DB, Southwestern (Kan.) . .1935
Bandison, Romeo, DT, Oregon 1995
Bandy, Don, G, Tulsa 1967–68
Banks, Carl, LB, Michigan State 1993
Banks, Willie, G, Alcorn A&M 1968–69
Banta, Jack, RB, USC 1941
Barber, Ernie, C, San Francisco 1945
Barber, Jim T, San Francisco 1935–41
Barefoot, Ken, E, Virginia Tech 1968
Barfield, Ken, T, Mississippi 1954
Barker, Ed, E, Washington State 1954
Barker, Tony, LB, Rice 1992

Barnes, Billy Ray, RB, Wake Forest . .1962–63
Barnes, Walt, DT, Nebraska 1966–68
Barnett, Doug, DE, Azusa Pacific 1985
Barnett, Steve, T, Oregon 1964
Barnhardt, Tom, P, North Carolina 1988
Barni, Roy, B, San Francisco 1955–56
Barnwell, Malcolm, WR, Virginia Union 1985
Barrington, Tom, B, Ohio State 1966
Barry, Paul, B, Tulsa 1953
Bartkowski, Steve, QB, California 1985
Bartos, Hank, G, North Carolina 1938
Bartos, Joe, B, Navy 1950
Bass, Mike, CB, Michigan 1969–75
Bassi, Dick, G, Santa Clara 1937
Battles, Cliff, B,
  West Virginia Wesleyan 1932–37
Baugh, Sam, QB, TCU 1937–52
Baughan, Maxie, LB, Georgia Tech 1971
Bausch, Frank (Pete), C, Kansas 1934–36
Bayless, Martin, S, Bowling Green 1994
Beasley, Tom, DL, Virginia Tech 1984–86
Beatty, Ed, C, Mississippi 1961
Beban, Gary, QB, UCLA 1968–69
Bedore, Tom, G, No College 1944
Beinor, Ed, T, Notre Dame 1942
Bell, Coleman, TE, Miami 1994–95
Bell, William, RB, Georgia Tech 1994–95
Benish, Dan, DT, Clemson 1987
Benson, Cliff, TE, Purdue 1987
Berrang, Ed, E, Villanova 1949–52
Berschet, Merve, G, Illinois 1954–55
Bigby, Keiron, WR, Brown 1987
Biggs, Verlon, DE, Jackson State 1971–75
Bingham, Guy, C, Montana 1992–93
Birlem, Keith, B, San Jose State 1939
Boensch, Fred, G, Stanford 1947–48
Boll, Don, T, Nebraska 1953–59
Bond, Chuck, T, Washington 1937–38
Bond, Randal, B, Washington 1938
Bonner, Brian, LB, Minnesota 1989
Bosch, Frank, DT, Colorado 1968–70
Bosseler, Don, B, Miami 1957–64
Bostic, Jeff, C, Clemson 1980–93
Boswell, Ben, T, TCU 1934
Boutte, Marc, DT, LSU 1994–95
Bowles, Todd, S, Temple 1986–90, 92–93
Boykin, Deral, S, Louisville 1994
Braatz, Tom, DE, Marquette 1957–59
Bradley, Harold, E, Elon 1938
Bragg, Mike, P, Richmond 1968–79
Branch, Reggie, RB, East Carolina . .1985–89
Brandes, John, TE, Cameron 1990–92
Brantley, John, LB, Georgia 1992–93
Breding, Ed, LB, Texas A&M 1967–68
Breedlove, Rod, LB, Maryland 1960–64
Brewer, Homer, B, Mississippi 1960
Briggs, Bill, DE, Iowa 1966–67
Briggs, Bob, B, Central Oklahoma State .1965
Brilz, Darrick, G, Oregon State 1987
Brito, Gene, DE,
  Loyola (CA)) 1951–53, 1955–58
Britt, Ed, B, Holy Cross 1937
Britt, Oscar, G, Mississippi 1946
Brohm, Jeff, QB, Louisville 1995
Brooks, Perry, DT, Southern 1978–84

Brooks, Reggie, RB, Notre Dame . . .1993–95
Brown, Buddy, G, Arkansas 1951–52
Brown, Charlie, WR,
  South Carolina State 1982–84
Brown, Dan, E, Villanova 1950
Brown, Eddie, S, Tennessee 1975–77
Brown, Hardy, LB, Tulsa 1950
Brown, Larry, RB, Kansas State 1969–76
Brown, Ray, G, Arkansas State 1989–95
Brown, Tom, DB, Maryland 1969
Brownlow, Darrick, LB, Illinois 1995
Brueckman, Charley, C, Pittsburgh 1958
Brundige, Bill, DE, Colorado 1970–77
Brunet, Bob, RB,
  Louisiana Tech 1968, 1970–77
Bryant, Kelvin, RB,
  North Carolina 1986–88, 1990
Bryant, Trent, CB, Arkansas 1981
Buck, Jason, DE, BYU 1991–93
Budd, Frank, WR, Villanova 1963
Buggs, Danny, WR, West Virginia . . .1976–79
Bukich, Rudy, QB, USC 1957–58
Buksar, George, B, Purdue 1951–52
Bunch, Derek, LB, Michigan State 1987
Burks, Shawn, LB, LSU 1986
Burkus, Carl, T, George Washington 1948
Burman, George, G, Northwestern . .1971–72
Burmeister, Danny, S, North Carolina . .1987
Burrell, John, WR, Rice 1966–67
Busich, Sam, E, Ohio State 1936
Butkus, Carl, T, George Washington 1948
Butsko, Harry, LB, Maryland 1963
Butz, Dave, DT, Purdue 1975–88
Byner, Earnest, RB, East Carolina . . .1989–93

Cafego, George, QB, Tennessee 1943
Caldwell, Ravin, LB, Arkansas 1987–92
Campiglio, Bob, B, W. Liberty State 1933
Campofreda, Nick, C,
  Western Maryland 1944
Campora, Don, T, Pacific 1953
Caravello, Joe, TE, Tulane 1987–88
Carlson, Mark, T, S. Connecticut State . .1987
Carpenter, Brian, CB, Michigan 1983–84
Carpenter, Preston, E, Arkansas 1964–66
Carr, Jim, LB, Morris Harvey 1964–65
Carroll, Jim, LB, Notre Dame 1966–68
Carroll, Leo, DE, San Diego State . . .1969–70
Carroll, Vic, T, Nevada 1936–42
Carson, John, E, Georgia 1954–59
Carter, Tom, CB, Notre Dame 1993–95
Casares, Rick, RB, Florida 1965
Caster, Rich, TE, Jackson State 1981–82
Castiglia, Jim, B, Georgetown 1947–48
Cherne, Hal, T, DePaul 1933
Cherry, Raphel, S, Hawaii 1985
Cheverko, George, B, Ohio State 1948
Christensen, Erik, E, Richmond 1956
Churchwell, Don, T, Mississippi 1959
Cichowski, Gene, B, Indiana 1958–59
Cifers, Ed, E, Tennessee 1941–42, 1946
Clair, Frank, E, Ohio State 1941
Claitt, Rickey, FB, Bethune–Cookman1980–81
Clark, Algy, DB, Ohio State 1932

Clark, Gary, WR, James Madison . . .1985–92
Clark, Jim, G, Oregon 1952–53
Clark, Mike, DE, Florida 1981
Clay, Billie, B, Mississippi 1966
Clay, Ozzie, B, Iowa State 1964
Clifton, Gregory, WR,
    Johnson C. Smith 1993
Cloud, John, B, William & Mary 1952–53
Cochran, Tom, B, Auburn 1949
Cofer, Joe, S, Tennessee 1987
Coffey, Ken, S, SW Texas State 1983–86
Coia, Angelo, WR, USC 1964–65
Coleman, Greg, P, Florida A&M 1988
Coleman, Monte, LB,
    Central Arkansas 1979–94
Collier, Jim, E, Arkansas 1963
Collins, Andre, LB, Penn State 1990–94
Collins, Paul, (Rip), E, Pittsburgh . . .1932–35
Collins, Shane, DE, Arizona State . . .1992–94
Concannon, Rick, G, NYU 1934–36
Condit, Merle, B, Carnegie Tech 1945
Conklin, Cary, QB, Washington 1990–93
Conkright, Bill, C, Oklahoma 1943
Connell, Mike, P, Cincinnati 1980–81
Copeland, Anthony, LB, Louisville 1987
Copeland, Danny, S,
    Eastern Kentucky 1991–93
Corbitt, Don, C, Arizona 1948
Coupee, Al, B, Iowa 1946
Cowne, John, C, Virginia Tech 1987
Cox, Bill, B, Duke 1951–52, 1955
Cox, Steve, P, Arkansas 1985–88
Coyle, Eric, C, Colorado 1987–88
Crabb, Claude, CB, Colorado 1962–63
Crane, Dennis, DT, USC 1968–69
Crews, Terry, LB, Western Michigan 1995
Crisler, Harold, E, San Jose State 1948–49
Crissy, Cris, WR, Princeton 1981
Croftcheck, Don, G, Indiana 1965–66
Cronan, Peter, LB, Boston College . .1981–85
Cronin, Gene, DE, Pacific 1961–62
Crossan, Dave, C, Maryland 1965–69
Crotty, Jim, B, Notre Dame 1960–61
Crow, Orien, C,
    Haskell Indian School 1933–34
Cudzik, Walt, C, Purdue 1954
Cunningham, Doug, RB, Mississippi . . .1974
Cunningham, Jim, RB, Pittsburgh . . .1961–63
Curtis, Bobby, LB, Savannah State 1987
Curtis, Mike, LB, Duke 1977–78
Curtis, Travis, S, West Virginia . . .1988, 1991
Cvercko, Andy, G, Northwestern 1963

Dale, Roland, E, Mississippi 1950
Daniels, Calvin, LB, North Carolina 1986
Darre, Bernie, G, Tulane 1961
Davidson, Ben, DT, Washington 1962–63
Davis, Andy, B, George Washington 1952
Davis, Brian, CB, Nebraska 1987–90
Davis, Fred, T, Alabama 1941–42, 1945
Davis, Jack, G, Maryland 1959
Davis, Wayne, DB, Indiana State 1989–90
Davlin, Mike, T, San Francisco 1955
Day, Eagle, QB, Mississippi 1959–60

Deal, Rufus, B, Auburn 1942
Dean, Fred, G, Texas Southern 1978–82
Dean, Vernon, CB, San Diego State .1982–87
DeCarlo, Art, DB, Georgia 1956–57
DeCorrevont, Bill, B, Northwestern 1945
Dee, Bob, DE, Holy Cross 1957–58
Deeks, Don, T, Washington 1947
DeFrance, Chris, WR, Arizona State 1979
DeFruiter, Bob, B, Nebraska 1945–47
Dekker, Al, WR, Michigan State 1953
Deloplaine, Jack, RB, Salem College 1978
Dennison, Glenn, TE, Miami 1987
Denson, Moses, RB,
    MD Eastern Shore 1974–75
DeMao, Al, C, Duquesne 1945–53
Dess, Darrell, G,
    North Carolina State 1965–66
Didier, Clint, TE, Portland State 1982–87
Didion, John, LB, Oregon State 1969–70
Doll, Don, DE, USC 1953
Donnalley, Rick, C, North Carolina .1984–85
Doolan, John, B, Georgetown 1945
Dorow, Al, QB, Michigan State 1954–56
Dow, Ken, B, Oregon State 1941
Dowda, Harry, DB, Wake Forest 1949–53
Dowler, Boyd, WR, Colorado 1971
Drazenovich, Chuck, LB, Penn State .1950–59
Dubinetz, Greg, G, Yale 1979
DuBois, Phil, TE, San Diego State . . .1979–80
Duckworth, Joe, E, Colgate 1947
Dudley, Bill, RB, Virginia 1950–51, 1953
Dugan, Fred, WR, Dayton 1961–63
Duich, Steve, G, San Diego State 1969
Duncan, Leslie, DB, Jackson State . . .1971–73
Dunn, Coye, B, USC 1943
Dunn, K.D., TE, Clemson 1987
Dupard, Reggie, RB, SMU 1989–90
Dusek, Brad, LB, Texas A&M 1974–81
Dwyer, Jack, DB, Loyola (CA) 1951
Dye, Les, E, Syracuse 1944–45
Dyer, Henry, RB, Grambling 1969–70

Ecker, Enrique, T, John Carroll 1952
Edwards, Brad, S, South Carolina . . .1990–93
Edwards, Turk, T, Washington State . .1932–40
Edwards, Weldon, T, TCU 1948
Eilers, Pat, DB, Notre Dame 1992–94
Elewonibi, Moe, T, BYU 1990–93
Ellard, Henry, WR, Fresno State 1994–95
Elliott, Matt, C, Michigan 1992
Ellstrom, Marv, B, Oklahoma 1943
Ellstrom, Swede, FB, Oklahoma 1934
Elmore, Doug, DB, Mississippi 1962
Elter, Leo, RB, Duquesne 1955–57
Erhardt, Clyde, C, Georgia 1946–49
Erickson, Carl, C, Washington 1938–39
Ervins, Ricky, RB, USC 1991–94
Etherly, David, CB, Portland State 1987
Evans, Charles, RB, USC 1974
Evans, Reggie, RB, Richmond 1983

Fanucci, Mike, DE, Arizona State 1972
Farkas, Andy, FB, Detroit 1938–44

Farman, Dick, G, Washington State .1939–43
Farmer, Tom, B, Iowa 1947–48
Faulkner, Jeff, DE, Southern 1993
Feagin, Tom, G, Houston 1963
Felber, Nip, E, North Dakota 1932
Felton, Ralph, LB, Maryland 1954–60
Ferris, Neil, DB, Loyola (CA) 1951–52
Filchock, Frank, QB, Indiana 1944–45
Fiorentino, Al, G, Boston College . . .1943–44
Fischer, Pat, CB, Nebraska 1968–77
Fisher, Bob, T, USC 1940
Flick, Tom, QB, Washington 1981
Flores, Mike, DT, Louisville 1995
Foltz, Vernon, C, St. Vincent's 1944
Forte, Ike, RB, Arkansas 1978–80
Foxx, Dion, LB, James Madison 1995
Frahm, Dick, B, Nebraska 1935
Frain, Todd, TE, Nebraska 1986
Francis, Dave, FB, Ohio State 1963
Frankian, Ike, E, St. Mary's 1933
Frazier, Frank, G, Miami 1987
Freeman, Bob, DB, Auburn 1962
Frerrote, Gus, QB, Tulsa 1994–95
Friesz, John, QB, Idaho 1994
Fritsch, Ted, C, St. Norbert 1976–79
Fryer, Brian, WR, Alberta (Canada) .1976–78
Fugett, Jean, TE, Amherst 1976–79
Fulcher, Bill, G, Georgia Tech 1956–58
Fuller, Larry, B, No College 1944–45

Gaffney, Jim, B, Tennessee 1945–46
Gage, Steve, S, Tulsa 1987–88
Gaines, William, DT, Florida 1995
Galbraith, Scott, TE, USC 1995
Gannon, Rich, QB, Delware 1993
Garner, Dwight, RB, California 1986
Garrett, Alvin, WR, Angelo State . . .1981–84
Garzoni, Mike, B, USC 1947
Geathers, James, DT, Wichita State . .1990–92
Gentry, Lee, B, Tulsa 1941
German, Jim, QB, Centre College 1939
Gesek, John, C,
    Cal State Sacramento 1994–95
Giaquinto, Nick, RB, Connecticut . .1981–83
Gibson, Alec, DT, Illinois 1987
Gibson, Joe, B, Tulsa 1943
Gilmer, Harry, QB, Alabama . .1948–52, 1954
Glick, Gary, DB, Colorado A&M . . .1959–61
Gob, Art, E, Pittsburgh 1959–60
Gogolak, Charlie, K, Princeton 1966–68
Goodburn, Kelly, P, Emporia State . .1990–93
Goode, Bob, RB, Texas A&M 1954–55
Goodnight, Clyde, E, Tulsa 1949–50
Goodyear, John, B, Marquette 1942
Goosby, Tom, G, Baldwin–Wallace 1966
Gouveia, Kurt, LB, BYU 1987–94
Graf, Dave, LB, Penn State 1981
Graf, Rick, LB, Wisconsin 1993
Graham, Don, LB, Penn Stte 1989
Grant, Alan, CB, Stanford 1994
Grant, Bob, LB, Wake Forest 1971
Grant, Darryl, DT, Rice 1981–90
Grant, Frank, WR,
    S. Colorado State 1973–78

Gray, Bill, G, Oregon State 1947–48
Green, Darrell, CB, Texas A&I 1983–95
Green, Tony, RB, Florida 1978
Green, Trent, QB, Indiana 1995
Griffin, Keith, RB, Miami 1984–88
Grimm, Dan, C, Colorado 1969
Grimm, Russ, G, Pittsburgh 1981–91
Guglielmi, Ralph, QB,
   Notre Dame 1955, 1958–60
Gulledge, David, FS, Jacksonville State ..1992
Gundlach, Herman, G, Harvard 1935

Hackbart, Dale, DB, Wisconsin 1961–63
Hageman, Fred, C, Kansas 1961–64
Haight, Mike, T, Iowa 1992
Haines, Kris, WR, Notre Dame 1979
Haji–Sheikh, Ali, K, Michigan 1987
Haley, Dick, Db, Pittsburgh 1959–60
Hall, Galen, QB, Penn State 1962
Hall, Windlan, DB, Arizona State 1977
Hamel, Dean, DT, Tulsa 1985–88
Hamilton, Rick, LB, Central Florida .1993–94
Hamilton, Steve, DE, East Carolina .1985–88
Hamlin, Gene, C, Western Michigan ...1970
Hammond, Bobby, RB,
   Morgan State 1979–80
Hanburger, Chris, LB,
   North Carolina 1965–78
Hancock, Mike, TE, Idaho State 1973–75
Hanna, Zip, G, South Carolina 1945
Hansen, Ron, G, Minnesota 1954
Harbour, Dave, C, Illinois 1988–89
Hardeman, Buddy, RB, Iowa State 1979–80
Hare, Cecil, FB, Gonzaga 1941–42, 1945
Hare, Ray, QB, Gonzaga 1940–43
Harlan, Jim, T, Howard Payne 1978
Harmon, Clarence, RB,
   Mississippi State 1977–82
Harold, George, B, Allen 1968
Harraway, Charley, RB,
   San Jose State 1969–73
Harris, Don, S, Rutgers 1978–79
Harris, Hank, G, Texas 1947–48
Harris, Jim, DB, Howard Payne 1970
Harris, Joe, LB, Georgia Tech 1977
Harris, Rickie, DB, Arizona 1965–70
Harrison, Kenny, WR, SMU 1980
Harry, Carl, WR, Utah 1989, 92
Hart, Jim, QB, Southern Illinois 1984
Hartley, Howard, B, Duke 1948
Hartman, Bill, B, Georgia 1938
Harvey, Ken, LB, California 1994–95
Harvin, Allen, RB, Cincinnati 1987
Hatcher, Ron, FB, Michigan State 1962
Hauss, Len, C, Georgia 1964–77
Haws, Kurt, TE, Utah 1994
Hayden, Ken, C, Arkansas 1943
Hayes, Jeff, P, North Carolina 1982–85
Haymond, Alvin, DB, Southern 1972
Haynes, Hall, DB,
   Santa Clara 1950, 1953–55
Haynes, Reggie, TE, UNLV 1978
Hazelwood, Ted, T, North Carolina 1953
Heath, Leon, FB, Oklahoma 1951–53

Hecker, Norb, DB,
   Baldwin–Wallace 1955–57
Heenan, Pat, E, Notre Dame 1960
Hegarty, Bill, T, Villanova 1960
Heinz, Bob, DT, Pacific 1978
Hendershot, Larry, LB, Arizona State ...1967
Henderson, Jon, WR, Colorado State ...1970
Hendren, Bob, T, USC 1949–51
Hennessey, Jerry, DE, Santa Clara ...1952–53
Hermeling, Terry, T, Nevada 1970–80
Hernandez, Joe, WR, Arizona 1964
Hickman, Dallas, DE, California 1976–81
Hickman, Donnie, G, USC 1978
Hill, Calvin, RB, Yale 1976–77
Hill, Irv, B, Trinity 1933
Hill, Nate, DE, Auburn 1989
Hitchcock, Ray, C, Minnesota 1987
Hoage, Terry, S, Georgia 1991
Hobbs, Stephen, WR,
   North Alabama 1990–92
Hochertz, Martin, DE,
   Southern Illinois 1993
Hodgson, Pat, TE, Georgia 1966
Hoffman, Bob, QB, USC 1940–41
Hoffman, John, DE, Hawaii 1969–70
Hokuf, Steve, B, Nebraska 1933–35
Hollar, John, B, Appalachian State ..1948–49
Hollinquest, Lamont, LB, USC 1993–94
Holloway, Derek, WR, Arkansas 1986
Holly, Bob, QB, Princeton 1982–83
Holman, Walter, RB,
   West Virginia State 1987
Holman, Willie, DE,
   South Carolina State 1973
Holmer, Walt, B, Northwestern 1933
Horner, Sam, B, VMI 1960–61
Horstmann, Roy, FB, Purdue 1933
Horton, Ethan, TE, North Carolina 1994
Houghton, Jerry, T, Washington State ..1950
Houston, Ken, S, Prairie View 1973–80
Houston, Walt, G, Purdue 1955
Hover, Don, LB, Washington State ..1978–79
Howard, Desmond, WR, Michigan ..1992–94
Howell, Dixie, B, Alabama 1937
Hudson, Bob, G, Clemson 1959
Huff, Ken, G, North Carolina 1983–85
Huff, Sam, LB, West Virginia ..1964–67, 1969
Hughley, George, FB,
   Central Oklahoma State 1965
Hull, Mike, RB, USC 1971–74
Humphries, Stan, QB, NE Louisiana 1989–91
Huntington, Greg, C, Penn State 1993
Hunter, Bill, DB, Syracuse 1965
Hurley, George, G, Washington State 1932–33
Hyatt, Fred, WR, Auburn 1973

Imhof, Martin, DE, San Diego State 1974
Intrieri, Marne, G, Loyola, Md. 1933–34
Irwin, Don, FB, Colgate 1936–39
Izo, George, QB, Notre Dame 1961–64

Jackson, Charles, S, Texas Tech 1987
Jackson, Leroy, RB, Western Illinois .1962–63

Jackson, Steve, LB, Texas–Arlington .1966–67
Jackson, Trenton, WR, Illinois 1967
Jackson, Wilbur, FB, Alabama 1980–82
Jacobs, Jack, QB, Oklahoma 1946
Jacoby, Joe, T/G, Louisville 1981–93
Jaffurs, John, G, Penn State 1946
Jagielski, Harry, T, Indiana 1956
James, Dick, RB, Oregon 1956–63
Janowicz, Vic, B, Ohio State 1954–55
Jaqua, Jon, S, Lewis & Clark 1970–72
Jefferson, Roy, WR, Utah 1971–76
Jencks, Bob, K/E, Miami (OH) 1965
Jenkins, Jacque, FB, Vanderbilt ...1943, 1946
Jenkins, James, TE, Rutgers 1991–95
Jenkins, Ken, RB, Bucknell 1985–86
Jessie, Tim, RB, Auburn 1987
Johnson, AJ, SW Texas State 1989–94
Johnson, Billy, WR, Widener 1988
Johnson, Dennis, DT, Delaware 1974–77
Johnson, Jimmie, TE, Howard 1989–91
Johnson(Howard), Joe, WR,
   Notre Dame 1989–91
Johnson, Larry, C,
   Haskell Indian 1933–35, 1944
Johnson, Mitch, T, UCLA 1966–68, 1972
Johnson, Randy, QB, Texas A&I 1975–76
Johnson, Richard, WR, Colorado 1987
Johnson, Sidney, CB, California 1990–92
Johnson, Tim, DT, Penn State 1990–95
Johnson, Tré, T, Temple 1994–95
Johnston, Jim, B, Washington 1939–40
Jones, Anthony, TE, Wichita State ...1984–88
Jones, Chuck, E, George Washington ...1955
Jones, David, C, Texas 1987
*Jones, Deacon, DE,
   Mississippi Vocational 1974*
Jones, Harvey, B, Baylor 1947
Jones, Jimmie, DE, Wichita State ...1971–73
Jones, Joe, DE, Tennessee State 1979–80
Jones, Larry, WR,
   NE Missouri State 1974–77
Jones, Larry, FB, Miami 1995
Jones, Melvin, G, Houston 1981
Jones, Stan, DT, Maryland 1966
Jordan, Curtis, FS, Texas Tech 1981–86
Jordan, Jeff, RB, Washington 1971–72
Junker, Steve, E, Xavier 1961–62
Junkin, Trey, LB, Louisiana Tech 1984
Jurgensen, Sonny, QB, Duke 1964–74
Justice, Charlie, RB,
   North Carolina 1950, 1952–54
Justice, Ed, B, Gonzaga 1936–42
Juzwik, Steve, B, Notre Dame 1942

Kahn, Ed, G, North Carolina 1935–37
Kalaniuvalu, Alai, G, Oregon State 1994
Kamp, Jim, T, Oklahoma City 1933
Kammerer, Carl, DE, Pacific 1963–69
Kane, Rick, RB, San Jose State 1984
Kantor, Joe, RB, Notre Dame 1966
Karamatic, George, B, Gonzaga 1938
Karas, Emil, E, Dayton 1959
Karcher, Jim, G, Ohio State 1936–39
Karras, Lou, T, Purdue 1950–51

Karras, Ted, DT, Northwestern 1987
Katrishen, Mike, T,
	Southern Mississippi 1948–49
Kaufman, Mel, LB, Cal Poly SLO . . .1981–88
Kawal, Ed, C, Illinois 1937
Keating, Chris, LB, Maine 1985
Keenan, Jack, T, South Carolina 1944–45
Kehr, Rick, G, Carthage 1987–88
Kelley, Gordon, LB, Georgia 1962–63
Kelly, John, T, Florida A&M 1966–67
Kenneally, Gus, E, St. Boneventure 1932
Kerr, Jim, DB, Penn State 1961–62
Khayat, Bob, K, Mississippi . . 1960, 1962–63
Khayat, Ed, DT, Tulane 1957, 1962–63
Kiick, Jim, RB, Wyoming 1977
Kilmer, Bill, QB, UCLA 1971–78
Kimball, Bruce, G, Massachusetts . . .1983–84
Kimble, Garry, CB,
	Sam Houston State 1987
Kimmel, J.D., T, Houston 1955–56
Kimmel, John, LB, Colgate 1987
Kincaid, Jim, B, South Carolina 1954
Kirk, Randy, LB, San Diego State 1990
Knight, Curt, K, Coast Guard 1969–73
Koch, Markus, DE, Boise State 1986–91
Koniszewski, John, T,
	Geo. Wash. 1945–46, 1948
Kopay, Dave, RB, Washington 1969–70
Kovatch, John, E, Notre Dame 1942–46
Krakoski, Joe, B, Illinois 1961
Krakoski, Joe, LB, Washington 1986
Krause, Max, FB, Gonzaga 1937–40
Krause, Paul, DB, Iowa 1964–67
Krause, Red, C, St. Louis 1938
Kresky, Joe (Mink), G, Wisconsin 1932
Kreuger, Al, RB, USC 1941–42
Krouse, Ray, T, Maryland 1960

Kruczek, Mike, QB, Boston College 1980
Kubin, Larry, LB, Penn State 1982–84
Kuchta, Frank, C, Notre Dame 1959
Kupp, Jake, G, Washington 1966
Kuziel, Bob, G, Pittsburgh 1975–80

Laaveg, Paul, G, Iowa 1970–75
Lachey, Jim, T, Ohio State 1988–95
Lane, Skip, S, Mississippi 1987
Lapka, Ted, E. St. Ambrose . . .1943–44, 1946
LaPresta, Benny, B, St. Louis 1933
Larson, Bill, TE, Colorado State 1977
Larson, Pete, RB, Cornell 1967–68
Lasse, Dick, LB, Syracuse 1960–61
Lathrop, Kit, DT, Arizona State 1987
Laster, Donald, T, Tennessee State . . .1982–83
Laufenberg, Babe, QB, Indiana 1983–85
Lavender, Joe, CB, San Diego State . .1976–82
Law, Dennis, WR,
	East Tennessee State 1979
Lawrence, Don, T, Notre Dame 1959–61
LeBaron, Eddie, QB,
	Pacific 1952–53, 1955–59
Lemek, Ray, T, Notre Dame 1957–61
Lennan, Reid, G, No College 1945
Leon, Tony, G, Alabama 1943
Lewis, Dan, RB, Wisconsin 1965
Lewis, Ron, G, Washington State 1995
Liebenstein, Todd, DE, UNLV 1982–85
Lipscomb, Paul, T, Tennessee 1950–54
Livingston, Howie, B, Fullerton JC . .1948–50
Lockett, J.W., B,
	Central Oklahoma State 1964
Logan, Marc, FB, Kentucky 1995
Lohmiller, Chip, K, Minnesota 1988–94
Lolatai, Al, G, Weber State 1945

Long, Bob, WR, Wichita State 1969
Lookabaugh, John, E, Maryland 1946–47
Looney, Joe Don, RB, Oklahoma . . .1966–67
Lorch, Karl, DT, USC 1976–81
Love, John, WR, North Texas State 1967
Lowe, Gary, B, Michigan State 1956–57
Lowry, Quentin, LB,
	Youngstown State 1981–83
Luce, Lew, B, Penn State 1961
Lynch, Dick, B, Notre Dame 1958

MacAfee, Ken, E, Alabama 1959
Macioszczck, Art, FB,
	Western Michigan 1948
MacMurdo, Jim, T, Pittsburgh 1932–33
Madarik, Elmer, B, Detroit 1948
Malinchak, Bill, WR, Indiana . 1970–74, 1976
Malone, Benny, RB, Arizona State . . .1978–79
Malone, Charley, E,
	Texas A&M 1934–40, 1942
Mandeville, Chris, DB, Cal–Davis 1989
Manley, Dexter, DE,
	Oklahoma State 1981–89
Mann, Charles, DE, Nevada–Reno . . .1983–93
Manton, Tillie, FB, TCU 1938
Manusky, Greg, LB, Colgate 1988–90
Marciniak, Ron, C, Kansas State 1955
Marcus, Pete, E, Kentucky 1944
Marshall, Leonard, DT, LSU 1994
Marshall, Rich, T, Stephen F. Austin 1966
Marshall, Wilber, LB, Florida 1988–92
Martin, Aaron, DB,
	North Carolina College 1968
Martin, Jim, K, Notre Dame 1964
Martin, Steve, DE, Jackson State 1987
Mason, Tommy, RB, Tulane 1971–72

Masterson, Bob, E, Miami 1938–43
Matich, Trevor, C, BYU 1994–95
Mattson, Riley, T, Oregon 1961–64
Mauti, Rich, WR, Penn State 1984
May, Mark, T, Pittsburgh 1981–89
Mayhew, Martin, CB, Florida State . .1989–92
Mays, Alvoid, CB, West Virginia 1990–94
Mazurek, Fred, B, Pittsburgh 1965–66
McCabe, Dick, B, Pittsburgh 1959
McChesney, Bob, E, UCLA 1936–42
McCrary, Greg, TE, Clark 1978, 1981
McDaniel, John, WR, Lincoln 1978–80
McDaniel, Le Charls, CB,
   Cal Poly SLO 1981–82
McDole, Ron, DE, Nebraska 1971–78
McDonald, Ray, RB, Idaho 1967–68
McEwen, Craig, TE, Utah 1987–88
McGee, Tim, WR, Tennessee 1993
McGee, Tony, DE, Bishop (TX) 1982–84
McGrath, Mark, WR,
   Montana State 1983–85
McGriff, Curtis, DT, Alabama 1987
McKee, Paul, E, Syracuse 1947–48
McKeever, Marlin, LB, USC 1968–70
McKenzie, Raleigh, G, Tennessee . . .1985–94
McKinney, Zion, WR, South Carolina . .1980
McLinton, Harold, LB, Southern . . .1969–78
McNeil, Clifton, WR, Grambling . . .1971–72
McPhail, Hal, FB, Xavier 1934–35
McQuaid, Dan, T, UNLV 1985–87
McQuilken, Kim, QB, Lehigh 1978–80
McRae, Stan, E, Michigan State 1946
Meade, Jim, B, Maryland 1939–40
Meads, Johnny, LB, Nicholls State 1992
Meadows, Ed, DB, Duke 1959
Melinger, Steve, E, Kentucky 1956–57
Mendenhall, Mat, DE, BYU 1981–82
Merkle, Ed, G, Oklahoma A&M 1944
Mercein, Chuck, RB, Yale 1969
Metcalf, Terry, RB, San Diego State 1981
Michaels, Ed, G, Villanova 1937
Micka, Mike, FB, Colgate 1944
Mickles, Joe, RB, Mississippi 1989
Middleton, Ron, TE, Auburn . .1988, 1990–93
Millen, Matt, LB, Penn State 1991
Miller, Allen, LB, Ohio 1962–63
Miller, Clark, DE, Utah State 1969
Miller, Dan, K, Florida 1982
Miller, Fred, T, Pacific 1955
Miller, John, T,
   Boston College 1956, 1958–59
Miller, Tom, B, Hampden–Sydney 1945
Millner, Wayne, E,
*   Notre Dame 1936–41, 1945*
Mills, Lamar, DT, Indiana 1994
Milot, Rich, LB, Penn State 1979–87
Mingo, Gene, K, No College 1967
Mitchell, Bobby, FL, Illinois 1962–68
Mitchell, Brian, RB, SW Louisiana . .1990–95
Mitchell, Michael, CB, Howard Payne . .1987
Modzelewski, Dick, DT, Maryland . .1953–54
Mojsiejenko, Ralf, P,
   Michigan State 1989–90
Momsen, Tony, C, Michigan 1952
Monachino, Jim, B, California 1955

Monaco, Ray, G, Holy Cross 1944
Monasco, Don, B, Texas 1954
Monk, Art, WR, Syracuse 1980–92
Mont, Tommy, QB, Maryland 1947–49
Moore, Chuck, G, Arkansas 1962
Moore, Darryl, G, UTEP 1992–93
Moore, Jeff, RB, Jackson State 1984
Moore, Wilbur, B, Minnesota 1939–46
Moran, Jim G, Holy Cross 1935–36
Morgan, Bob, DT, Maryland 1954
Morgan, Boyd, S, USC 1939–40
Morgan, Mike, LB, LSU 1968
Morley, Sam, E, Stanford 1954
Morris, Jamie, RB, Michigan 1988–89
Morrison, Darryl, S, Arizona 1993–95
Morrison, Tim, CB,
   North Carolina 1986–87
Mortensen, Fred, QB, Arizona State 1979
Morton, Michael, RB, UNLV 1985
Moseley, Mark, K, Stephen F. Austin .1974–86
Moss, Eddie, RB, SE Missouri State 1977
Moss, Joe, T, Maryland 1952
Muhammad, Calvin, WR,
   Texas Southern 1984–85
Mul–Key, Herb, RB, No College 1972–74
Murphy, Mark, S, Colgate 1977–84
Murray, Eddie, K, Tulane 1995
Musgrove, Spain, DT, Utah State . . .1967–69
Musick, Jim, FB, USC 1932–33, 1935–36
Myslinski, Tom, G, Tennessee 1992

Natowich, Andy, B, Holy Cross 1944
Nelms, Mike, KR, Baylor 1980–84
Nelson, Ralph, RB, No College 1975
Niemi, Laurie, T, Washington State .1949–53
Nichols, Gerald, DT, FloridaState 1993
Ninowski, Jim, QB, Michigan State . .1967–68
Nisby, John, G, Pacific 1962–64
Nix, Doyle, B, SMU 1958–59
Nobile, Leo, G, Penn State 1947
Noble, James, WR, Stephen F. Austin . . .1986
Nock, George, RB, Morgan State 1972
Noga, Al, DE, Hawaii 1993
Norman, Jim, T, No College 1955
Norris, Hal, B, California 1955–56
North, Jim T, Central Washington 1944
Norton, Jim, T, Washington 1969
Nott, Doug, B, Detroit 1935
Nottage, Dexter, DE, Florida A&M . .1994–95
Nugent, Dan, G, Auburn 1976–78, 1980
Nussbaumer, Bob, E, Michigan 1947–48

O'Brien, Fran, T, Michigan State 1960–66
O'Brien, Gail, T, Nebraska 1934–36
O'Dell, Stu, LB, Indiana 1974–76
Ogrin, Pat, DT, Wyoming 1981–82
Oliphant, Mike, RB, Puget Sound 1988
Oliver, Muhammad, CB, Oregon 1995
Olkewicz, Neal, LB, Maryland 1979–89
Olsson, Les, G, Mercer 1934–38
Olszewski, John, B, California 1958–60
Orr, Terry, TE, Texas 1986–92
Osborne, Tom, WR, Hastings (NE) .1960–61

Ostrowski, Chet, E, Notre Dame 1954–59
Owen, Tom, QB, Wichita State 1982
Owens, Brig, DB, Cincinnati 1966–77
Owens, Don, T, Southern Mississippi . . .1957
Owens, Rich, DE, Lehigh 1995

Paine, Jeff, LB, San Jose State 1986
Paluck, John, DE, Pittsburgh . .1956, 1959–65
Palmer, Sterling, DE, Florida State . .1993–95
Papit, John, B, Virginia 1951–53
Pardee, Jack, LB, Texas A&M 1971–72
Parks, Mickey, C, Oklahoma 1938–40
Parrish, Lemar, CB, Lincoln 1978–81
Pasqua, Joe, T, SMU 1943
Paternoster, Angelo, G, Georgetown 1943
Patton, Joe, G, Alabama A&M 1994–95
Patton, Marvcus, LB, UCLA 1995
Pebbles, Jim, E, Vanderbilt . . .1946–49, 1951
Peiffer, Dan, C, Southeast Missouri State 1980
Pellegrini, Bob, LB, Maryland 1962–65
Pepper, Gene, G, Missorui 1950–53
Pergine, John, LB, Notre Dame 1973–75
Perrin, Lonnie, RB, Illinois 1979
Peters, Floyd, T, San Francisco State 1970
Peters, Tony, S,
   Oklahoma 1979–82, 1984–85
Peters, Volney, T, USC 1954–57
Peterson, Nelson, RB,
   West Virginia Wesleyan 1937
Pettey, Phil, G, Missouri 1987
Petitbon, Richie, S, Tulane 1971–72
Phillips, Joe, WR, Kentucky 1985–87
Piasecky, Al, E, Duke 1943–45
Pierce, Dan, RB, Memphis State 1970
Pinckert, Erny, FB, USC 1932–40
Planutis, Jerry, B, Michigan State 1956
Podoley, Jim, RB,
   Central Michigan 1957–60
Poillon, Dick, B, Canisius 1942, 1946–49
Polsfoot, Fran, E, Washington State 1953
Pounds, Darryl, CB, Nicholls State 1995
Pottios, Myron, LB, Notre Dame . . .1971–73
Presley, Leo, C, Oklahoma 1945
Prestel, Jim, T, Idaho 1966–67
Promuto, Vince, G, Holy Cross 1960–70

Query, Jeff, WR, Millikin 1995
Quinlan, Bill, DE, Michigan State 1965
Quirk, Ed, B, Missouri 1948–51

Raab, Marc, C, USC 1993
Raba, Bob, TE, Maryland 1981
Rae, Mike, QB, USC 1981
Ramsey, Knox, G, William & Mary . .1952–53
Raymer, Cory, C, Wisconsin 1995
Reaves, Willard, RB, Northern Arizona .1989
Rector, Ron, B, Northwestern 1966
Reed, Alvin, TE, Prairie View 1973–75
Reed, Bob, G, Tennessee State 1965
Reger, John, LB, Pittsburgh 1964–66
Renfro, Will, T, Memphis State 1957–59
Reynolds, Mack, QB, LSU 1960

Ribar, Frank, G, Duke 1943
Ricca, Jim, C, Georgetown 1951–54
Richard, Stanley, S, Texas 1995
Richardson, Grady, TE,
    Cal St. Fullerton 1979–80
Richardson, Huey, LB, Florida 1992
Richter, Pat, WR, Wisconsin 1963–70
Riggins, John, RB,
    Kansas 1976–79, 1981–85
Riggs, Gerald, RB,
    Arizona State 1989–91
Riggs, Jim, TE, Clemson 1993
Riley, Jack, T, Northwestern 1933
Roberts, Jack, B, Georgia 1932
Roberts, Walter, WR,
    San Jose State 1969–70
Robinson, Dave, LB, Penn State 1973–74
Robinson, Lybrant, DE,
    Delaware State 1989
Robinson, Tony, QB, Tennessee 1987
Roby, Reggie, P, Iowa 1993–94
Rock, Walter, T, Maryland 1968–73
Rocker, Tracy, DT, Auburn 1989–90
Roehnelt, Bill, LB, Bradley 1960
Rogers, George, RB,
    South Carolina 1985–87
Rosato, Sal, B, Villanova 1945–47
Rose, Carlton, LB, Michigan 1987
Rosso, George, B, Ohio State 1954
Roussel, Tom, LB,
    Southern Mississippi 1968–70
Roussos, Mike, T, Pittsburgh 1948–49
Rowe, Ray, TE, San Diego State 1992
Rubbert, Ed, QB, Louisville 1987
Runnels, Tom, RB,
    North Texas State 1956–57
Rush, Tyrone, RB, North Alabama 1994
Russell, Bo, T, Auburn 1939–40
Rutgens, Joe, DT, Illinois 1961–69
Ruthstrom, Ralph, B, SMU 1947
Rutledge, Jeff, QB, Alabama 1990–92
Ryan, Frank, QB, Rice 1969–70
Ryczek, Dan, C, Virginia 1973–75
Rykovich, Jules, B, Illinois 1952–53
Rymkus, Lou, T, Notre Dame 1943
Rypien, Mark, QB,
    Washington State 1987–93
Rzempoluch, Ted, DB, Virginia 1963

Saenz, Eddie, RB, USC 1946–51
Sagnella, Anthony, DT, Rutgers 1987
Salem, Ed, B, Alabama 1951
Salter, Bryant, S, Pittsburgh 1974–75
Sample, Johnny, DB,
    Maryland State 1963–65
Sanchez, John, T, San Francisco 1947–49
Sanders, Lonnie, DB,
    Michigan State 1963–67
Sanders, Ricky, WR, SW Texas State .1986–93
Sandifer, Dan, DB, LSU 1948–49
Sanford, Haywood, E, Alabama 1940
Sarboe, Phil, DB, Washington State 1934
Sardisco, Tony, G, Tulane 1956
Saul, Ron, G, Michigan State 1976–81

Savage, Sebastian, CB,
    North Carolina State 1995
Sawyer, John, TE, Southern Mississippi .1983
Scafide, John, T, Tulane 1933
Scanlan, Jerry, T, Hawaii1 980–81
Scarbath, Jack, QB, Maryland 1953–54
Schick, Doyle, LB, Kansas 1961
Schilling, Ralph, E, Oklahoma City 1946
Schlereth, Mark, G, Idaho 1989–94
Schmidt, Kermit (Dutch), E,
    Cal Poly–Pomona 1932
Schoenke, Ray, G, SMU 1966–75
Schrader, Jim, C,
    Notre Dame 1954, 1956–61
Schroeder, Jay, QB, UCLA 1984–88
Scissum, Williard, G, Alabama 1987
Scott, Jake, S, Georgia 1976–78
Scotti, Ben, DB, Maryland 1959–61
Scudero, Joe, B, San Francisco 1954–58
Scully, Mike, C, Illinois 1988
Seals, George, G, Missouri 1964
Seay, Virgil, WR, Troy State 1981–84
Sebek, Nick, B, Indiana 1950
Seedborg, John, E, Arizona State 1965
Seno, Frank, B,
    George Washington 1943–44, 1949
Settles, Tony, LB, Elon 1987
Severson, Jeff, DB, Long Beach State . . .1972
Seymour, Bob, B, Oklahoma 1940–45
Sharp, Everett, T, California Tech . . .1944–45
Shepard, Derrick, WR, Oklahoma . .1987–88
Shepherd, Bill, FB, Western Maryland . .1935
Shepherd, Leslie, WR, Temple 1994–95
Shiner, Dick, QB, Maryland 1964–66
Shoener, Herb, E, Iowa 1948–49
Shorter, Jim, DB, Detroit 1964–67
Shugart, Clyde, G, Iowa State 1939–43
Shula, Don, DB, John Carroll 1957
Shuler, Heath, QB, Tennessee 1994–95
Siano, Tony, C, Fordham 1932
Siegert, Herb, G, Illinois 1949–51
Siemering, Larry, C, San Francisco . .1935–36
Siever, Paul, T, Penn State 1992–93
Simmons, Ed, T,
    Eastern Washington 1987–95
Simmons, Roy, G, Georgia Tech 1983
Sinko, Steve, T, Duquesne 1934–36
Sistrunk, Manny, DT,
    Arkansas AM&N 1970–75
Slivinski, Steve, G, Washington 1939–43
Smith, Ben, E, Alabama 1937
Smith, Cedric, FB, Florida 1994–95
Smith, Dick, DB, Northwestern 1967–68
Smith, Ed, FB, NYU 1936
Smith, George, C, California . .1937, 1941–43
Smith, Hugh, E, Kansas 1962
Smith, Jack, E, Stanford 1943
Smith, Jerry, TE, Arizona State 1965–77
Smith, Jim, DB, Oregon 1968
Smith, Jimmy, RB, Elon 1984
Smith, John, WR, North Texas State 1978
Smith, Larry, RB, Florida 1974
Smith, Paul, DE, New Mexico 1979–80
Smith, Ricky, CB, Alabama State 1984
Smith, Riley, QB, Alabama 1936–38

Smith, Timmy, RB, Texas Tech 1987–88
Smith, Vernice, G, Florida A&M 1993–95
Snead, Norm, QB, Wake Forest 1961–63
Sneddon, Bob, B, St. Mary's (CA) 1944
Snidow, Ron, DE, Oregon 1963–67
Snipes, Angelo, LB, West Georgia 1986
Snowden, Jim, T, Notre Dame 1965–72
Sobolenski, Joe, G, Michigan 1949
Sommer, Mike, B, Geo. Wash. .1958–59, 1961
Sommers, John, C, UCLA 1947
Spaniel, Frank, B, Notre Dame 1950
Sparks, Dave, G, South Carolina 1954
Spirida, John, E, St. Anselm's 1939
Stacco, Ed, T, Colgate 1948
Stallings, Don, E, North Carolina 1960
Stanfel, Dick, G, San Francisco 1956–58
Stanley, Walter, WR, Mesa (CO) 1990
Starke, George, T, Columbia 1973–84
Stasica, Leo, B, Colorado 1943
Staton, Jim, T, Wake Forest 1951
Steber, John, G, Georgia Tech 1946–50
Steffen, Jim, DB, UCLA 1961–65
Stenn, Paul, T, Villanova 1946
Stensrud, Mike, DT, Iowa State 1989
Stephens, Louis, G, San Francisco . . .1955–60
Stephens, Rod, LB, Georgia Tech 1995
Steponovich, Mike, G, St. Mary's 1933
Stief, Dave, WR, Portland State 1983
Stits, Bill, DB, UCLA 1959
Stock, Mark, WR, VMI 1993
Stokes, Fred, DE,
    Georgia Southern 1989–92
Stokes, Tim, T, Oregon 1975–77
Stone, Ken, S, Vanderbilt 1973–75
Stout, Pete, B, TCU 1949–50
Stovall, Dick, C, Abilene Christian 1949
Stowe, Tyronne, LB, Rutgers 1994
Stralka, Clem, G,
    Georgetown 1938–42, 1945–46
Stuart, Jim, T, Oregon 1938
Sturt, Fred, G, Bowling Green 1974
Stynchula, Andy, DT, Penn State 1960–63
Suminski, Dave, G, Wisconsin 1953
Sutton, Ed, B, North Carolina 1957–59
Sweeney, Walt, G, Syracuse 1974–75
Sykes, Bob, B, San Jose State 1952
Szafaryn, Len, T, North Carolina 1949

Talbert, Diron, DT, Texas 1971–80
Tamm, Ralph, T, West Chester 1991
Taylor, Charley, WR, Arizona State . .1964–77
Taylor, Hugh (Bones), E,
    Oklahoma City 1947–54
Taylor, Keith, S, Illinois 1994–95
Taylor, Mike, T, USC 1971
Taylor, Roosevelt, DB, Grambling 1972
Temple, Mark, B, Oregon 1936
Tereshinski, Joe, E, Georgia 1947–54
Theismann, Joe, QB, Notre Dame . . .1974–85
Theofiledes, Harry, QB, Waynesburg . . .1968
Thielemann, R.C., G, Arkansas 1985–88
Thomas, Duane, RB,
    West Texas State 1973–74
Thomas, George, B, Oklahoma 1950–51

Thomas, Johnny, CB,
Baylor 1988–90, 92–94
Thomas, Mike, RB, UNLV 1975–78
Thomas, Ralph, E, San Francisco . . .1955–56
Thomas, Spencer, S, Washburn 1975
Thompson, Ricky, WR, Baylor 1978–81
Thompson, Steve, DT, Minnesota 1987
Thure, Brian, T, California 1995
Thurlow, Steve, RB, Stanford 1966–68
Tice, Mike, TE, Maryland 1989
Tillman, Rusty, LB,
Northern Arizona 1970–77
Tilton, Ron, G, Tulane 1986
Titchenal, Bob, C, San Jose State 1940–42
Todd, Dick, RB,
Texas A&M 1939–42, 1945–48
Toibin, Brendan, K, Richmond 1987
Toneff, Bob, DT, Notre Dame 1959–64
Torgeson, LaVern, LB,
Washington State 1955–57
Tosi, Flavio, E, Boston College 1934–36
Towns, Morris, T, Missouri 1984
Tracy, Tom, B, Tennessee 1963–64
Truitt, Dave, TE, North Carolina 1987
Truitt, Olanda, WR,
Mississippi State 1994–95
Tuckey, Dick, FB, Manhattan 1938
Turk, Matt, P, Wisconsin–Whitewater . .1995
Turley, Doug, E, Scranton 1944–48
Turner, J.T., G, Duke 1984
Turner, Jay, B, George Washington . .1938–39
Turner, Kevin, LB, Pacific 1981
Turner, Scott, CB, Illinois 1995
Tyrer, Jim, T, Ohio State 1974

Ucovich, Mitchell, T, San Jose State 1944
Ulinski, Harry, C,
Kentucky 1950–51, 1953–56
Ungerer, Joe, T, Fordham 1944–45

Vactor, Ted, DB, Nebraska 1969–74
Vanderbeek, Matt, LB, Michigan State . .1995
Varty, Mike, LB, Northwestern 1974
Vaughn, Clarence, S,
Northern Illinois 1987–91
Venuto, Sam, B, Guilford 1952
Verdin, Clarence, WR,
SW Louisiana 1986–87
Vereb, Ed, RB, Maryland 1960
Vital, Lionel, RB, Nicholls State 1987
Voytek, Ed, G, Purdue 1957–58

Waddy, Ray, CB, Texas A&I 1979–80
Wade, Bob, DB, Morgan State 1969
Ward, David (Nubbin), E,
Haskell Indian 1933
Waechler, Henry, DT, Nebraska 1987
Wahler, Jim, DT, UCLA 1992–93
Walker, Rick, TE, UCLA 1980–85
Walters, Tom, DB,
Southern Mississippi 1964–67
Walton, Alvin, S, Kansas 1986–91

Walton, Frank, G, Pittsburgh 1944–45
Walton, Joe, E, Pittsburgh 1957–60
Watters, Dale (Muddy), T, Florida . .1932–33
Ward, Bill, G, Washington State 1946–47
Warren, Don, TE, San Diego State . .1979–92
Washington, Anthony, CB,
Fresno State 1983–84
Washington, Fred, T, North Texas State .1968
Washington, James, S, UCLA 1995
Washington, Joe, RB, Oklahoma 1981–84
Washington, Mickey, CB, Texas A&M . . .1992
Watson, Jim, C, Pacific 1945
Watson, Sid, B, Northwestern 1958
Watts, George, T, Appalachian State 1942
Weatherall, Jim, T, Oklahoma 1958
Weaver, Charlie, LB, USC 1981
Weil, Jack, P, Wyoming 1989
Weisenbaugh, Heinie, B,
Pittsburgh 1935–36
Welch, Herb, DB, UCLA 1989
Weldon, Larry, QB, Presbyterian 1944–45
Weller, Rabbit (Bub), B, Haskell Indian .1933
Wells, Billy, B, Michigan State .1954, 1956–57
Westbrook, Michael, WR, Colorado 1995
Westfall, Ed, B, Ohio Wesleyan 1932–33
Whisenhunt, Ken, TE, Georgia Tech 1990
White, Jeris, CB, Hawaii 1980–82
Whited, Marvin, G, Oklahoma 1942–45
Whitfield, A.D., RB,
North Texas State 1966–68
Whitlow, Bob, C, Arizona 1960–61
Wilbur, John, G, Stanford 1971–73
Wilburn, Barry, CB, Mississippi 1985–89
Wilde, George, B, Texas A&M 1947
Wilder, James, RB, Missouri 1990
Wilkerson, Basil, E, Oklahoma City 1932
Wilkin, Willie, T, St. Mary's (CA) . . .1939–43
Wilkins, Roy, LB, Georgia 1960–61
Williams, Clarence, RB,
South Carolina 1982
Williams, Doug, QB, Grambling 1986–89
Williams, Eric, DT,
Washington State 1990–93
Williams, Fred, T, Arkansas 1964–65
Williams, Gerard, DB, Langston 1976–78
Williams, Greg, FS,
Mississippi State 1982–84
Williams, Jeff, T, Rhode Island 1978–80
Williams, John, B, USC 1952–53
Williams, Kevin, CB, Iowa State . .1985, 1988
Williams, Marvin, TE, Fullerton State . .1987
Williams, Michael, TE,
Alabama A&M 1982–84
Williams, Robert, CB, Baylor 1993
Williams, Sid, LB, Southern 1967
Williamson, Ernie, T, North Carolina . . .1947
Willis, Keith, DT, Northeastern 1993
Willis Larry, S, Texas–El Paso 1973
Wilson, Bobby, DT, Michigan State .1991–94
Wilson, Eric, LB, Maryland 1987
Wilson, Ted, WR, Central Florida 1987
Wilson, Wayne, RB, Shepard 1987
Winans, Tydus, WR, Fresno State 1994–95
Windham, David, LB, Jackson State 1987
Wingate, Heath, C, Bowling Green 1967

Winslow, Doug, WR, Drake 1976–77
Witucki, Casimir, G, Indiana 1953–56
Wonsley, Otis, RB, Alcorn State 1981–85
Woodberry, Dennis, CB,
S. Arkansas 1987–88
Woodruff, Lee, FB, Mississippi 1932
Woods, Tony, DE, Pittsburgh 1994–95
Woodward, Dick, C, Iowa 1952
Wooten, John, G, Colorado 1968
Wooten, Mike, C, VMI 1987
Wright, Steve, T, Alabama 1970
Wrigth, Ted, B, North Texas State . . .1934–35
Wulff, Jim, B, Michigan State 1960–61
Wyant, Fred, QB, West Virginia 1956
Wyche, Sam, QB, Furman 1971–73
Wycheck, Frank, TE–FB, Maryland .1993–94
Wycoff, Doug, FB, Georgia Tech 1934
Wynne, William, DE, Tennessee State . . .1977
Wysocki, Pete, LB,
Western Michigan 1975–80

Yarber, Eric, WR, Idaho 1986–87
Yehobah–Kodie, Phil, LB, Penn State . . .1995
Yonaker, John, E, Notre Dame 1952
Youel, Jim, B, Iowa 1946–48
Young, Bill, T, Alabama 1937–42, 1946
Young, Roy, T, Texas A&M 1938
Young, Wilburn, DE, William Penn 1981
Youngblood, Jim, LB, Tennessee Tech . . .1984
Yowarsky, Walt, E, Kentucky 1951–54

Zagers, Bert, B,
Michigan State 1955, 1957–58
Zendejas, Max, K, Arizona 1986
Zeno, Joe, G, Holy Cross 1942–44
Zimmerman, Roy, B, San Jose State .1940–42

Hall of Famers in Italics

COACHING RECORDS

Coach	REGULAR SEASON				PLAYOFFS		
	W	L	T	Pct.	W	L	Yrs.
Ray Flaherty	47	16	3	.735	2	1	1937-42
Arthur "Dutch" Bergman	6	3	1	.650	1	1	1943
Dud DeGroot	14	5	1	.725	0	1	1944-45
A.G. "Turk" Edwards	16	18	1	.471	0	0	1946-48
John Whelchel	3	3	1	.500	0	0	1949
Herman Ball	4	16	0	.200	0	0	1949-51
Dick Todd	5	4	0	.556	0	0	1951
Earl "Curly" Lambeau	10	13	1	.438	0	0	1952-53
Joe Kuharich	26	32	2	.450	0	0	1954-58
Mike Nixon	4	18	2	.208	0	0	1959-60
Bill McPeak	21	46	3	.321	0	0	1961-65
Otto Graham	17	22	3	.440	0	0	1966-68
Vince Lombardi	7	5	2	.571	0	0	1969
Bill Austin	6	8	0	.429	0	0	1970
George Allen	67	30	1	.689	2	5	1971-77
Jack Pardee	24	24	0	.500	0	0	1978-80
Joe Gibbs	124	60	0	.674	16	5	1981-92
Richie Petitbon	4	12	0	.250	0	0	1993
Norv Turner	9	23	0	.281	0	0	1994-95

(Washington Redskins)

ASSISTANT COACHES

Aldrich, Charles "Ki" 1947
Arapoff, Jason 1992–95
Austin, Bill 1969–70, 1973–77

Baker, Ray 1937–39
Ball, Herman 1952–54
Bass, Marvin 1952
Banker, Chuck 1987–88
Bielski , Dick 1973–76
Bowser, Bob 1978–80
Breaux, Don 1981–93
Bugel, Joe 1981–89
Burns, Jack 1989–91

Cabrelli, Larry 1951
Callahan, Ray 1978–80
Cameron, Cam 1994–95
Carpenter, Ken 1968
Carpenter, Lew 1969–70
Cherundolo, Charles 1964–65

DePaul, Bobby 1989–93
Diange, Joe 1987
Dickson, George . .1969–70, 1978–80
Doll, Don 1966–70
Dowhower, Rod 1990–93
Dowler, Boyd 1971–72
Dudley, Bill 1953
Dunn, John 1984–86

Edwards, Glenn "Turk" 1940–45, 1949
Evans, Dick 1955–58

Gibron, Abe 1960–64
Grimm, Russ 1992–95

Haluchak, Mike 1994–95
Hanifan, Jim 1990–95
Hayes, Tom 1995
Hawkins, Ralph 1972–77
Hefferle, Ernie 1959
Henning, Dan 1981–82, 1987–88
Hickman, Bill 1973–77, 1981–88
Hilton, John 1978–80
Hilyer, Jim 1975–76
Horton, Ray 1994–95
Huff, Sam 1969–70
Hughes, Ed 1964–67

Jackson, Bobby 1994–95
Karmelowicz, Bob 1994–95

Kilroy, Frank 1962–64
Kuharich, Joe 1954

Lanham, Paul 1973–77, 1987–88
Levy, Marv 1971–72
Lynn, Ron 1994–95

Marchibroda, Ted 1961–65,
1971–74
Mathews, Ray 1968
Matuszak, Marv 1977
McCormack, Mike 1966–72
McCulley , Pete 1977
McPeak, Bill 1959
Mee, Kirk 1974–77
Millner, Wayne 1946–48, 1954
Moore, Wilber 1947–50

Neri, Jerry 1952
Nixon, Mike 1954–58

O'Connor, Fred 1979–80

Pardee, Jack 1973
Peccatiello, Larry 1981–93
Petitbon, Richie 1978–92

Reed, Max 1950
Raines, Frank 1988–89
Renfro, Ray 1966–67
Rhome, Jerry 1983–87
Riley, Dan 1982–95

Robiskie, Terry 1994–95
Rodriguez, Pete 1994–95

Scarry, Mike 1966–68
Sevier, Wayne 1981–86, 1989–93
Siemering, Larry 1953
Simmons, Warren "Rennie" .1981–93
Speros, Jim 1982–83
Sullivan, Joe 1971–72
Stautner, Ernie 1965
Svare, Harland 1969–70

Taylor, Charley 1981–93
Temerario, Tim 1960–65
Tereshinski, Joe 1955–59
Thomas, Emmitt 1986–94
Todd, Dick 1951
Torgeson, Torgy 1959–61,
1971–77, 1981–93
Tuttle, Orville 1951

Urich, Richard "Doc" 1978–80

Waller, Charlie 1972–77
Walton, Frank 1948
Walton, Joe 1974–80
Wetzel, Steve 1990–91
Wilson, George 1965
Willsey, Ray 1962–63
Winner, Charley 1971–72

ANNUAL RESULTS 1932–1995

1932
Won 4, Lost 4, Tied 2

Head Coach–Lud Wray

L	Oct. 2	0	Brooklyn 14	(H)
W	Oct. 9	14	Giants...................6	(H)
L	Oct. 16	0	Cardinals..............9	(H)
T	Oct. 23	0	Giants...................0	(A)
T	Oct. 30	7	Bears 7	(H)
W	Nov. 6	19	Staten Island........6	(H)
L	Nov. 13	0	Packers 21	(H)
L	Nov. 20	0	Portsmouth 10	(A)
W	Nov. 27	8	Cardinals..............6	(A)
W	Dec. 4	7	Brooklyn 0	(A)
Season Ttls		**55***		**79***

1933
Won 5, Lost 5, Tied 2

Head Coach–Lone Star Dietz

T	Sept. 17	7	Packers 7	(A)
L	Sept. 24	0	Bears 7	(A)
W	Oc. 1	21	Pirates 6	(A)
W	Oct. 8	21	Giants...................20	(H)
L	Oct. 15	0	Portsmouth 13	(H)
W	Oct. 22	10	Cardinals..............0	(H)
L	Oct. 29	14	Pirates 16	(H)
W	Nov. 5	10	Bears 0	(H)
L	Nov. 12	0	Giants...................7	(A)
W	Nov. 19	20	Packers 7	(H)
L	Nov. 26	0	Brooklyn 14	(A)
T	Dec. 3	0	Cardinals...............0	(A)
		103		97

1934
Won 6, Lost 6

Head Coach–Lone Star Dietz

W	Sept. 16	7	Pirates 0	(A)
L	Sept. 30	6	Brooklyn 10	(A)
L	Oct. 7	13	Giants...................16	(A)
W	Oct. 14	39	Pirates 0	(H)
L	Oct. 17	0	Lions 24	(A)
W	Oct. 21	6	Eagles 0	(H)
W	Oct. 28	9	Cardinals..............0	(H)
L	Nov. 4	0	Packers 10	(H)
L	Nov. 11	0	Bears 21	(H)
W	Nov. 18	14	Eagles 7	(A)
L	Nov. 25	0	Giants...................3	(A)
W	Dec. 2	13	Brooklyn 3	(H)
		107		94

1935
Won 2, Lost 8, Tied 1

Head Coach–Eddie Casey

W		7	Brooklyn 3	(H)
L		12	Giants...................20	(H)
L		7	Lions 17	(H)
L		6	Giants...................17	(A)
L		0	Pirates 6	(A)
L		0	Lions 14	(A)
L		6	Eagles 7	(H)

L		14	Bears 30	(H)
L		0	Cardinals...............6	(H)
W		13	Pirates 3	(H)
T		0	Brooklyn 0	(A)
		65		123

1936
Won 7, Lost 5

Head Coach–Ray Flaherty

L		0	Pirates 10	(A)
W		26	Eagles 3	(A)
W		14	Brooklyn 3	(A)
L		0	Giants...................7	(H)
L		2	Packers 31	(A)
W		17	Eagles 7	(H)
W		13	Cardinals..............10	(H)
L		3	Packers 7	(H)
L		0	Bears 26	(H)
W		30	Brooklyn 6	(H)
W		30	Pirates 0	(H)
W		14	Giants...................0	(A)
		149		110

World Championship

L		6	Packers 21	*(N)

* *Game played at Polo Grounds*

1937
Won 8, Lost 3

Head Coach Ray Flaherty

W	Sept. 15	13	Giants...................3	(H)
L	Sept. 24	14	Cardinals..............21	(H)
W	Oct. 3	11	Brooklyn 7	(A)
L	Oct. 10	0	Eagles 14	(H)
W	Oct. 17	34	Steelers 20	(H)
W	Oct. 24	10	Eagles 7	(A)
W	Oct. 31	21	Brooklyn 0	(H)
L	Nov. 14	13	Steelers 21	(A)
W	Nov. 21	16	Rams 7	(A)
W	Nov. 28	14	Packers 6	(A)
W	Dec. 5	49	Giants...................14	(A)
		195		120

World Championship

W	Dec. 12	28	Bears 21	(A)

1938
Won 6, Lost 3, Tied 2

Head Coach–Ray Flaherty

W	Sept. 11	26	Eagles 23	(A)
T	Sept. 18	16	Brooklyn 16	(H)
W	Sept. 25	37	Rams 13	(H)
L	Oct. 9	7	Giants...................10	(H)
W	Oct. 16	7	Lions 5	(A)
W	Oct. 23	20	Eagles 14	(H)
T	Oct. 30	6	Brooklyn 6	(A)
W	Nov. 6	7	Steelers 0	(A)
L	Nov. 13	7	Bears 31	(A)
W	Nov. 27	15	Steelers 0	(H)
L	Dec. 4	0	Giants...................36	(A)
		148		154

1939
Won 8, Lost 2, Tied 1

Head Coach–Ray Flaherty

W	Sept. 17	7	Eagles 0	(A)
T	Oct. 1	0	Giants...................0	(H)
W	Oct. 8	41	Brooklyn 13	(H)
W	Oct. 15	44	Steelers 14	(H)
W	Oct. 22	21	Steelers 14	(A)
L	Oct. 29	14	Packers 24	(A)
W	Nov. 5	7	Eagles 6	(H)
W	Nov. 12	42	Brooklyn 0	(A)
W	Nov. 19	28	Cardinals..............7	(H)
W	Nov. 26	31	Lions 7	(H)
L	Dec. 3	7	Giants....................9	(A)
		242		94

1940
Won 9, Lost 2

Head Coach–Ray Flaherty

W	Sept. 15	24	Brooklyn 17	(H)
W	Sept. 22	21	Giants....................7	(H)
W	Oct. 6	40	Steelers 10	(A)
W	Oct. 13	28	Cardinals..............21	(H)
W	Oct. 20	34	Eagles 17	(H)
W	Oct. 27	20	Lions 14	(A)
W	Nov. 3	37	Steelers 10	(H)
L	Nov. 10	14	Brooklyn 16	(A)
W	Nov. 17	7	Bears 3	(H)
L	Nov. 24	7	Giants...................21	(A)
W	Dec. 1	13	Eagles 6	(H)
		245		142

World Championship

L	Dec. 8	0	Bears 73	(H)

1941
Won 6, Lost 5

Head Coach–Ray Flaherty

L	Sept. 28	10	Giants...................17	(H)
W	Oct. 5	3	Brooklyn 0	(H)
W	Oct. 12	24	Steelers 20	(A)
W	Oct. 19	21	Eagles 17	(A)
W	Oct. 26	17	Rams 13	(H)
W	Nov. 2	23	Steelers 3	(H)
L	Nov. 9	7	Brooklyn 13	(A)
L	Nov. 16	21	Bears 35	(A)
L	Nov. 23	13	Giants...................20	(A)
L	Nov. 30	17	Packers 22	(H)
W	Dec. 7	20	Eagles 14	(H)
		176		174

1942
Won 10, Lost 1

Head Coach–Ray Flaherty

W	Sept. 20	28	Steelers 14	(H)
L	Sept. 27	7	Giants...................14	(H)
W	Oct. 4	14	Eagles 10	(A)
W	Oct. 11	33	Rams 14	(H)
W	Oct. 18	21	Brooklyn 10	(A)
W	Oct. 25	14	Steelers 0	(A)
W	Nov. 1	30	Eagles 27	(H)

* Season totals points scored, allowed

W Nov. 8   28   Cardinals..............0   (H)
W Nov. 15 14   Giants..................7   (A)
W Nov. 22 23   Brooklyn..............3   (H)
W Nov. 29 15   Lions 3   (A)
                227   102

World Championship

W Dec. 13 14   Bears 6   (H)

1943   Won 6, Lost 3, Tied 1

Head Coach–Arthur "Dutch" Bergman

W Oct. 10 27   Brooklyn...............0   (H)
W Oct. 17 33   Packers 7   (A)
W Oct. 24 13   Cardinals..............7   (H)
W Oct. 31 48   Brooklyn.............10   (A)
T Nov. 7   14   Phil–Pitt..............14   (A)
W Nov. 14 42   Lions 20   (H)
W Nov. 21 21   Bears 7   (H)
L Nov. 28 14   Phil–Pitt..............27   (H)
L Dec. 5   10   Giants..................14   (A)
L Dec. 12   7   Giants..................31   (H)
                229   137

Eastern Title Playoff

W Dec. 19 28   Giants....................0   (A)

World Championship

L Dec. 26 21   Bears 41   (A)

1944   Won 6, Lost 3, Tied 1

Head Coach–Dudley DeGroot

T Oct. 8   31   Eagles 31   (A)
W Oct. 15 21   Yanks 14   (A)
W Oct. 22 17   Brooklyn.............14   (H)
W Oct. 29 42   Card–Pitt 20   (H)
W Nov. 5   14   Rams 10   (H)
W Nov. 12 10   Brooklyn 0   (A)
L Nov. 19   7   Eagles 37   (H)
W Nov. 26 14   Yanks 7   (H)
L Dec. 3   13   Giants..................16   (A)
L Dec. 10   0   Giants..................31   (H)
                169   180

1945   Won 8, Lost 2

Head Coach–Dudley DeGroot

L Oct. 7   20   Yanks 28   (A)
W Oct. 14 14   Steelers 0   (A)
W Oct. 21 24   Eagles 14   (H)
W Oct. 28 24   Giants..................14   (H)
W Nov. 4   24   Cardinals.............21   (H)
W Nov. 11 34   Yanks 7   (H)
W Nov. 18 28   Bears 21   (H)
L Nov. 25   0   Eagles 16   (A)
W Dec. 2   24   Steelers 0   (H)
W Dec. 9   17   Giants....................0   (H)
                209   121

World Championship

L Dec. 16 14   Rams 15   (A)

1946   Won 5, Lost 5, Tied 1

Head Coach–A.G. "Turk" Edwards

T Sept. 29 14   Steelers 14   (H)
W Oct. 6   17   Lions 16   (H)
W Oct. 13 24   Giants..................14   (H)
W Oct. 20 14   Yanks 6   (A)
L Oct. 27 24   Eagles 28   (H)
L Nov. 3   7   Steelers 14   (A)
W Nov. 10 17   Yanks 14   (H)
L Nov. 17 20   Bears 24   (A)
W Nov. 24 27   Eagles 10   (A)
L Dec. 1   7   Packers 20   (H)
L Dec. 8   0   Giants..................31   (A)
                171   191

1947   Won 4, Lost 8

Head Coach–A.G. "Turk" Edwards

L Sept. 28 42   Eagles 45   (A)
W Oct. 5   27   Steelers 26   (H)
W Oct. 12 28   Giants..................20   (H)
L Oct. 19 10   Packers 27   (A)
L Oct. 26 20   Bears 56   (H)
L Nov. 2   14   Eagles 38   (H)
L Nov. 9   14   Steelers 21   (A)
L Nov. 16 21   Lions 38   (A)
W Nov. 23 45   Cardinals.............21   (H)
L Nov. 30 24   Yanks 27   (A)
L Dec. 7   10   Giants..................35   (A)
W Dec. 14 40   Yanks 13   (H)
                295   367

1948   Won 7, Lost 5

Head Coach–A.G. "Turk" Edwards

W Sept. 26 17   Steelers 14   (H)
W Oct. 3   41   Giants..................10   (H)
L Oct. 10   7   Steelers 10   (H)
L Oct. 17   0   Eagles 45   (H)
W Oct. 24 23   Packers 7   (A)
W Oct. 31 59   Yanks 21   (H)
W Nov. 7   23   Yanks 7   (H)
W Nov. 14 46   Lions 21   (H)
L Nov. 21 21   Eagles 42   (A)
L Nov. 28 13   Bears 48   (A)
L Dec. 5   13   Rams 41   (H)
W Dec. 12 28   Giants..................21   (A)
                291   287

1949   Won 4, Lost 7, Tied 1

Head Coach–John Whelchel (7 games)
Head Coach–Herman Ball

L Sept. 26   7   Cardinals.............38   (A)
W Oct. 3   27   Steelers 14   (A)
L Oct. 9   35   Giants..................45   (H)
W Oct. 16 38   Bulldogs 14   (H)
L Oct. 23 14   Eagles 49   (H)
T Oct. 30 14   Bulldogs 14   (A)
W Nov. 6   27   Steelers 14   (H)
L Nov. 13 21   Eagles 44   (H)
L Nov. 20 21   Bears 31   (H)
L Nov. 27   7   Giants..................23   (A)

W Dec. 4   30   Packers 0   (H)
L Dec. 11 27   Rams 53   (A)
                268   339

1950   Won 3, Lost 9

Head Coach–Herman Ball

W Sept. 17 38   Colts 14   (A)
L Sept. 24 21   Packers 35   (A)
L Oct. 1   7   Steelers 26   (H)
L Oct. 8   17   Giants..................21   (H)
L Oct. 22 28   Cardinals.............38   (H)
L Oct. 29   3   Eagles 35   (A)
L Nov. 5   21   Giants..................24   (A)
L Nov. 12   0   Eagles 33   (H)
L Nov. 19 14   Browns 20   (A)
W Nov. 26 38   Colts 28   (H)
W Dec. 3   24   Steelers 7   (A)
L Dec. 10 21   Browns 45   (H)
                232   326

1951   Won 5, Lost 7

Head Coach–Herman Ball (3 games)
Head Coach–Dick Todd

L Sept. 30 17   Lions 35   (A)
L Oct. 7   14   Giants..................35   (H)
L Oct. 14   0   Browns 45   (A)
W Oct. 21   7   Cardinals..............3   (H)
W Oct. 28 27   Eagles 23   (A)
L Nov. 4   0   Bears 27   (H)
L Nov. 11 14   Giants..................28   (A)
W Nov. 18 22   Steelers 7   (A)
W Nov. 25 31   Rams 21   (H)
L Dec. 2   21   Eagles 35   (H)
W Dec. 9   20   Cardinals.............17   (A)
L Dec. 16 10   Steelers 20   (H)
                183   296

1952   Won 4, Lost 8

Head Coach–Earl "Curly" Lambeau

W Sept. 28 23   Cardinals..............7   (A)
L Oct. 5   20   Packers 35   (A)
L Oct. 12   6   Cardinals.............17   (H)
W Oct. 19 28   Steelers 24   (A)
L Oct. 26 15   Browns 19   (A)
L Nov. 2   23   Steelers 24   (H)
L Nov. 9   20   Eagles 38   (A)
L Nov. 16 17   49ers 23   (H)
W Nov. 23 10   Giants..................14   (H)
L Nov. 30 24   Browns 48   (H)
W Dec. 7   27   Giants..................17   (A)
W Dec. 14 27   Eagles 21   (H)
                240   287

1953   Won 6, Lost 5, Tied 1

Head Coach–Earl "Curly" Lambeau

W Sept. 27 24   Cardinals.............13   (A)
T Oct. 2   21   Eagles 21   (A)
W Oct. 11 13   Giants....................9   (H)
L Oct. 18 14   Browns 30   (H)
L Oct. 25 17   Colts 27   (A)

L　Nov. 1　3　Browns.............27　(A)
W　Nov. 8　28　Cardinals...........17　(H)
L　Nov. 15　24　Bears ....27　(H)
W　Nov. 22　24　Giants............21　(A)
W　Nov. 29　17　Steelers.............9　(A)
W　Dec. 6　10　Eagles.............0　(H)
L　Dec. 13　13　Steelers............14　(H)
　　　　208　　　　215

1954　Won 3, Lost 9

Head Coach–Joe Kuharich

L　Sept. 26　7　49ers.............41　(A)
L　Oct. 2　7　Steelers............37　(A)
L　Oct. 10　21　Giants.............51　(H)
L　Oct. 17　21　Eagles............49　(H)
L　Oct. 24　7　Giants.............24　(A)
W　Oct. 31　24　Colts.............21　(H)
L　Nov. 7　3　Browns.............62　(A)
W　Nov. 14　17　Steelers............14　(H)
L　Nov. 21　16　Cardinals...........38　(A)
L　Nov. 28　33　Eagles............41　(A)
L　Dec. 5　14　Browns.............34　(H)
W　Dec. 12　37　Cardinals...........20　(H)
　　　　207　　　　432

1955　Won 8, Lost 4

Head Coach–Joe Kuharich

W　Sept. 25　27　Browns.............17　(A)
W　Oct. 1　31　Eagles............30　(A)
L　Oct. 9　10　Cardinals...........24　(H)
L　Oct. 16　14　Browns.............24　(H)
W　Oct. 23　14　Colts.............13　(A)
L　Oct. 30　7　Giants.............35　(A)
W　Nov. 6　34　Eagles............21　(H)
W　Nov. 13　7　49ers.............0　(A)
W　Nov. 20　31　Cardinals...........0　(A)
W　Nov. 27　23　Steelers............14　(A)
L　Dec. 4　20　Giants.............27　(H)
W　Dec. 11　28　Steelers............17　(H)
　　　　246　　　　222

1956　Won 6, Lost 6

Head Coach–Joe Kuharich

L　Sept. 30　13　Steelers.............30　(A)
L　Oct. 6　9　Eagles.............13　(A)
L　Oct. 14　3　Cardinals...........31　(H)
W　Oct. 21　20　Browns.............9　(H)
W　Oct. 28　17　Cardinals...........14　(A)
W　Nov. 11　18　Lions ....17　(H)
W　Nov. 18　33　Giants.............7　(H)
W　Nov. 25　20　Browns.............17　(A)
L　Dec. 2　14　Giants.............28　(A)
W　Dec. 9　19　Eagles.............17　(H)
L　Dec. 16　0　Steelers.............23　(H)
L　Dec. 23　17　Colts.............19　(A)
　　　　183　　　　225

1957　Won 5, Lost 6, Tied 1

Head Coach–Joe Kuharich

L　Sept. 29　7　Steelers.............28　(A)
W　Oct. 6　37　Cardinals...........14　(A)
L　Oct. 13　20　Giants.............24　(H)
L　Oct. 20　14　Cardinals...........44　(H)
W　Oct. 27　31　Giants.............14　(A)
L　Nov. 3　17　Browns.............21　(A)
L　Nov. 10　17　Colts.............21　(H)
T　Nov. 17　30　Browns.............30　(H)
L　Nov. 24　12　Eagles.............21　(H)
W　Dec. 1　14　Bears ....3　(A)
W　Dec. 8　42　Eagles.............7　(H)
W　Dec. 15　10　Steelers.............3　(H)
　　　　251　　　　230

1958　Won 4, Lost 7, Tied 1

Head Coach–Joe Kuharich

W　Sept. 18　24　Eagles.............14　(A)
L　Oct. 4　10　Cardinals...........37　(A)
L　Oct. 12　14　Giants.............21　(H)
W　Oct. 19　37　Packers.............21　(H)
L　Oct. 26　10　Colts.............35　(A)
L　Nov. 2　16　Steelers.............24　(A)
W　Nov. 9　45　Cardinals...........31　(H)
L　Nov. 16　10　Browns.............20　(H)
L　Nov. 23　0　Giants.............30　(A)
L　Nov. 30　14　Browns.............21　(A)
T　Dec. 7　14　Steelers.............14　(H)
W　Dec. 14　20　Eagles.............0　(H)
　　　　214　　　　268

1959　Won 3, Lost 9

Head Coach–Mike Nixon

L　Sept. 17　21　Cardinals...........49　(A)
W　Oct. 4　23　Steelers.............17　(A)
W　Oct. 11　23　Cardinals...........14　(H)
L　Oct. 18　6　Steelers.............27　(H)
L　Oct. 25　7　Browns.............34　(A)
L　Nov. 1　23　Eagles.............30　(A)
W　Nov. 8　27　Colts.............24　(H)
L　Nov. 15　17　Browns.............31　(H)
L　Nov. 22　0　Packers.............21　(A)
L　Nov. 29　14　Giants.............45　(A)
L　Dec. 6　14　Eagles.............34　(H)
L　Dec. 13　10　Giants.............24　(H)
　　　　185　　　　350

1960　Won 1, Lost 9, Tied 2

Head Coach–Mike Nixon

L　Sept. 25　0　Colts.............20　(A)
W　Oct. 9　26　Cowboys ....14　(H)
T　Oct. 16　24　Giants.............24　(H)
T　Oct. 23　27　Steelers.............27　(A)
L　Oct. 30　10　Browns.............31　(H)
L　Nov. 6　7　Cardinals...........44　(A)
L　Nov. 13　13　Eagles.............19　(A)
L　Nov. 20　14　Cardinals...........26　(H)
L　Nov. 27　10　Steelers.............22　(A)
L　Dec. 4　16　Browns.............27　(A)
L　Dec. 11　3　Giants.............17　(H)
L　Dec. 18　28　Eagles.............38　(H)
　　　　178　　　　309

1961　Won1, Lost 12, Tied 1

Head Coach–Bill McPeak

L　Sept. 17　3　49ers.............35　(A)
L　Sept. 24　7　Eagles ....14　(A)
L　Oct. 1　21　Giants.............24　(H)
L　Oct. 8　7　Browns.............31　(A)
L　Oct. 15　0　Steelers.............20　(A)
L　Oct. 22　0　Cardinals...........24　(H)
L　Oct. 29　24　Eagles.............27　(H)
L　Nov. 5　0　Giants.............53　(A)
L　Nov. 12　6　Browns.............17　(H)
T　Nov. 19　28　Cowboys.............28　(A)
L　Nov. 26　6　Colts.............27　(H)
L　Dec. 3　24　Cardinals...........38　(A)
L　Dec. 10　14　Steelers.............30　(H)
W　Dec. 17　34　Cowboys.............24　(H)
　　　　174　　　　392

1962　Won 5, Lost 7, Tied 2

Head Coach–Bill McPeak

T　Sept. 16　35　Cowboys ....35　(A)
W　Sept. 23　17　Browns.............16　(A)
W　Sept. 30　24　Cardinals...........14　(H)
W　Oct. 8　20　Rams ....14　(H)
T　Oct. 14　17　Cardinals...........17　(A)
W　Oct. 21　27　Eagles.............21　(A)
L　Oct. 28　34　Giants.............49　(A)
L　Nov. 4　10　Cowboys.............38　(H)
W　Nov. 11　17　Browns.............9　(H)
L　Nov. 18　21　Steelers.............23　(A)
L　Nov. 25　24　Giants.............42　(H)
L　Dec. 2　14　Eagles.............37　(H)
L　Dec. 8　21　Colts.............34　(A)
L　Dec. 15　24　Steelers.............27　(H)
　　　　305　　　　376

1963　Won 3, Lost 11

Head Coach–Bill McPeak

L　Sept. 15　14　Browns.............37　(A)
W　Sept. 21　37　Rams ....14　(A)
W　Sept. 29　21　Cowboys ....17　(H)
L　Oct. 6　14　Giants.............24　(H)
L　Oct. 13　24　Eagles.............37　(H)
L　Oct. 20　27　Steelers.............38　(A)
L　Oct. 27　7　Cardinals...........21　(H)
L　Nov. 3　20　Cowboys.............35　(A)
L　Nov. 10　20　Cardinals...........24　(A)
L　Nov. 17　28　Steelers.............34　(H)
W　Nov. 24　13　Eagles.............10　(A)
L　Dec. 1　20　Colts.............36　(H)
L　Dec. 8　14　Giants.............44　(A)
L　Dec. 15　20　Browns.............27　(H)
　　　　279　　　　398

1964
Won 6, Lost 8

Head Coach–Bill McPeak

L	Sept. 13	13	Browns..............27	(H)
L	Sept. 20	18	Cowboys 24	(A)
L	Sept. 25	10	Giants................13	(A)
L	Oct. 4	17	Cardinals...........23	(H)
W	Oct. 11	35	Eagles 20	(H)
L	Oct. 18	24	Cardinals...........38	(A)
W	Oct. 25	27	Bears 20	(H)
W	Nov. 1	21	Eagles 10	(A)
L	Nov. 8	24	Browns..............34	(A)
W	Nov. 15	30	Steelers 0	(A)
W	Nov. 22	28	Cowboys 16	(H)
W	Nov. 29	36	Giants................21	(H)
L	Dec. 6	7	Steelers 14	(H)
L	Dec. 13	17	Colts.................45	(A)
		307	305	

1965
Won 6, Lost 8

Head Coach–Bill McPeak

L	Sept. 19	7	Browns..............17	(H)
L	Sept. 26	7	Cowboys 27	(A)
L	Oct. 3	10	Lions 14	(A)
L	Oct. 10	16	Cardinals...........37	(H)
L	Oct. 17	7	Colts.................38	(H)
W	Oct. 24	24	Cardinals...........20	(A)
W	Oct. 31	23	Eagles 21	(H)
W	Nov. 7	23	Giants..................7	(A)
L	Nov. 14	14	Eagles 21	(A)
W	Nov. 21	31	Steelers 3	(A)
W	Nov. 28	34	Cowboys 31	(H)
L	Dec. 5	16	Browns..............24	(A)
L	Dec. 12	10	Giants................27	(H)
W	Dec. 19	35	Steelers 14	(H)
		257	301	

1966
Won 7, Lost 7

Head Coach–Otto Graham

L	Sept. 11	14	Browns..............38	(H)
L	Sept. 18	7	Cardinals...........23	(A)
W	Sept. 25	33	Steelers 27	(A)
W	Oct. 2	24	Steelers 10	(H)
W	Oc.t 9	33	Falcons..............20	(A)
L	Oct. 16	10	Giants................13	(A)
W	Oct. 23	26	Cardinals...........20	(H)
W	Oct. 30	27	Eagles 13	(A)
L	Nov. 6	10	Colts.................37	(A)
L	Nov. 13	30	Cowboys 31	(H)
L	Nov. 20	3	Browns..............14	(A)
W	Nov. 27	72	Giants................41	(H)
W	Dec. 11	34	Cowboys 31	(A)
L	Dec. 18	28	Eagles 37	(H)
		351	355	

1967
Won 5, Lost 6, Tied 3

Head Coach–Otto Graham

L	Sept. 17	24	Eagles 35	(A)
W	Sept. 24	30	Saints.................10	(A)
W	Oct. 1	38	Giants................34	(H)
L	Oct. 8	14	Cowboys 17	(H)
T	Oct. 15	20	Falcons..............20	(A)
T	Oct. 22	28	Rams 28	(A)
L	Oct. 29	13	Colts.................17	(H)
L	Nov. 5	21	Cardinals...........27	(H)
W	Nov. 12	31	49ers.................28	(H)
W	Nov. 19	27	Cowboys 20	(A)
L	Nov. 26	37	Browns..............42	(A)
T	Dec. 3	35	Eagles 35	(H)
W	Dec. 10	15	Steelers 10	(A)
L	Dec. 17	14	Saints................30	(H)
		347	353	

1968
Won 5, Lost 9

Head Coach–Otto Graham

W	Sept. 15	38	Bears 28	(A)
L	Sept. 22	17	Saints................37	(A)
L	Sept. 29	21	Giants................48	(A)
W	Oct. 6	17	Eagles 14	(H)
W	Oct. 13	16	Steelers 13	(H)
L	Oct. 20	14	Cardinals...........41	(A)
L	Oct. 27	10	Giants................13	(H)
L	Nov. 3	14	Vikings..............27	(A)
W	Nov. 10	16	Eagles 10	(A)
L	Nov. 17	24	Cowboys 44	(H)
L	Nov. 24	7	Packers..............27	(H)
L	Nov. 28	20	Cowboys 29	(A)
L	Dec. 8	21	Browns..............24	(H)
W	Dec. 15	14	Lions 3	(H)
		249	358	

1969
Won 7, Lost 5, Tied 2

Head Coach–Vince Lombardi

W	Sept. 21	26	Saints................20	(A)
L	Sept. 28	23	Browns..............27	(A)
T	Oct. 5	17	49ers.................17	(A)
W	Oct. 12	33	Cardinals...........17	(H)
W	Oct. 19	20	Giants................14	(H)
W	Oct. 26	14	Steelers 7	(A)
L	Nov. 2	17	Colts.................41	(A)
T	Nov. 9	28	Eagles 28	(H)
L	Nov. 16	28	Cowboys 41	(H)
W	Nov. 23	27	Falcons..............20	(H)

(Washington Redskins)

L	Nov. 30	13	Rams 24	(H)
W	Dec. 7	34	Eagles 29	(A)
W	Dec. 14	17	Saints................14	(H)
L	Dec. 21	10	Cowboys 20	(A)
		307	319	

1970
Won 6, Lost 8

Head Coach – Bill Austin

Sept 20	L	17–26	at San Francisco
Sept 27	L	17–27	at St. Louis
Oct 4	W	33–21	at Philadelphia
Oct 11	W	31–10	Detroit
Oct 19	L	20–34	at Oakland
Oct 25	W	20–0	Cincinnati
Nov 1	W	19–3	at Denver
Nov 8	L	10–19	Minnesota
Nov 15	L	33–35	at New York Giants
Nov 22	L	21–45	Dallas
Nov 29	L	24–27	New York Giants
Dec 6	L	0–34	at Dallas
Dec 13	W	24–6	Philadelphia
Dec 20	W	28–27	St. Louis

1971
Won 9, Lost 4, Tie 1

Head Coach – George Allen

Sept 19	W	24–17	at St. Louis
Sept 26	W	30–3	at New York Giants
Oct 3	W	20–16	at Dallas
Oct 10	W	22–13	Houston
Oct 17	W	20–0	St. Louis
Oct 24	L	20–27	at Kansas City
Oct 31	W	24–14	New Orleans
Nov 7	T	7–7	Philadelphia
Nov 14	L	15–16	at Chicago
Nov 21	L	0–13	Dallas
Nov 28	W	20–13	at Philadelphia
Dec 5	W	23–7	New York Giants
Dec 13	W	38–24	at Los Angeles
Dec 19	L	13–20	Cleveland

Playoffs

Dec 26	L	20–24	at San Francisco

1972   Won 11, Lost 3

Head Coach – George Allen

Sept 18	W	24–21	at Minnesota
Sept 24	W	24–10	St. Louis
Oct 1	L	23–24	at New England
Oct 8	W	14–0	Philadelphia
Oct 15	W	33–3	at St. Louis
Oct 22	W	24–20	Dallas
Oct 29	W	23–16	at New York Giants
Nov 5	W	35–17	at New York Jets
Nov 12	W	27–13	New York Giants
Nov 20	W	24–13	Atlanta
Nov 26	W	21–16	Green Bay
Dec 3	W	23–7	at Philadelphia
Dec 9	L	24–34	at Dallas
Dec 17	L	17–24	Buffalo

Playoffs

Dec 24	W	16–3	Green Bay
Dec 31	W	26–3	Dallas

Super Bowl VII, Los Angeles, CA

Jan 14	L	7–14	Miami

1973   Won 10, Lost 4

Head Coach – George Allen

Sept 16	W	38–0	San Diego
Sept 23	L	27–34	at St. Louis
Sept 30	W	28–7	at Philadelphia
Oct 8	W	14–7	Dallas
Oct 14	W	21–3	at New York Giants
Oct 21	W	31–13	St. Louis
Oct 28	L	3–19	at New Orleans
Nov 5	L	16–21	at Pittsburgh
Nov 11	W	33–9	San Francisco
Nov 18	W	22–14	Baltimore
Nov 22	W	20–0	at Detroit
Dec 2	W	27–24	New York Giants
Dec 9	L	7–27	at Dallas
Dec 16	W	38–20	Philadelphia

Playoffs

Dec 22	L	20–27	at Minnesota

1974   Won 10, Lost 4

Head Coach – George Allen

Sept 15	W	13–10	at New York Giants
Sept 22	L	10–17	St. Louis
Sept 30	W	30–3	Denver
Oct 6	L	17–28	at Cincinnati
Oct 13	W	20–17	Miami
Oct 20	W	24–3	New York Giants
Oct 27	L	20–23	at St. Louis
Nov 3	W	17–6	at Green Bay
Nov 10	W	27–20	at Philadelphia
Nov 17	W	28–21	Dallas
Nov 24	W	26–7	Philadelphia
Nov 28	L	23–24	at Dallas
Dec 9	W	23–17	at Los Angeles
Dec 15	W	42–0	Chicago

Playoffs

Dec 22	L	10–19	at Los Angeles

1975   Won 8, Lost 6

Head Coach – George Allen

Sept 21	W	41–3	New Orleans
Sept 28	W	49–13	New York Giants
Oct 5	L	10–26	at Philadelphia
Oct 13	W	27–17	St. Louis
Oct 19	L	10–13	at Houston
Oct 26	W	23–7	at Cleveland
Nov 2	W	30–24	* Dallas
Nov 9	W	21–13	at New York Giants
Nov 16	L	17–20	* at St. Louis
Nov 23	L	23–26	* Oakland
Nov 30	W	31–30	Minnesota
Dec 7	W	30–27	at Atlanta
Dec 13	L	10–31	at Dallas
Dec 21	L	3–26	Philadelphia

* overtime

1976   Won 10, Lost 4

Head Coach – George Allen

Sept 12	W	19–17	New York Giants
Sept 19	W	31–7	Seattle
Sept 27	W	20–17	* at Philadelphia
Oct 3	L	7–33	at Chicago
Oct 10	L	30–33	Kansas City
Oct 17	W	20–7	Detroit
Oct 25	W	20–10	St. Louis
Oct 31	L	7–20	Dallas
Nov 7	W	24–21	at San Francisco
Nov 14	L	9–12	at New York Giants
Nov 21	W	16–10	at St. Louis
Nov 28	W	24–0	Philadelphia
Dec 5	W	37–16	at New York Jets
Dec 12	W	27–14	at Dallas

Playoffs

Dec 18	L	20–35	at Minnesota

1977   Won 9, Lost 5

Head Coach –George Allen

Sept 18	L	17–20	at New York Giants
Sept 25	W	10–6	Atlanta
Oct 2	W	24–14	St. Louis
Oct 9	W	10–0	at Tampa Bay
Oct 16	L	16–34	at Dallas
Oct 23	L	6–17	New York Giants
Oct 30	W	23–17	Philadelphia
Nov 7	L	3–10	at Baltimore
Nov 13	W	17–14	at Philadelphia
Nov 21	W	10–9	Green Bay
Nov 27	L	7–14	Dallas
Dec 4	W	10–0	at Buffalo
Dec 10	W	26–20	at St. Louis
Dec 17	W	17–14	Los Angeles Rams

1978   Won 8, Lost 8

Head Coach – Jack Pardee

Sept 3	W	16–14	at New England
Sept 10	W	35–30	Philadelphia
Sept 17	W	28–10	at St. Louis
Sept 24	W	23–3	New York Jets
Oct 2	W	9–5	Dallas
Oct 8	W	21–19	at Detroit
Oct 15	L	10–17	at Philadelphia
Oct 22	L	6–17	at New York Giants
Oct 29	W	38–20	San Francisco
Nov 6	L	17–21	at Baltimore
Nov 12	W	16–13	* New York Giants
Nov 19	L	17–27	St. Louis
Nov 23	L	10–37	at Dallas
Dec 3	L	0–16	Miami
Dec 10	L	17–20	at Atlanta
Dec 16	L	10–14	Chicago

* overtime

1979   Won 10, Lost 6

Head Coach – Jack Pardee

Sept 2	L	27–29	Houston
Sept 9	W	27–24	at Detroit
Sept 17	W	27–0	New York Giants
Sept 23	W	17–7	at St. Louis
Sept 30	W	16–7	at Atlanta
Oct 7	L	17–28	at Philadelphia
Oct 14	W	13–9	at Cleveland
Oct 21	W	17–7	Philadelphia
Oct 28	L	10–14	New Orleans
Nov 4	L	7–38	at Pittsburgh
Nov 11	W	30–28	St. Louis
Nov 18	W	34–20	Dallas
Nov 25	L	6–14	at New York Giants
Dec 2	W	38–21	Green Bay
Dec 9	W	28–14	Cincinnati
Dec 16	L	34–35	at Dallas

1980   Won 6, Lost 10

Head Coach – Jack Pardee

Sept 8	L	3–17	Dallas
Sept 14	W	23–21	at New York Giants
Sept 21	L	21–24	at Oakland
Sept 28	L	0–14	Seattle
Oct 5	L	14–24	at Philadelphia
Oct 13	L	17–20	at Denver
Oct 19	W	23–0	St. Louis
Oct 26	W	22–14	New Orleans
Nov 2	L	14–39	Minnesota
Nov 9	L	21–35	at Chicago
Nov 15	L	0–24	Philadelphia
Nov 23	L	10–14	at Dallas
Nov 30	L	6–10	at Atlanta
Dec 7	W	40–17	San Diego
Dec 13	W	16–13	New York Giants
Dec 21	W	31–7	at St. Louis

1981   Won 8, Lost 8

Head Coach – Joe Gibbs

Sept 6	L	10–26	Dallas
Sept 13	L	7–17	New York Giants
Sept 20	L	30–40	at St. Louis Cardinals
Sept 27	L	13–36	at Philadelphia
Oct 4	L	17–30	San Francisco
Oct 11	W	24–7	at Chicago
Oct 18	L	10–13	at Miami
Oct 25	W	24–22	New England
Nov 1	W	42–21	St. Louis

Nov 8	W	33–31	Detroit
Nov 15	W	30–27	* at New York Giants
Nov 22	L	10–24	at Dallas
Nov 29	L	14–21	at Buffalo
Dec 6	W	15–13	Philadelphia
Dec 13	W	38–14	Baltimore Colts
Dec 20	W	30–7	at Los Angeles Rams

* overtime

1982   Won 8, Lost 1

Head Coach – Joe Gibbs

Sept 12	W	37–34	* at Philadelphia
Sept 19	W	21–13	at Buccaneers
Nov 21	W	27–17	at New York Giants
Nov 28	W	13–9	Philadelphia
Dec 5	L	10–24	Dallas
Dec 12	W	12–7	at St. Louis
Dec 19	W	15–14	New York Giants
Dec 26	W	27–10	at New Orleans
Jan 2	W	28–0	St. Louis

DNP: (Home): Cleveland, Pittsburgh, San Francisco, Minnesota; (Away): Dallas, Houston, Cincinnati.

* overtime

Playoffs

Jan 8	W	31–7	Detroit
Jan 15	W	21–7	Minnesota
Jan 22	W	31–17	Dallas

Super Bowl XVII, Pasadena, CA

Jan 30	W	27–17	Miami

1983   Won 14, Lost 2

Head Coach – Joe Gibbs

Sept 5	L	30–31	Dallas
Sept 11	W	23–13	at Philadelphia
Sept 18	W	27–12	Kansas City
Sept 25	W	27–17	at Seattle
Oct 2	W	37–35	Los Angeles Raiders
Oct 9	W	38–14	at St. Louis
Oct 17	L	47–48	at Green Bay
Oct 23	W	38–17	Detroit
Oct 31	W	27–24	at San Diego
Nov 6	W	45–7	St. Louis
Nov 13	W	33–17	at New York Giants
Nov 20	W	42–20	at Los Angeles Rams
Nov 27	W	28–24	Philadelphia
Dec 4	W	37–21	Atlanta Falcons
Dec 11	W	31–10	at Dallas
Dec 17	W	31–22	New York Giants

Playoffs

Jan 1	W	51–7	Los Angeles Rams
Jan 8	W	24–21	San Francisco

Super Bowl XVIII, Tampa, FL

Jan 22	L	9–38	Los Angeles Raiders

1984   Won 11, Lost 5

Head Coach – Joe Gibbs

Sept 2	L	17–35	Miami
Sept 10	L	31–37	at San Francisco
Sept 16	W	30–14	New York Giants

Sept 23	W	26–10	at New England
Sept 30	W	20–0	Philadelphia
Oct 7	W	35–7	at Indianapolis
Oct 14	W	34–14	Dallas
Oct 21	L	24–26	at St. Louis
Oct 28	L	13–37	at New York Giants
Nov 5	W	27–14	Atlanta
Nov 11	W	28–14	Detroit
Nov 18	L	10–16	at Philadelphia
Nov 25	W	41–14	Buffalo
Nov 29	W	31–17	at Minnesota
Dec 9	W	30–28	at Dallas
Dec 16	W	29–27	St. Louis

Playoffs

Dec 30	L	19–23	Chicago

1985   Won 10, Lost 6

Head Coach – Joe Gibbs

Sept 9	L	14–44	at Dallas
Sept 15	W	16–13	Houston
Sept 22	L	6–19	Philadelphia
Sept 29	L	10–45	at Chicago
Oct 7	W	27–10	St. Louis
Oct 13	W	24–3	Detroit
Oct 20	L	3–17	at New York Giants
Oct 27	W	14–7	at Cleveland
Nov 3	W	44–10	at Atlanta
Nov 10	L	7–13	Dallas
Nov 18	W	23–21	New York
Nov 24	W	30–23	at Pittsburgh
Dec 1	L	8–35	San Francisco
Dec 8	W	17–12	at Philadelphia
Dec 15	W	27–24	Cincinnati
Dec 21	W	27–16	at St. Louis

1986   Won 12, Lost 4

Head Coach – Joe Gibbs

Sept 7	W	41–14	Philadelphia
Sept 14	W	10–6	LA Raiders
Sept 21	W	30–27	at San Diego
Sept 28	W	19–14	Seattle
Oct 5	W	14–6	at New Orleans
Oct 12	L	6–30	at Dallas
Oct 19	W	28–21	St. Louis
Oct 27	L	20–27	at New York Giants
Nov 2	W	44–38	* Minnesota
Nov 9	W	16–7	at Green Bay
Nov 17	W	14–6	San Francisco
Nov 23	W	41–14	Dallas
Nov 30	W	20–17	at St. Louis
Dec 7	L	14–24	New York Giants
Dec 13	L	30–31	at Denver
Dec 21	W	21–14	at Philadelphia

Playoffs

Dec 28	W	19–7	Los Angeles Rams
Jan 3	W	27–13	at Chicago
Jan 11	L	0–17	at New York Giants

1987   Won 11, Lost 4

Head Coach – Joe Gibbs

Sept 13	W	34–24	Philadelphia
Sept 20	L	20–21	at Atlanta
Sept. 27			New England
Oct 4	W	28–21	St. Louis
Oct 11	W	38–12	at New York Giants
Oct 19	W	13–7	at Dallas
Oct 25	W	17–16	New York Jets
Nov 1	W	27–7	at Buffalo
Nov 8	L	27–31	at Philadelphia
Nov 15	W	20–13	Detroit
Nov 23	L	26–30	Los Angeles Rams
Nov 29	W	23–19	New York Giants
Dec 6	W	34–17	at St. Louis
Dec 13	W	24–20	Dallas
Dec 20	L	21–23	at Miami
Dec 26	W	27–24	* at Minnesota

* overtime

Playoffs

Jan 10	W	21–17	at Chicago
Jan 17	W	17–10	Minnesota

Super Bowl XXII, San Diego, CA

Jan 31	W	42–10	Denver

1988   Won 7, Lost 9

Head Coach – Joe Gibbs

Sept 5	L	20–27	at Giants
Sept 11	W	30–29	Pittsburgh
Sept 18	W	17–10	Philadelphia
Sept 25	L	21–30	at Phoenix
Oct 2	L	23–24	Giants
Oct 9	W	35–17	at Dallas
Oct 16	W	33–17	Phoenix
Oct 23	W	20–17	at Green Bay
Oct 30	L	17–41	at Houston
Nov 6	W	27–24	New Orleans
Nov 13	L	14–34	Chicago
Nov 21	L	21–37	at San Francisco
Nov 27	L	13–17	Cleveland
Dec 4	W	20–19	at Philadelphia
Dec 11	L	17–24	Dallas
Dec 17	L	17–20	* at Cincinnati

* overtime

1989   Won 10, Lost 6

Head Coach – Joe Gibbs

Sept 11	L	24–27	New York Giants
Sept 17	L	37–42	Philadelphia
Sept 24	W	30–7	at Dallas
Oct 1	W	16–14	at New Orleans
Oct 8	W	30–28	Phoenix
Oct 15	L	17–20	at New York Giants
Oct 22	W	32–28	Tampa Bay
Oct 29	L	24–37	at Los Angeles Raiders
Nov 5	L	3–13	Dallas
Nov 12	W	10–3	at Philadelphia
Nov 20	L	10–14	Denver
Nov 26	W	38–14	Chicago
Dec 3	W	29–10	at Phoenix
Dec 10	W	26–21	San Diego

(Nate Fine)

Dec 17	W	31–30	at Atlanta
Dec 23	W	29–0	at Seattle

1990　　　Won 10, Lost 6

Head Coach – Joe Gibbs

Sept 9	W	31–0	Phoenix
Sept 16	L	13–26	at San Francisco
Sept 23	W	19–15	Dallas
Sept 30	W	38–10	at Phoenix
Oct 14	L	20–24	Giants
Oct 21	W	13–7	Philadelphia
Oct 28	L	10–21	at Giants
Nov 4	W	41–38	* at Detroit
Nov 12	L	14–28	at Philadelphia
Nov 18	W	31–17	New Orleans
Nov 22	L	17–27	at Dallas
Dec 2	W	42–20	Miami
Dec 9	W	10–9	Chicago
Dec 15	W	25–10	at New England
Dec 22	L	28–35	at Indianapolis
Dec 30	W	29–14	Buffalo

*overtime

Playoffs

Jan 4	W	20–6	at Philadelphia
Jan 12	L	10–28	at San Francisco

1991　　　Won 14, Lost 2

Head Coach – Joe Gibbs

Sept 1	W	45–0	Detroit
Sept 9	W	33–31	at Dallas
Sept 15	W	34–0	Phoenix
Sept 22	W	34–27	at Cincinnati
Sept 30	W	23–0	Philadelphia
Oct 6	W	20–7	at Chicago
Oct 13	W	42–17	Cleveland
Oct 27	W	17–13	at Giants
Nov 3	W	16–13	* Houston
Nov 10	W	56–17	Atlanta
Nov 17	W	41–14	at Pittsburgh
Nov 24	L	21–24	Dallas
Dec 1	W	27–6	at Rams
Dec 8	W	20–14	at Phoenix

Dec 15	W	34–17	Giants
Dec 22	L	22–24	at Philadelphia

Playoffs

Jan 4	W	24–7	Atlanta
Jan 12	W	41–10	Detroit

Super Bowl XXVI, Minneapolis, MN

Jan 26	W	37–24	Buffalo

1992　　　Won 9, Lost 7

Head Coach – Joe Gibbs

Sept 7	L	10–23	at Dallas
Sept 13	W	24–17	Atlanta
Sept 20	W	13–10	Detroit
Oct 4	L	24–17	at Phoenix
Oct 12	W	34–3	Denver
Oct 18	W	16–12	Philadelphia
Oct 25	W	15–13	at Minnesota
Nov 1	L	7–24	New York Giants
Nov 8	W	16–3	at Seattle
Nov 15	L	15–35	at Kansas City
Nov 23	L	3–20	at New Orleans
Nov 29	W	41–3	Phoenix
Dec 6	W	28–10	at New York Giants
Dec 13	W	20–17	Dallas
Dec 20	L	13–17	at Philadelphia
Dec 26	L	20–21	Los Angeles Raiders

Playoffs

Jan 2	W	24–7	at Minnesota
Jan 9	L	13–20	at San Francisco

1993　　　Won 4, Lost 12

Head Coach – Richie Petitbon

Sept 6	W	35–16	Dallas
Sept 12	L	10–17	Phoenix
Sept 19	L	31–34	at Philadelphia
Oct 4	L	10–17	at Miami
Oct 10	L	7–41	New York Giants
Oct 17	L	6–36	at Phoenix
Nov 1	L	10–24	at Buffalo
Nov 7	W	30–24	Indianapolis

Nov 14	L	6–20	at New York Giants
Nov 21	L	6–10	at L.A. Rams
Nov 28	L	14–17	Philadelphia
Dec 5	W	23–17	at Tampa Bay
Dec 11	L	0–3	New York Jets
Dec 19	W	30–17	Atlanta
Dec 26	L	3–38	at Dallas
Dec 31	L	9–14	Minnesota

1994　　　Won 3, Lost 13

Head Coach – Norv Turner

Sept. 4	L	7–28	Seattle
Sept. 11	W	38–24	at New Orleans
Sept. 18	L	23–31	at New York Giants
Sept. 25	L	20–27	Atlanta
Oct. 2	L	7–34	Dallas
Oct. 9	L	17–21	at Philadelphia
Oct. 16	L	16–19	* Arizona
Oct. 23	W	41–27	Indianapolis
Oct. 30	L	29–31	Philadelphia
Nov. 6	L	22–37	San Francisco
Nov. 20	L	7–31	at Dallas
Nov. 27	L	19–21	New York Giants
Dec. 4	L	21–26	at Tampa Bay
Dec. 11	L	15–17	at Arizona
Dec. 18	L	14–17	Tampa Bay
Dec. 24	W	24–21	at L.A. Rams

* Overtime

1995　　　Won 6, Lost 10

Head Coach – Norv Turner

Sept. 3	W	27–7	Arizona
Sept. 10	L	8–20	Oakland
Sept. 17	L	31–38	at Denver
Sept. 24	L	6–14	at Tampa Bay
Oct. 1	W	27–23	Dallas
Oct. 8	L	34–37	* at Philadelphia
Oct. 15	L	20–24	at Arizona
Oct. 22	W	36–30	* Detroit
Oct. 29	L	15–24	NYGiants
Nov. 5	L	3–24	at Kansas City
Nov. 19	L	20–27	Seattle
Nov. 26	L	7–14	Philadelphia
Dec. 3	W	24–17	at Dallas
Dec. 10	L	13–20	at NYGiants
Dec. 17	W	35–23	at St. Louis
Dec. 24	W	20–17	Carolina

* Overtime

TEAM RECORDS

SCORING

Most Points, Season

* 541	1983
485	1991
426	1984
386	1989
381	1990
379	1987

*NFL Record

Fewest Points, Season

55	1932

Most Points, Game

72	vs Giants (41)	11/27/66
59	vs Yanks (21)	10/31/48
56	vs Falcons (17)	11/10/91
49	@ Giants (14)	12/05/37
49	vs Giants (13)	09/28/75

Most Points, One Half

38	vs Giants	11/27/66
35	vs Lions	09/01/91

Most Points, One Quarter

24	vs Giants	11/27/66

Most Points, Both Teams, Game

* 113	Redskins, 72 vs Giants, 41	11/27/66
95	Redskins, 47 @ Packers, 48	10/17/83
87	Redskins, 42 @ Eagles, 45	09/28/47

*NFL Record

Fewest Points, Both Teams, Game

0 ...... 4 times

Most TDs, Season

63	1983
56	1991
51	1984
47	1987
47	1967

Fewest TDs, Season

6	1932

Most TDs, Game

* 10	vs Giants	11/27/66
8	vs Falcons	11/10/91
8	vs Yanks	10/31/48

*NFL Record

Most TDs, Both Teams, Game

* 16	Redskins, 10 vs Giants, 6	11/27/66
12	Redskins, 6 @ Eagles, 6	09/28/47
11	Redskins, 5 vs Eagles, 6	09/17/89

*NFL Record

Most PATs, Season

62	1983
56	1991
48	1984
43	1987
42	1967

Most PATs, Game

9	vs Giants	11/27/66
8	vs Falcons	11/10/91
8	vs Yanks	10/31/48

Most PATs, Both Teams, Game

* 14	Redskins, 9 vs Giants, 5	11/27/66

*NFL Record

Most FG Attempts, Season

* 49	1971
47	1983
43	1991
42	1973

* NFL Record

Fewest FG Attempts, Season

5	1940

Most FGs, Season

33	1983
31	1991
30	1992
30	1990
29	1971
29	1989

Fewest FGs, Season

0	1935

Most FGs, Game

5 .... 7 times
Most recently ...... @ Vikings 10/25/92

Most FG Attempts, Game

7	vs Oilers	10/10/71 (5 made)
6	most recently @ Eagles	12/22/91

Most FG Attempts, Both Teams, Game

* 11	Redskins, 6 @ Bears, 5	11/14/71
11	Redskins, 6 @ Giants, 5	11/14/76

* NFL Record

Most FGs, Both Teams, Game

* 8	Redskins, 5 @ Bears, 3	11/14/71

* NFL Record

FIRST DOWNS

Most First Downs, Season

353	(165, 173, 15)	1983
339	(154, 164, 21)	1984
338	(101, 217, 20)	1989
334	(136, 173, 25)	1980

Fewest First Downs, Season

95	1935

Most First Downs, Game

* 39	@ Lions	11/04/90
	(14 rush, 25 pass, 0 pen)	
35	vs Bears	11/26/89
	(9 rush, 22 pass, 4 pen)	
33	@ Packers	10/17/83
	(12 rush, 21 pass, 0 pen)	
33	@ Browns	11/26/67
	(9 rush, 22 pass, 2 pen)	
30	vs 49ers	11/12/67
	(8 rush, 16 pass, 6 pen)	

* NFL Record

Fewest First Downs, Game

...... 4	@ Browns	11/07/54
	(2 rush, 1 pass, 1 pen)	

Most First Downs, Rushing, Season

165	1983
154	1984
147	1985
136	1981

Fewest First Downs, Rushing, Season

55	1943
55	1961

Most First Downs, Passing, Season

217	1989
202	1988
193	1990
179	1991
173	1981
173	1983

Fewest First Downs, Passing, Season

55	1961

Most First Downs, Penalty, Season

29	1987
28	1978
27	1979
26	1947
26	1962

Fewest First Downs, Penalty, Season

4	1944

TOTAL YARDS

Most Yards Gained, Season

6,253	1989
6,139	1983
5,741	1991
5,679	1988
5,623	1981

Fewest Yards Gained, Season

2,015	1935

Most Yards Gained, Game

676	vs Lions	11/04/90
	(194 rush, 482 pass)	
625	vs Yanks	10/31/48
	(124 rush, 501 pass)	

Fewest Yards Gained, Game

64	@ Browns	11/07/54
	(33 rush, 31 pass)	

Most Yards Gained, Both Teams, Game

1,027	Redskins, 676 @ Lions, 351	11/04/90
1,025	Redskins, 552 @ Packers, 473	10/17/83
1,013	Redskins, 487 vs Vikings, 526	11/02/86
988	Redskins, 419 @ Cardinals, 569	09/17/59

Most Total Plays, Season

1,135	1985
1,127	1983
1,121	1984
1,116	1989
1,083	1981

Fewest Total Plays, Season

639	1936

RUSHING

Most Yards Gained, Season

2,625	1983
2,523	1985
2,328	1979
2,274	1984
2,157	1981

Fewest Yards Gained, Season

904	1944

Most Yards Gained, Game

352.............vs Rams 11/25/51
307.............@ Falcons 11/03/85
299.............@ Bills.........................11/01/87
296.............vs Giants.....................12/09/45

Fewest Yards Gained, Game

10.............@ Buccaneers 12/04/94
14.............@ Eagles.......................09/28/47

Most Yards Gained, Both Teams, Game

531 ....Redskins, 255 vs Browns, 276
....11/15/59

Most Attempts, Season

629...1983
609...1979
588...1984
571...1985
548...1976

Fewest Attempts, Season

320...1943

Most Attempts, Game

64 ....vs Rams....................11/25/51

Highest Avg., Season

4.7...1959
4.6...1970
4.4...1943
4.4...1945

Most TDs, Season

30...1983
23...1986
21...1991
20...1984
20...1985

Fewest TDs, Season

4...1977

PASSING

Most Net Yards, Season

4,349...1989
4,136...1988
3,869...1986
3,730...1967
3,692...1991

Fewest Net Yards, Season

752...1935

Fewest Net Yards, Game

−28 ....vs Steelers 12/07/58

Most Net Yards, Game

501.................vs Yanks 10/31/48

Most Net Yards, Both Teams, Game

849........................Redskins, 378; Vikings, 471
....11/02/86
731 ....Redskins, 411; Bears, 320
....10/26/47
711.......................Redskins, 368; Packers, 403
....10/17/83

Most Attempts, Season

592...1988
581...1989
546...1994
542...1986
536...1990

Fewest Attempts, Season

113...1933
152...1934

Most Attempts, Game

63 ....(43 comp) .....@ Lions.............11/04/90
63.........(32) ....@ Raiders...........10/29/89
58.........(30) ....vs 49ers 12/01/85
57.........(33) ....vs Bears.............10/25/64
54..........(26) ....@ Cowboys........11/22/90

Fewest Attempts, Game

7 ....vs Giants............12/11/60

Most Attempts, Both Teams, Game

100 ....Redskins, 40 vs 49ers, 60 ......11/17/86

Most Completions, Season

337...1989
327...1988
307...1981
301...1990
301...1967

Fewest Completions, Season

34...1933
44...1934

Most Completions, Game

43 ....@ Lions 11/04/90
33 ....vs Bears 10/25/64
32 ....@ Browns 11/26/67
32 ....@ Raiders.............10/29/89
32 ....@ Giants 09/18/94

Fewest Completions, Game

0 ....vs Giants.....................12/11/60

Most Completions, Both Teams, Game

57.......Redskins, 20 vs Cardinals, 37...12/16/84
56......Redskins, 43 @ Lions, 13 ...11/04/90
54......Redskins, 17 vs Colts, 37 ...11/07/93
52......Redskins, 22 @ Eagles, 30 ...10/08/95
51......Redskins, 21, vs Lions, 30 ...10/22/95
51......Redskins, 26 vs Bears, 25 ....10/26/47

Highest Completion Pct., Season

64.0 ....(253 atts/162 comp) 1982
64.0 ....(228 atts/146 comp) 1945
61.9 ....(444 atts/275 comp) 1969
61.5 ....(413 atts/254 comp) 1974

Most TD Passes, Season

33...1988
31...1967
30...1991
29...1983
28...1966
28...1947
28...1975

Fewest TD Passes, Season

1...1933

Most TD Passes, Game

6...................vs Falcons......................11/10/91
6...................vs Cardinals 11/23/47
6...................@ Brooklyn 10/31/43

Most Passes Intercepted, Season

34...1963
32...1954

Fewest Passes Intercepted, Season

9...................(253 attempts) 1982
10...............(228 attempts) 1945
10...............(342 attempts) 1970

Most Passes Intercepted, Game

7...................@ Steelers 12/03/50
7...................@ Giants 12/08/63

Most Passes Intercepted, Both Teams, Game

11...........Redskins, 7 @ Giants, 4........12/08/63

SACKS

Most Sacks, Season

66...1984
55...1986
53...1987
53...1973
51...1983

Most Sacks, Game

10.................@ Buccaneers 10/09/77
8...................vs Cowboys 09/23/90

Fewest Times Sacked, Season

9...1991
11...1972
17...1971
19...1967

Most Times Sacked, Season

52...1977
52...1985
48...1984

TURNOVERS/TAKEAWAYS

Most Opponents' Fumbles, Season

46...1983

Most Opponents' Fumbles Recovered, Season

32...1936

Fewest Opponents' Fumbles Recovered, Season

6...1945
6...1994

Most Opponents' Fumbles Recovered, Game

* 8.....................vs Cardinals 10/25/76
* NFL Record

Most Own Fumbles Recovered, Season

26...1940

Fewest Own Fumbles Recovered, Season

* 2...1958
* NFL Record

Most Total Fumbles Recovered, Game

* 10 ....vs Cardinals 10/25/76
* NFL Record

Most Fumbles, Both Teams, Game

13 ....Redskins, 8 @ Steelers, 5 ....11/14/37
13 ....Redskins, 6 @ Giants, 7 ....11/06/60
13 ....Redskins, 4 vs Cardinals, 9......10/25/76

Most TD Fumble Recoveries, Game

* 2 ....vs Chargers 09/16/73
2 ....vs Vikings...................11/29/84
* NFL Record

Most Interceptions, Season

34...1966
34...1983
33...1980

Fewest Interceptions, Season

11...1982
11...1991
13...1959
14...1988

Most Takeaways, Season

61...1983

Fewest Turnovers, Season

    16..1982

    18..1983

Highest Turnover/Takeaway Ratio, Season

    * +43 1983

    * NFL Record

PENALTIES

Most Penalties, Season

    122..1948

    117..1978

114..1980

105..1989

102..1990

Fewest Penalties, Season

    40..1958

Most Penalties, Game

    17 ....@ Steelers 10/10/48

    16 ....vs Yanks...................11/11/45

    16 ....vs Eagles 11/02/47

    16 ....vs Giants 10/03/48

Most Penalty Yards, Season

    1,110...1948

    1,009...1980

    999..1978

    940..1981

Fewest Penalty Yards, Season

    332..1939

Most Penalty Yards, Game

    160..................@ Steelers 10/10/48

    152................vs Giants 10/13/46

    150..................@ Eagles 11/24/46

INDIVIDUAL RECORDS

SCORING

Most Points, Career

    Mark Moseley 1974–86 1,207

    Chip Lohmiller 1988–94 787

    Charley Taylor............1964–77 540

    John Riggins...............1976–79, 81–85 510

    Curt Knight 1969–73 475

    Art Monk 1980–93 390

    Jerry Smith 1965–77 360

    Gary Clark..................1985–92 348

    Hugh Taylor 1947–54 348

    Larry Brown 1969–76 330

    Bobby Mitchell..........1962–68 330

Most Points, Season

    Mark Moseley ....1983.........................161

    Chip Lohmiller ....1991.........................149

    John Riggins..............1983.........................144

    Chip Lohmiller ....1990.........................131

    Chip Lohmiller ....1989.........................128

    Chip Lohmiller ....1992.........................120

    Mark Moseley ....1984.........................120

    Curt Knight...............1971.........................114

    Mark Moseley ....1979.........................114

    George Rogers ....1986.........................108

    Charlie Gogolak........1966.........................105

Most Points, No TDs, Season

    Mark Moseley ....1983.......................*161

    Chip Lohmiller ....1991.........................149

    Chip Lohmiller ....1990.........................131

    Chip Lohmiller ....1989.........................128

    Chip Lohmiller ....1992.........................120

    Mark Moseley ....1984.........................120

    * NFL Record

Most Points, Game

    24...........Dick James vs Cowboys 12/17/61

    ....(4 TDs)

    24...........Larry Brown vs Eagles..........12/16/73

    ....(4 TDs)

    20...........Andy Farkas vs Rams 09/25/38

    ....(3 TDs, 2 PATs)

Most Consecutive Games Scoring

    Chip Lohmiller..92

    .... (1st in 1988–13th in 1993)

    Mark Moseley 91

    ....(12th in 1980–5th in 1986)

    Mark Moseley 70

    ....(1st in 1974–14th in 1978)

Most TDs, Career

    Charley Taylor.............1964–77 90

    John Riggins................1976–79, 81–85 85

    Art Monk 1980–93 65

    Jerry Smith..................1965–77 60

Gary Clark ....1985–92...................58

Hugh Taylor ....1947–54...................58

Larry Brown ....1969–76...................55

Bobby Mitchell ....1962–68...................55

Andy Farkas ....1938–44...................35

Most TDs, Season

    John Riggins ....1983....................24

    George Rogers ....1986....................18

    Charley Taylor ....1966....................15

    Larry Brown ....1973....................14

    John Riggins ....1984....................14

    John Riggins ....1981....................13

Most TDs, Game

    4...........Dick James vs Cowboys 12/17/61

    4...........Larry Brown vs Eagles 12/16/73

Most Consecutive Games TD Scored

    John Riggins ....1982–83...............13

    George Rogers ....1985–86................12

KICKING

Most PATs, Career

    Mark Moseley.................1974–86.......417

    Chip Lohmiller..............1988–94.......262

Most PATs, Season

    Mark Moseley.................1983....................62

    Chip Lohmiller..............1991....................56

    Mark Moseley.................1984....................48

    Chip Lohmiller..............1990....................41

    Chip Lohmiller..............1989....................41

    Curt Knight ....1972....................40

    Chip Lohmiller..............1988....................40

Most PATs, Game

    9 ....Charlie Gogolak vs Giants.......11/27/66

    8 ....Chip Lohmiller vs Falcons.......11/10/91

    8 ....Dick Poillon vs Yanks...............10/31/48

Most PAT Attempts, Career

    Mark Moseley.................1974–86.......442

    Chip Lohmiller..............1988–94.......267

    Curt Knight ....1969–73.......176

Most PAT Attempts, Season

    Mark Moseley.................1983....................63

    Chip Lohmiller..............1991....................56

    Mark Moseley.................1984....................51

    Charlie Gogolak ....1966....................42

    Curt Knight ....1972....................42

    Mark Moseley.................1981....................42

Most PAT Attempts, Game

    10 ....Charlie Gogolak vs Giants.......11/27/66

Most Consecutive PATs, Career

    Chip Lohmiller..............1988–93................213

Most FGs, Career

    Mark Moseley................1974–86.................263

    Chip Lohmiller..............1988–94.................175

    Curt Knight ....1969–73.................101

    Sam Baker.....................1953, 56–59...........54

    Bob Khayat ....1960, 62–63...........38

Most FGs, Season

    Mark Moseley................1983........................33

    Chip Lohmiller..............1991........................31

    Chip Lohmiller..............1992........................30

    Chip Lohmiller..............1990........................30

    Chip Lohmiller..............1989........................29

    Curt Knight ....1971........................29

Most FGs, Game

    5 ....Chip Lohmiller @ Vikings 10/25/92

    ....(22, 42, 25, 45, 49)

    5 ....Chip Lohmiller @ Eagles 12/22/91

    ....(21, 35, 47, 47, 38, missed 49)

    5 ....Chip Lohmiller vs Bills 12/30/90

    ....(37, 24, 19, 43, 32)

    5 ....Curt Knight vs Oilers...............10/10/71

    ....(15, 36, 13, 17, 39, missed 47, 33)

    5 ....Curt Knight @ Bears................11/14/71

    ....(30, 12, 37, 9, 27, missed 45)

    5 ....Curt Knight vs Colts...............11/18/73

    ....(35, 18, 37, 42, 29)

    5 ......Mark Moseley vs Saints 10/26/80

    ....(50, 28, 35, 52, 38, missed 50)

Most FG Attempts, Career

    Mark Moseley................1974–86.................397

    Chip Lohmiller..............1988–94.................245

    Curt Knight ....1969–73.................175

Most FG Attempts, Season

    Curt Knight ....1971........................49

    Mark Moseley................1983........................47

    Chip Lohmiller..............1991........................43

    Curt Knight ....1973........................42

    Chip Lohmiller..............1992........................40

    Chip Lohmiller..............1990........................40

    Chip Lohmiller..............1989........................40

Most FG Attempts Game

    7 ....Curt Knight vs Oilers...........10/10/71

Most Consecutive FGs

    Mark Moseley................1981–82.................23

Most Consecutive FGs, Season

    Mark Moseley................1982........................20

Most Consecutive Games, FG Made
Chip Lohmiller..............1988–90.................28
Mark Moseley................1976–77.................15

Best FG Pct., Season (20 Atts)
Mark Moseley.................1982.....*.952 (20–21)
Mark Moseley.................1984 ....774 (24–31)
Mark Moseley.................1979 ....759 (25–33)
Chip Lohmiller.................1990 ....750 (30–40)
Chip Lohmiller.................1992 ..... .750 (30–40)
Eddie Murray ....1995 ....750 (27–36)
* NFL Record

Longest Field Goals
57.......Steve Cox vs Seahawks 09/28/86
56.......Chip Lohmiller @ Colts 12/22/90
55.......Chip Lohmiller vs Cowboys 09/23/90
55.......Steve Cox vs Eagles.................09/07/86
54.......Chip Lohmiller vs Eagles 10/30/94
54.......Mark Moseley @ Eagles 11/13/77
53.......Chip Lohmiller vs Lions 09/20/92
53.......Chip Lohmiller vs Cowboys 09/09/91
53.......Chip Lohmiller @ Colts 12/22/90
53.......Mark Moseley @ Falcons 09/30/79
53.......Mark Moseley @ Cowboys.......10/16/77

RUSHING

Most Yards Gained, Career
John Riggins...............1976–79, 81–85.....7,472
Larry Brown ....1969–76.................5,875
Earnest Byner ....1989–93.................3,950
Mike Thomas ....1975–78.................3,360
Don Bosseler ....1957–64.................3,112
Cliff Battles................1933–37.................3,037
George Rogers ....1985–87.................2,909
Charley Harraway ......1969–73.................2,659
Rob Goode ....1949–51, 54–55....2,247
Joe Washington ....1981–84.................2,070

Most Yards Gained, Season
John Riggins...............1983.....................1,347
Terry Allen.................1995.....................1,309
John Riggins...............1984.....................1,239
Earnest Byner ....1990.....................1,219
Larry Brown ....1972.....................1,216
George Rogers ....1986.....................1,203
John Riggins...............1979.....................1,153
Larry Brown ....1970.....................1,125
Mike Thomas ....1976.....................1,101
George Rogers ....1985.....................1,093
Reggie Brooks ....1993.....................1,063
Earnest Byner ....1991.....................1,048
John Riggins...............1978.....................1,014

Most Yards Gained, Game
221 (29 atts) ....Gerald Riggs vs Eagles
....09/17/89
215 (16 atts)....................Cliff Battles vs Giants
....10/08/33
206 (34 atts) ....George Rogers @ Cardinals
....12/21/85
195 (31 atts) ....Mike Thomas @ Cardinals
....11/21/76
191 (29 atts) ....Larry Brown vs Giants
....10/29/72
190 (18 atts) ....John Olszewski @ Browns
....11/15/59

Most Rushing Attempts, Career
John Riggins...............1976–79, 81–85....1, 988
Larry Brown ....1969–76.................1,530
Earnest Byner ....1989–93.....................990
Mike Thomas ....1975–78.....................877
Cliff Battles................1933–37.....................725
Charley Harraway ......1969–73.....................719
George Rogers ....1985–87.....................697
Andy Farkas ....1938–44.....................556

Most Rushing Attempts, Season
John Riggins ....1983.....................374
Terry Allen ....1995.....................338
John Riggins ....1984.....................327
George Rogers ....1986.....................303
Earnest Byner ....1990.....................297
Larry Brown ....1972.....................285
Earnest Byner ....1991.....................274
Earnest Byner ....1992.....................262
John Riggins ....1979.....................260

Most Rushing Attempts, Game
* 45 ......Jamie Morris @ Bengals............12/17/88
39 ......Earnest Byner @ Patriots 12/15/90
36 ......John Riggins vs Cowboys 1/22/83
36 ....George Rogers @ Eagles.........12/08/85
* NFL Record

Most 100–Yard Games, Career
John Riggins...............1976–79, 81–85..........19
Larry Brown ....1969–76.........................19
Earnest Byner ....1989–92..........................12
George Rogers ....1985–87..........................12

Most 100–Yard Games, Season
Rob Goode.................1951...............................7
Larry Brown ....1970...............................6
Larry Brown ....1972...............................6
Earnest Byner ....1990...............................5
John Riggins ....1984...............................5
George Rogers ....1986...............................5

Most TDs Rushing, Career
John Riggins ....1976–79, 81–85......79
Larry Brown ....1969–76..................35
George Rogers ....1985–87..................31

Most TDs Rushing, Season
John Riggins ....1983.....................24
George Rogers ....1986.....................18
John Riggins ....1984.....................14
John Riggins ....1981.....................13
Gerald Riggs ....1991.....................11

Most TDs Rushing, Game
3 .....Cliff Battles vs Giants 10/17/37
3 ....Andy Farkas @ Brooklyn 11/12/39
3 ......Dick James vs Cowboys 12/17/61
3 ......John Riggins @ Cardinals 10/09/83
3 ......John Riggins vs Lions 10/13/85
3 ......Earnest Byner vs Dolphins 12/02/90
3 ......Gerald Riggs @ Bengals 09/22/91

Most Consecutive Games, Rushing TDs
John Riggins ....1982–83................*13
George Rogers ....1985–86..................12
John Riggins 1983–84 8
* NFL Record

Longest Run From Scrimmage
88t ....Billy Wells @ Cardinals 11/21/54
85t.........Reggie Brooks @ Eagles 09/19/93
80t ....Rob Goode @ Packers...........09/24/50

Highest Avg. Gain, Career (min 250 carries)
Joe Theismann ....1974–85.................5.1
Charley Justice ....1950, 52–54..............4.8
Joe Washington ....1981–84...................4.6
Rob Goode ....1949–51, 54–55.......4.3
Dick Todd.................1939–42, 45–48.......4.3

Highest Avg. Gain, Season (min 100 carries)
Frank Atkins ....1945 ......5.42 (147–797)
Don Bosseler ....1959.......5.41 (119–644)
Charley Justice ....1953......5.36 (115–616)
Joe Washington ....1983.......5.32 (145–772)

PASSING

Most Yards Gained Passing, Career
Joe Theismann ....1974–85...........25,206
Sonny Jurgensen ....1964–74...........22,585
Sammy Baugh ....1937–52...........22,085
Mark Rypien ....1987–93...........15,928
Billy Kilmer...................1971–78...........12,352

Most Yards Gained Passing, Season
Jay Schroeder ....1986...................4,109
Mark Rypien ....1989...................3,768
Sonny Jurgensen ....1967...................3,747
Joe Theismann ....1983...................3,714
Joe Theismann ....1981...................3,568
Mark Rypien ....1991...................3,564
Joe Theismann ....1984...................3,391
Mark Rypien ....1992...................3,282
Sonny Jurgensen ....1966...................3,209
Sonny Jurgensen ....1969...................3,102
Norm Snead ....1963...................3,043

Most Yards Gained Passing, Game
446 (17–24) ....Sammy Baugh vs Yanks
....10/31/48
442 (16–31)................Mark Rypien vs Falcons
....11/10/91
430 (30–52) ....Doug Williams vs Steelers
....09/11/88
424 (23–40) ....Norm Snead vs Steelers
....11/17/63
420 (22–40) ....Jay Schroeder @ Giants
....10/27/86
418 (32–50)...........Sonny Jurgensen @ Browns
....11/26/67
417 (23–39) ....Joe Theismann vs Raiders
....10/02/83
411 (26–43)........Sonny Jurgensen vs Cowboys
....11/28/65

Most Pass Attempts, Career
Joe Theismann.............1974–85 3,602
Sonny Jurgensen 1964–74 3,155
Sammy Baugh..............1937–52 3,016
Mark Rypien 1987–93 2,207
Billy Kilmer 1971–78 1,104
Eddie LeBaron ....1952–53, 55–59 ...1,104
Norm Snead 1961–63 1,092
Jay Schroeder 1984–87 1,017

Most Pass Attempts, Season
Jay Schroeder................1986....541 (276 comp)
Sonny Jurgensen..........1967............508 (288)
Joe Theismann ....1981 ....496 (293)
Mark Rypien ....1992 ....479 (269)
Joe Theismann ....1984 ....477 (283)
Mark Rypien ....1989 ....476 (280)
Joe Theismann ....1983 ....459 (276)
Joe Theismann ....1980 ....454 (262)
Sonny Jurgensen..........1969 ....442 (274)

Most Pass Attempts, Game
58 (30 comp) ....Jay Schroeder vs 49ers
....12/01/85
54 (26) ....Mark Rypien @Cowboys
....11/22/90
53 (27) ....Mark Rypien @ Raiders
....10/29/89
52 (30) ....Doug Williams vs Steelers
....09/11/88
51 (20) ....Jay Schroeder vs Giants
....12/07/86
50 (32) ....John Friesz @ Giants
....09/18/94
50 (32) ....Sonny Jurgensen @ Browns
....11/26/67
50 (30)....................Sonny Jurgensen vs Eagles
....12/03/67

Most Pass Completions, Career

Joe Theismann 1974–85 2,044
Sonny Jurgensen 1964–74 1,831
Sammy Baugh 1937–52 1,709
Mark Rypien 1987–93 1,244
Billy Kilmer 1971–78 953

Most Pass Completions, Season

Joe Theismann 1981 293
Sonny Jurgensen 1967 288
Joe Theismann 1984 283
Mark Rypien 1989 280
Joe Theismann 1983 276
Jay Schroeder 1986 276
Sonny Jurgensen 1969 274
Mark Rypien 1992 269
Joe Theismann 1980 262
Sonny Jurgensen 1966 254

Most Pass Completions, Game

32 (50 atts)...........Sonny Jurgensen @ Browns
....11/26/67
32 (50) ....John Friesz @ Giants
....09/18/94
30 (47) ....Mark Rypien vs Bears
....11/26/89
30 (50) ....Sonny Jurgensen vs Eagles
....12/03/67
30 (52) ....Doug Williams vs Steelers
....09/11/88
30 (58) ....Jay Schroeder vs 49ers
....12/01/85
30 (42) ....Jeff Rutledge @ Lions
....11/04/90

Highest Completion Pct., Career
(min 1,000 atts)

Sonny Jurgensen ......1964–74 ....58.0
Joe Theismann ....1974–85 ....56.7
Mark Rypien ....1987–93 ....56.4
Sammy Baugh ....1937–52 ....56.7
Billy Kilmer ....1971–78 ....53.2

Highest Completion Pct., Season
(min 150 atts)

Sammy Baugh ....1945.......70.3 (128–182)
Sonny Jurgensen ......1974.......64.1 (107–167)
Joe Theismann ....1982.......63.9 (161–252)
Sammy Baugh ....1947.......62.7 (111–177)
Sonny Jurgensen ......1969.......62.0 (274–442)
Joe Theismann ....1983.......60.1 (276–459)

Highest Completion Pct., Game
(min 15 atts)

87.5 (14–16)Sammy Baugh vs Steelers
....11/03/40

Longest Pass Completion

* 99t.....................Frank Filchock to Andy Farkas
....vs Steelers 10/15/39
99t.....................George Izo to Bobby Mitchell
....@ Browns 09/15/63
99t ....Sonny Jurgensen to Gerry Allen
....@ Bears 09/15/68
* NFL Record (tied)

Highest QB Rating, Career (min 1,000 atts)

Sonny Jurgensen.............1964–74 ....85.0
Mark Rypien ....1987–93 ....80.2
Joe Theismann ....1974–85 ....77.4
Billy Kilmer...................1971–78 ....77.0
Jay Schroeder ....1984–87 ....72.6
Sammy Baugh ....1937–52 ....72.0

Highest QB Rating, Season

Sammy Baugh ....1945 ....109.7

Mark Rypien ....1991 ....97.9
Joe Theismann ....1983 ....97.0
Sonny Jurgensen ....1974 ....94.6
Sammy Baugh ....1947 ....92.3
Joe Theismann ....1982 ....91.3
Eddie LeBaron ....1957 ....88.6
Mark Rypien ....1989 ....88.1
Sonny Jurgensen ....1967 ....87.6
Joe Theismann ....1984 ....86.6

Most TD Passes, Career

Sammy Baugh 1937–52 187
Sonny Jurgensen 1964–74 179
Joe Theismann 1974–85 160
Billy Kilmer 1971–78 103
Mark Rypien 1987–92 98

Most TD Passes, Season

Sonny Jurgensen 1967 31
Joe Theismann 1983 29
Mark Rypien 1991 28
Sonny Jurgensen 1966 28
Sammy Baugh 1947 25
Sammy Baugh 1943 24
Sonny Jurgensen 1964 24
Joe Theismann 1984 24

Most TD Passes, Game

6.............Mark Rypien vs Falcons 11/10/91
6.............Sammy Baugh vs Cardinals11/23/47
6.............Sammy Baugh @ Brooklyn10/31/43

Most Consecutive Games, TD Pass

Sonny Jurgensen.............1966–68 23
Joe Theismann 1982–83 15

Most Consecutive Passes, No Interceptions

Joe Theismann 1983 162

Most Consecutive Games, No Interceptions

Joe Theismann 1983 5

Lowest Interception Pct., Career
(min 1,000 atts)

Mark Rypien ....1987–93 ....3.3
Jay Schroeder ....1984–87 ....3.6
Joe Theismann ....1974–85 ....3.8
Sonny Jurgensen............1964–74 ....5.9
Eddie LeBaron..............1952–53, 55–59 ....6.3
Norm Snead ....1961–63 ....6.5
Sammy Baugh ....1937–52 ....6.7

Lowest Interception Pct., Season

Sammy Baugh.........1945.......2.1 .....(4–182)
Jay Schroeder ....1985 ......2.3 ... (5–209)
Joe Theismann.......1983.......2.3 .....(11–459)
Mark Rypien ....1991.......2.6 .....(11–421)
Joe Theismann ....1984.......2.7 ...(13–477)
Mark Rypien ....1989.......2.7 ... (13–476)
Sonny Jurgensen......1970.......2.9 ...(10–337)
Sonny Jurgensen ....1974.......2.9 .....(5–167)

Most Interceptions, Career

Sammy Baugh 1937–52 205
Joe Theismann 1974–85 138
Sonny Jurgensen 1964–74 116
Eddie LeBaron............1952–53, 55–59 88
Mark Rypien 1987–93 75
Billy Kilmer 1971–78 75

Most Interceptions, Season

Norm Snead 1963 27
Sammy Baugh 1948 23
Norm Snead 1962 22
Norm Snead 1961 22
Jay Schroeder 1986 22
Sammy Baugh 1943 21

Most Interceptions, Game

6 ....Sammy Baugh @ Giants 11/11/51
6 ....Jay Schroeder vs Giants 12/07/86

RECEIVING

Most Receptions, Career

Art Monk 1980–93 888
Charley Taylor 1964–77 649
Gary Clark 1985–92 549
Jerry Smith 1965–77 421
Ricky Sanders 1986–93 414
Bobby Mitchell 1962–68 393
Hugh Taylor 1947–54 272
Don Warren 1979–92 244
Larry Brown 1969–76 238
Roy Jefferson 1971–76 208

Most Receptions, Season

Art Monk 1984 106
Art Monk 1985 91
Art Monk 1989 86
Ricky Sanders 1989 80
Gary Clark 1989 79
Charlie Brown 1983 78
Gary Clark 1990 75
Gary Clark 1986 74
Henry Ellard 1994 74
Ricky Sanders 1988 73
Art Monk 1986 73
Bobby Mitchell 1962 72
Art Monk 1988 72
Charley Taylor 1966 72
Gary Clark 1985 72
Art Monk 1991 71
Charley Taylor 1969 71
Gary Clark 1991 70
Charley Taylor 1967 70
Joe Washington 1981 70

Most Receptions, Game

13 (168 yards) ....Art Monk @ Lions
....11/04/90
13 (230) ....Art Monk vs Bengals
....12/15/85
13 (130) ....Kelvin Bryant vs Giants
....12/07/86
12 (158) ....Ricky Sanders @ Raiders
....10/29/89
12 (118).........Clarence Harmon vs Chargers
....12/07/80
12 (183)...................Bobby Mitchell vs Eagles
....10/11/64

Most Yards Gained Receiving, Career

Art Monk.......................1980–93...........13,026
Charley Taylor ....1964–77............9,140
Gary Clark ....1985–92............8,742
Bobby Mitchell ....1962–68............6,491
Ricky Sanders ....1986–93............5,854
Jerry Smith ....1965–77............5,496
Hugh Taylor ....1947–54............5,233
Roy Jefferson ....1971–76............3,119
Bill Anderson ....1958–63............2,930
Don Warren....................1979–92............2,536

Most Yards Gained Receiving, Season

Bobby Mitchell ....1963.................1,436
Henry Ellard ....1994.................1,397
Bobby Mitchell ....1962.................1,384
Art Monk ....1984.................1,372
Gary Clark ....1991.................1,340
Gary Clark ....1986.................1,265
Gary Clark ....1989.................1,229
Art Monk ....1985.................1,226
Charlie Brown ....1983.................1,225

Art Monk.....................1989.................1,186
Ricky Sanders...............1988.................1,143
Ricky Sanders...............1989.................1,138
Charley Taylor..............1966.................1,119
Gary Clark..................1990.................1,112
Art Monk.....................1986.................1,068
Gary Clark..................1987.................1,066
Art Monk.....................1991.................1,049
Henry Ellard................1995.................1,005

Most Yards Gained Receiving, Game
255 (7 rec)...........Anthony Allen vs Cardinals
....10/04/87
241 (11)...........................Gary Clark @ Giants
....10/27/86
230 (13)...................Art Monk vs Bengals
....12/15/85
218 (11).................Bobby Mitchell vs Steelers
....11/17/63
213 (7)................Wilbur Moore vs Brooklyn
....10/31/43
212 (8).........................Hugh Taylor @ Eagles
....09/28/47
203 (4)..........................Gary Clark vs Falcons
....11/10/91
200 (11)..........................Frank Grant vs 49ers
....11/07/76
200 (10)..............................Art Monk vs 49ers
....09/10/84

Most TD Receptions, Career
Charley Taylor..............1964–77.................79
Art Monk.....................1980–93.................65
Jerry Smith..................1965–77.................60
Gary Clark...................1985–92.................58
Hugh Taylor..................1947–54.................58

Most TD Receptions, Season
Ricky Sanders...............1988.........................12
Charley Taylor..............1966.........................12
Hugh Taylor..................1952.........................12
Jerry Smith..................1967.........................12
Bobby Mitchell..............1962.........................11

Most TD Receptions, Game
3............Gary Clark vs Falcons.........11/10/91
3............Art Monk @ Colts..............10/07/84
3............Anthony Allen vs Cardinals.10/04/87
3............Larry Brown vs Eagles........12/16/73
3............Jerry Smith vs Cowboys......11/16/69
3............Pat Richter @ Bears............09/15/68
3............Jerry Smith @ Rams...........10/22/67
3............Hugh Taylor vs Cardinals....12/12/54
3............Hugh Taylor @ Giants.........12/07/52
3............Hugh Taylor vs Cardinals....10/22/50
3............Hugh Taylor @ Colts..........10/17/50
3............Hal Crisler vs Bulldogs.......10/16/49
3............Hugh Taylor @ Eagles.........09/28/47

INTERCEPTIONS

Most Interceptions, Career
Darrell Green.................1983–95.................40
Brig Owens....................1966–77.................36
Sammy Baugh................1937–52.................31
Mike Bass....................1969–75.................30
Joe Lavender.................1976–82.................29
Paul Krause..................1964–67.................28
Pat Fischer...................1968–77.................27
Mark Murphy.................1977–83.................27

Most Interceptions, Season
Dan Sandifer..................1948.........................13
Paul Krause..................1964.........................12
Sammy Baugh................1943.........................11
Don Doll.......................1953.........................10
Dick Alban...................1954...........................9
Lemar Parrish................1979...........................9

Mark Murphy.................1983...........................9
Barry Wilburn................1987...........................9

Most Interceptions, Game
4............Sammy Baugh vs Lions........11/14/43
4............Dan Sandifer vs Yanks.........10/31/48

Consecutive Games, with Interception
Paul Krause...................1964...........................7
Lemar Parrish................1978–79......................6
Barry Wilburn................1987...........................6

Most Yards Interception Returns, Career
Brig Owens....................1966–77.................686
Mike Bass....................1969–75.................478
Pat Fischer...................1968–77.................412
Darrell Green.................1983–95.................350
Chris Hanburger.............1965–78.................347

Most Yards Interception Returns, Season
Dan Sandifer..................1948.......................258
George Cheverko.............1948.......................168
Brig Owens....................1966.......................165
Mike Bass....................1973.......................161
Brad Edwards.................1992.......................157

Longest Interception Return
100t........Barry Wilburn @ Vikings.....12/26/87
93t........Dick Poillon @ Eagles..........11/21/48

Most Interception Returns for TDs, Career
Darrell Green.................1983–95.......................3
Andre Collins................1990–94.......................3
Brig Owens....................1966–77.......................3
Mike Bass....................1969–75.......................3

Most Interception Ret. for TDs, Season
Dan Sandifer..................1948...........................2
Dale Hackbart................1961...........................2
Vernon Dean..................1984...........................2
Andre Collins................1994...........................2

SACKS

Most Sacks, Career
Dexter Manley................1981–89.................97.5
Charles Mann................1983–93.................82.0
Dave Butz....................1975–88.................59.5
Monte Coleman..............1979–94.................56.5
Diron Talbert.................1971–80.................56.0
Bill Brundige.................1970–77.................48.5

Most Sacks, Season
Dexter Manley................1986.......................18.0
Coy Bacon....................1979.......................15.0
Dexter Manley................1985.......................15.0
Charles Mann................1985.......................14.5
Ken Harvey...................1994.......................13.5
Dexter Manley................1984.......................13.5
Verlon Biggs.................1973.......................13.0
Bill Brundige.................1973.......................13.0

Most Sacks, Game
4.0........Diron Talbert vs Giants........09/28/75
4.0........Dexter Manley vs Giants......10/02/88

PUNTING

Most Punts, Career
Mike Bragg....................1968–79.................896
Pat Richter...................1963–70.................338
Sammy Baugh................1937–52.................334

Most Punts, Season
Mike Bragg....................1978.......................103
Mike Bragg....................1977.........................91
Mike Bragg....................1976.........................90
Pat Richter...................1964.........................90

Most Punts, Game
14.........Sammy Baugh vs Eagles.......11/05/39

Longest Punt
85.........Sammy Baugh vs Eagles.......12/01/40
81.........Sammy Baugh vs Lions.........11/14/43
77.........Steve Cox @ Bills.................11/01/87
76.........Sammy Baugh vs Rams.........11/04/44
76.........Dick Poillon @ Packers........10/24/48

Highest Punting Avg., Career
Sammy Baugh................1937–52...........*45.1
Sam Baker....................1953, 55–59........44.9
* NFL Record

Highest Punting Avg., Season
Sammy Baugh................1940...................*51.4
Sammy Baugh................1941.......................48.7
Sam Baker....................1959.......................45.5
Sam Baker....................1958.......................45.4
* NFL Record

Highest Punting Avg., Game
59.4........Sammy Baugh vs Lions........10/27/40

Most Punts Inside 20, Season
Mike Bragg....................1977.........................29
Jeff Hayes....................1983.........................29
Matt Turk....................1995.........................29

KICKOFF RETURNS

Most KO Returns, Career
Brian Mitchell................1990–95.................216
Mike Nelms...................1980–84.................174
Dick James...................1956–63.................155
Rickie Harris.................1965–70.................101
Eddie Saenz..................1946–51...................81

Most KO Returns, Season
Brian Mitchell................1994.........................58
Brian Mitchell................1995.........................55
Larry Jones...................1975.........................47
Mike Nelms...................1984.........................42
Ken Jenkins...................1985.........................41

Longest KO Return
102t........Larry Jones vs Eagles...........11/24/74
99t........Joe Johnson @ Raiders.........10/29/89
99t........Dale Atkeson vs Eagles.........10/17/54
99t........Tony Green @ Cardinals......09/17/78

Most Yards, Career
Brian Mitchell................1990–95.............5,367
Mike Nelms...................1980–84.............4,128
Dick James...................1956–63.............3,959
Rickie Harris.................1965–70.............2,305
Eddie Saenz..................1946–51.............1,995

Most Yards, Season
Brian Mitchell................1994.................1,478
Brian Mitchell................1995.................1,408
Mike Nelms...................1981.................1,099
Larry Jones...................1975.................1,086
Ken Jenkins...................1985.................1,018

Highest Avg. Return, Career
Bobby Mitchell...............1962–68.................28.5
Herb Mul–Key................1972–74.................27.8
Joe Scudero..................1954–58.................25.9
Dick James...................1956–63.................25.5
Brian Mitchell................1990–95.................24.9

Highest Avg. Return, Season
(min 20 returns)
Mike Nelms...................1981.......................29.7
Dick James...................1961.......................29.4
Larry Jones...................1974.......................29.2

Herb Mul–key ....1973...................28.1
Joe Scudero..................1955...................28.0

PUNT RETURNS

Most Punt Returns, Career
Mike Nelms ....1980–84.................212
Brian Mitchell ....1990–95.................172
Rickie Harris..................1965–70.................118
Eddie Brown ....1975–77.................111
Dick James ....1956–63...................99

Most Punt Returns, Season
Eddie Brown ....1977.......................57
Larry Jones ....1975.......................53
Mike Nelms ....1984.......................49
Eddie Brown ....1976.......................48
Mike Nelms ....1980.......................48

Most Punt Returns, Game
* 11..........Eddie Brown vs Bucs............10/09/77
9.............Mike Nelms vs Cardinals 12/21/80
* NFL Record

Longest Punt Return
96t..........Bill Dudley vs Steelers..........12/03/50
86t..........Rickie Harris vs Giants 10/19/69

Most Yards, Career
Mike Nelms ....1980–84.............1,948
Brian Mitchell ....1990–95.............1,938
Eddie Brown ....1975–77.............1,150
Rickie Harris..................1965–70.............1,012
Dick James ....1956–63...............805

Most Yards, Season
Eddie Brown ....1976.....................646
Brian Mitchell ....1991.....................600
Mike Nelms ....1981.....................492
Brian Mitchell ....1994.....................452
Eddie Brown ....1977.....................452

Highest Avg. Return, Career (min 40 ret.)
John Williams..................1952–53................12.8
Bill Dudley....................1950–51, 53........11.4
Darrell Green..................1983–95................11.3
Brian Mitchell ....1990–95................11.3
Eddie Saenz ....1946–51................11.2

Highest Avg. Return, Season (min 20 ret.)
John Williams..................1952...................15.3
Brian Mitchell ....1994...................14.1
Eddie Brown ....1976...................13.5
Brian Mitchell ....1991...................13.3
Eddie Saenz ....1947...................12.8
Rickie Harris..................1965...................12.8

Most TD Returns, Career
Brian Mitchell ....1990–95...................6
Mike Nelms ....1980–84...................3
Rickie Harris..................1965–70...................3

Most TD Returns, Season
Brian Mitchell ....1994.......................2
Brian Mitchell ....1991.......................2
Mike Nelms ....1981.......................2
Bert Zagers....................1957.......................2
John Williams..................1952.......................2

COMBINED RETURNS

Most Combined Returns, Career
Brian Mitchell ....1990–95.................388
Mike Nelms ....1980–84.................386
Dick James ....1956–63.................254
Rickie Harris..................1965–70.................219

Most Combined Returns, Season
Larry Jones ....1975...................*100
Eddie Brown ....1977.......................91
Mike Nelms ....1984.......................91
Brian Mitchell ....1994.......................90
Mike Nelms ....1980.......................86
* NFL Record

Most Combined Yards, Career
Brian Mitchell ....1990–95............6,942
Mike Nelms ....1980–84............6,076
Dick James ....1956–63............4,874
Rickie Harris..................1965–70............3,317

Most Combined Yards, Season
Brian Mitchell ....1994...................1,930
Brian Mitchell ....1995...................1,723
Mike Nelms ....1981...................1,594
Larry Jones ....1975...................1,493
Tony Green ....1978...................1,313

COMBINED NET YARDS

Most Combined Net Yards, Career
(Rushing, Receiving, Returns)
Art Monk 1980–93 12,358
..................................(332–12,026–0)
Charley Taylor 1964–77 10,833
..................................(1,488–9,140–205)
Gary Clark 1985–1992 8,845
..................................(41–8,742–62)
Brian Mitchell........1990–95 8,717
..................................(1,023–752–6,942)
John Riggins 1976–79, 81–85 8,400
..................................(7,472–928–0)
Larry Brown...........1969–76 8,360
..................................(5,875–2,485–0)
Bobby Mitchell 1962–68 8,162
..................................(438–6,492–1,232)
Dick James 1956–63 8,153
..................................(1,741–1,528–4,874)
Mike Nelms............1980–84 6,076
..................................(0–0–6,076)
Ricky Sanders 1986–93 5,970
..................................(94–5,854–22)
Jerry Smith.............1965–77 5,552
..................................(56–5,496–0)

Most Combined Net Yards, Season
Brian Mitchell........1994 2,477
..................................(311–236–1,930)
Brian Mitchell........1995 2,348
..................................(301–324–1,723)
Bobby Mitchell 1963 1,852
..................................(24–1,436–392)
Bobby Mitchell 1962 1,794
..................................(5–1,384–405)
Dick James 1963 1,713
..................................(384–262–1,067)
Larry Brown...........1972 1,689
..................................(1,216–473–0)
Mike Nelms............1981 1,594
..................................(0–0–1,594)
Charley Taylor 1964 1,589
..................................(755–814–20)
Charley Taylor 1966 1,542
..................................(262–1,119–151)
Larry Jones............1975 1,526
..................................(0–33–1,493)

SERVICE

Most Seasons, Redskin
Sammy Baugh ....1937–52..................16
Monte Coleman ....1979–94..................16
Art Monk.......................1980–93..................14
Don Warren....................1979–92..................14
Dave Butz......................1975–88..................14

Jeff Bostic.......................1980–93..................14
Len Hauss ....1964–77..................14
Charley Taylor ....1964–77..................14
Chris Hanburger ....1965–78..................14
Darrell Green...................1983–95..................13
Joe Jacoby ....1981–93..................13
Jerry Smith ....1965–77..................13
Mark Moseley..................1974–86..................13
Brig Owens ....1966–77..................12
George Starke ....1973–84..................12
Joe Theismann ....1974–85..................12

Most Consecutive Games Played, Redskin
Len Hauss ....1964–77.................196
Mark Moseley..................1974–86.................170
Joe Theismann ....1974–85.................163
Brig Owens ....1966–77.................154

Most Games Played, Redskin
Monte Coleman ....1979–94.................216
Art Monk ....1980–93.................205
Dave Butz.......................1975–88.................203
Len Hauss ....1964–77.................196
Don Warren....................1979–92.................194
Chris Hanburger ....1965–78.................187
Darrell Green...................1983–95.................186
Jeff Bostic.......................1980–93.................184
Mark Moseley..................1974–86.................182
Mike Bragg ....1968–79.................172
Joe Jacoby ....1981–93.................170
Jerry Smith ....1965–77.................168
Joe Theismann ....1974–85.................167
Charley Taylor ....1964–77.................165
Charles Mann ....1983–93.................163
Brig Owens ....1966–77.................158
George Starke ....1973–84.................156

Most Consecutive Games Started
Len Hauss ....1964–77.................192

Most Consecutive Pro Bowl Appearances
Ken Houston ....1973–79...................7
........................(10 overall, 1970–72 Houston)

Most Pro Bowl Appearances
Chris Hanburger ....1966–69, 72–76.........9
Charley Taylor ....1964–67, 72–75........8
Ken Houston ....1973–79...................7